HTML5 Games Most Wanted

Egor Kuryanovich

Shy Shalom

Russell Goldenberg

Mathias Paumgarten

David Strauß

Seb Lee-Delisle

Gaëtan Renaudeau

Jonas Wagner

Jonathan Bergknoff

Brian Danchilla

Rob Hawkes

friendsof

DESIGNER TO DESIGNER™

an Apress® company

HTML5 GAMES MOST WANTED

ISBN-13 (pbk): 978-1-4302-3978-9

ISBN-13 (electronic): 978-1-4302-3979-6

Distributed to the book trade worldwide by Springer Science+Business Media New York, 233 Spring Street, 6th Floor, New York, NY 10013. Phone 1-800-SPRINGER, fax (201) 348-4505, e-mail orders-ny@springer-sbm.com, or visit www.springeronline.com.

For information on translations, please e-mail rights@apress.com or visit www.apress.com.

Apress and friends of ED books may be purchased in bulk for academic, corporate, or promotional use. eBook versions and licenses are also available for most titles. For more information, reference our Special Bulk Sales–eBook Licensing web page at www.apress.com/bulk-sales.

Any source code or other supplementary materials referenced by the author in this text are available to readers at www.apress.com. For detailed information about how to locate your book's source code, go to www.apress.com/source-code/.

Credits

President and Publisher: Paul Manning	**Coordinating Editor:** Jessica Belanger
Lead Editor: Ben Renow-Clarke	**Copy Editors**: Kimberly Burton
Technical Reviewer: Andrew Zack	**Compositor:** Mary Sudul
Editorial Board: Steve Anglin, Ewan Buckingham, Gary Cornell, Louise Corrigan, Morgan Ertel, Jonathan Gennick, Jonathan Hassell, Robert Hutchinson, Michelle Lowman, James Markham, Matthew Moodie, Jeff Olson, Jeffrey Pepper, Douglas Pundick, Ben Renow-Clarke, Dominic Shakeshaft, Gwenan Spearing, Matt Wade, Tom Welsh	**Indexer:** SPi Global **Artist:** SPi Global **Cover Image Artist:** Corné van Dooren **Cover Designer:** Anna Ishchenko

Contents at a Glance

Contents

About the Authors

Egor Kuryanovich is a web developer from Belarus living in Minsk. He goes by the name of Sontan on the web, and his game, Far7, won the Best Technology category of Google's 2010 Game On competition.

Shy Shalom is an Israeli software engineer living in Tel Aviv. While his day job consists of writing enterprise applications in C++, his true passion is the aesthetics of 3D rendering. Shy has been active in the field of computer graphics throughout his career.

He has published several papers in the field of geometry processing while completing his graduate degree and has tutored courses on graphics and OpenGL at Tel Aviv University. Shy started working with WebGL at a very early stage in its conception and participated in the beta testing of its early implementations in Firefox and Google Chrome.

Some of Shy's projects in graphics, which are available online, include *CycleBlob*, a 3D lightcycle game that runs in the web browser; the *Happy Cube Solver*, an aid to solving 3D foam puzzles; and *KawaiiGL*, a small IDE for writing GLSL shaders and basic geometric modeling.

Russell Goldenberg is a candidate for a master's degree in interactive media at Emerson College in Boston. He is currently finishing up his final semester while teaching an undergraduate course in web design and development at Emerson. In 2009, he graduated from Union College with an interdepartmental degree in computer science and visual arts. If he's not coding, he's cooking or playing basketball.

His creative work primarily uses computer programming to create art. He investigates ideas in a variety of methods: games, data visualizations, interactive installations, and generative animation. Both form and topic tend to change. His process is to dive in and see what works and emerges along the way.

Mathias Paumgarten is a web developer that focuses on front-end and interaction development. Starting with a background in Flash development, he now focuses mainly on JavaScript. He found his passion for the web and code-based animation at a very young age and made his way from a small town in Austria all the way to New York City. He currently works for Firstborn Multimedia as a creative developer.

David Strauß is a creative programmer who discovered the magic of creating things at a very young age through his father's passion for working with wood. David mainly uses CoffeeScript and the Ruby on Rails framework to create beautiful web applications. One of his first projects, *Marble Run*, won Mozilla's Game On 2010 Challenge, beating teams like Fantasy Interactive and the Google Chrome Team.

Seb Lee-Delisle is a creative coder, speaker and teacher, working across platforms including JavaScript, Processing and openFrameworks. He works to bring people together with large scale installations like PixelPhones, interactive firework displays or glow-stick voting systems.

His work has pushed the boundaries of what is possible both on and off the web, and won two BAFTAs with Plug-in Media, the agency he co-founded in 2004.

A sought-after speaker, his recent Creative JavaScript / HTML5 workshop series sold out within hours. He co-hosts the Creative Coding Podcast, his blog can be found at seb.ly and he tweets @seb_ly.

Gaëtan Renaudeau (aka gre) is a web enthusiast studying towards a master's degree in computer science in France. Since 2009, he has worked for Zenexity in Paris as a web developer, building web applications, web services, and mobile applications. He enjoys working both in front-end (JavaScript, HTML5, CSS3) and server-side (mainly Play framework) development.

For fun you'll find him making web experiments, applications, and libraries— such as the recently completed HTML5 game called *Same Game Gravity*, available on six different platforms.

Jonas Wagner is a software engineer from Zurich, Switzerland, working on one of the biggest Swiss web sites. When not at work, he likes to explore the boundaries of what's possible with web technology.

Jonathan Bergknoff is a hobbyist programmer from New Jersey. He graduated from Cornell University in 2006 with degrees in math and physics and is currently earning a PhD in theoretical physics at UCLA. His programming projects include the JavaScript tower defense game *Picnic Defender*, a *Minesweeper* clone for the Nintendo DS, an NES emulator, and the iPod manager *jPod*.

Brian Danchilla is a freelance PHP and Java developer and author. He is the coauthor of *Pro PHP Programming* (Apress, 2011), a technical reviewer of *Foundation HTML5 Animation with JavaScript* (friends of ED, 2011), and the author of the upcoming *Beginning WebGL* (Apress, 2012). Brian has worked with OpenGL for several years and has a passion for graphics, art, and mathematics. His other interests include playing guitar, listening to music, and enjoying the outdoors.

Rob Hawkes is a serial experimenter who specializes in JavaScript development. He works for Mozilla as a Technical Evangelist and takes a strong interest in the game-related events and projects that happen within Mozilla and the wider developer community.

About the Technical Reviewer

Andrew Zack is the CEO of ZTMC, Inc. (www.ztmc.com), which specializes in search engine optimization (SEO) and internet marketing strategies. His project background includes almost 20 years of site development and project management experience and over 15 years as an SEO and internet marketing expert.

Andrew has been very active in the publishing industry, having coauthored *Flash 5 Studio* (Apress, 2001) and serving as a technical reviewer on more than 10 books and industry publications.

Having started working on the internet close to its inception, Andrew continually focuses on the cutting edge and beyond, concentrating on new platforms and technology to stay at the forefront of the industry.

About the Cover Image Artist

Corné van Dooren designed the front cover image for this book. After taking a brief hiatus from friends of ED to create a new design for the Foundation series, Corné worked at combining technological and organic forms with the results now appearing on this and other book covers.

Corné spent his childhood drawing on everything at hand, and then he began exploring the infinite world of multimedia—His journey of discovery hasn't stopped since! His mantra has always been, "The only limit to multimedia is the imagination," a saying that keeps him constantly moving forward.

Corné works for many international clients, writes features for multimedia magazines, reviews and tests software, authors multimedia studies, and works on many other friends of ED books. You can see more of his work and contact him through his website at: www.cornevandooren.com.

Introduction

HTML5 is a "game changer," allowing web browsers on such diverse hardware as smartphones, tablets, and personal computers to display the same games, interactive ads, and rich-media applications that were previously only possible as long as the end-user had downloaded the appropriate third-party plug-ins, most notably Flash. With the advent of HTML5, programmers are able to create cross-platform web applications.

The authors of this book are all real-world games programmers who have come together to share their HTML5 expertise, tips, and tricks with you.

In the first chapter of the book, Rob Hawkes, a Mozilla evangelist, discusses the state of open web gaming today. He explores the core technologies of HTML5 and JavaScript and the new APIs that have been introduced.

In Chapter 2, Russell Goldenberg will walk you through the design implementation and coding of his game *A to B*. This physics-based game involves a ball that must be manipulated by a series of modifiers, including walls and speed boosters, from point A to point B. It was written in Processing.js, a tool with which Goldenberg was very familiar, allowing him to quickly and easily create the game. For this project, Goldenberg was not looking to create a scalable, multi-author game, but instead was looking for a "quick and dirty" approach. The resulting game was a finalist in the Mozilla Game On 2010 competition.

In Chapter 3, Gaëtan Renaudeau shows us how to make multi-platform HTML games from scratch. He introduces us to the use of CSS, JavaScript, the canvas element, and DOM within HTML5 applications as demonstrated in a chess game that he has coded.

Chapter 4 is an in-depth walk-though of the use of the canvas element in HTML5. David Strauss and Mathias Paumgarten show us some of the techniques behind their massively popular *Marble Run* game.

We see how to create a three-dimensional iPhone/iPad game using HTML5 and CSS in Chapter 5. Seb Lee-Delisle of the BAFTA-winning Plug-in Media, will show you how to use CSS 3D transformations to move HTML elements in three-dimensional space. The example game in this chapter involves puffer fish that are to be exploded on touch.

Chapter 6, by Jonas Wagner, focuses on particle systems to create effects such as fire, rain, and smoke. You'll create a high-performance particle system that can deal with tens of thousands of particles, and find many code examples that you can use in your own projects.

Chapters 7 and 8 introduce the reader to WebGL. In Chapter 7, Brian Danchilla uses the example of a darts game to walk the reader through checking for WebGL support, understanding 3D coordinate systems, drawing basic shapes, animating 3D objects, and adding textures.

Chapter 8 advances from the previous chapter and shows how Shy Shalom used WebGL to create a three-dimensional, *TRON*-inspired, lightcycle game called *CycleBlob*.

in Chapter 9, learn how Jonathan Bergknoff used canvas, netcode, and WebSockets to create a real-time, multiplayer, bumper cars game. Bergknoff demonstrates the complexities of the game logic needed to enable his game to handle glancing collisions of several vehicles and their resulting trajectories in a multiplayer environment.

Finally, we round off the book with Chapter 10, where Egor Kuryanovich introduces us to the decision-making process when assessing which technologies to include in our HTML5 application. He outlines the benefits and disadvantages of the HTML5 canvas element, SVG, web sockets, server-sent events, and web fonts, preparing us for understanding the implications of the choices made by the other authors in subsequent chapters.

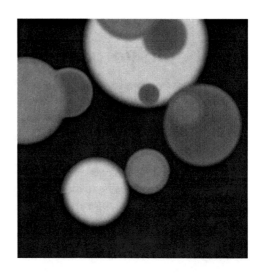

Chapter 1

The State of Open Web Games

In this chapter, I introduce the concept of open web game development using technologies such as HTML5 and JavaScript. I cover the various features that these technologies provide, including such gems as the Gamepad API, which allows you to break away from keyboard and mouse input. Towards the end of the chapter, I cover the current method of distributing and making money from your games, as well as highlighting the events that must happen for the web to become a viable platform for game development.

A brief introduction

My name is Rob Hawkes. I am a serial experimenter who specializes in JavaScript development. I work for Mozilla as a Technical Evangelist and take a strong interest in the game-related events and projects that happen within Mozilla and the wider developer community.

I'm a hobbyist game developer and I have worked on a variety of game-related projects using a variety of programming languages (Unity, ActionScript, PHP, Processing, and JavaScript) and technologies (augmented reality, mobile phones, desktop, and browsers).

Most recently I have been working on a multiplayer HTML5 game called Rawkets (http://rawkets.com) that acts as my test bed for experimenting with the various game-related technologies that I will be covering further on.

You can get in touch with me through my personal blog (http://rawkes.com) or through Twitter (@robhawkes). I'm always happy to help where I can.

Why should you care about open web games?

Open web games are by nature games created with open web technologies; as of today, these technologies are HTML5, CSS3, and JavaScript. In this chapter, I will be referring to these technologies under the umbrella term "open web games," as I feel it sums up the importance of the technologies quite well while also being easier to write multiple times—rather than listing every single individual technology, which I think we'll both appreciate in the long run.

The beauty of the technologies behind open web games is that they are the same ones that countless developers are already using to create web sites and web apps (arguably the same thing, but in this case it is worth defining them separately). These are technologies that have evolved since the dawn of the internet and have been proven as reliable and stable while other technologies rise and fall beside them.

Easy to get started

There is also an almost non-existent barrier to entry to develop games or anything else with these technologies. First off, they are completely free to use in all senses of the word. Secondly, the tools needed to develop and host games with these technologies can also be found for free or extremely low cost. In short, very little investment needs to be made to begin developing games using open web technologies. This is a massive plus point for indie developers who might be used to more restrictive environments like Flash, where you are required to buy into the proprietary technology and related development tools.

Excellent documentation

On top of the low barrier to entry is the well-written and free documentation that exists to help developers learn about every minor detail of these technologies. Web sites like the Mozilla Developer Network (https://developer.mozilla.org) have provided services like this for many years, with numerous other web sites and personal blogs doing the same.

Large and friendly community

Complimenting the documentation effort is a thriving community of developers and designers who care for nothing more but to further the web and share their experience with others. This is a community that can be found nearly everywhere you look; from the HTML5 group on Facebook, to Twitter, to dedicated forums like SitePoint, all the way to real-time chatrooms on IRC. For example, there is a growing community of open web game developers hanging out in the #bbg channel on irc.freenode.net—and we would love for you to come along and take part.

Write once, use anywhere

On a more technical level, the beauty of developing games with open web technologies is that it's very much a "write once, use anywhere" kind of approach. Now this isn't entirely true, as there are always nuances and exceptions to the rule; however, what is true is that this approach is inherently cross-platform and the technology has been created to work on a variety of operating systems and browsers with little to no platform-specific code.

What you *can* be certain of is that if a platform supports HTML5 and the JavaScript APIs that your game requires, then it's likely that your game will function in the way that you expect. Obviously things like hardware performance will cause issues on a per-device level, but that is something you'll experience using any technology anyway.

Uncompiled and open

Something that many proprietary developers find uncomfortable about the move to open web technologies is that the code is completely uncompiled and open for users to view. If you right-click on any web site within your browser, you will be able to view the source code and assets with relative ease—and the same is the case for open web games.

This behavior is core to the strength and purpose of the open web and it is unlikely to change— however much developers from other platforms would like it to. It is unlikely that digital rights management (DRM) will make its way onto the web in a non-proprietary way, and the same can be said for the compilation of code and assets, so that others can't see them in a readable fashion.

In my eyes, this clash of cultures is one of the major sticking points for game developers coming from platforms like mobile, console, and desktop. Traditional game development in that sense has been built around the idea of protecting intellectual property and making code and assets as difficult to access as possible. Now, one could argue that such moves are fruitless (I've yet to see a method of DRM that *hasn't* been eventually cracked), but I get why they exist and the motives behind their use. Unfortunately, all browsers are unlikely to accommodate this way of thinking, so it's not a viable way to look at game development on the web.

Instead, I believe that it is important for the web to prove itself as a viable platform to these developers and show that open assets and code does not mean rampant theft and a loss of control. History tells us that this won't happen and I'm confident that the benefits of the web as a platform will far outweigh the (minor) issues. In other words, how many web sites have you seen get stolen, replicated, and then perform better than the original?

Everyone has control

Something that still amazes me to this day is how no single entity controls the technologies and platform that the web is built on. This idea is another foreign concept to developers coming from a proprietary background, as there isn't a single point of contact to reach for when you want something added or changed. Instead, the technologies behind the web are defined by a set of specifications that are each managed by either the World Wide Web Consortium (W3C) or the Web Hypertext Application Technology Working Group (WHATWG).

Both of these groups are made up of a variety of stakeholders ranging from browser manufacturers, to technology companies, to general web developers. Anyone can be a part of these groups and that is why everyone has control. If you want something added or changed, then all you need do is take part in the discussions and have your say. For example, if you'd like to be a part of the discussions surrounding open web gaming technologies, then you should get involved in the W3C Games Community Group (www.w3.org/community/games/).

Access to the world's biggest audience

If anything, this is perhaps one of the most important aspects of the web as a platform for games. By building for browser technologies, you have access to practically every web user out there—all 6.9 billion of them! OK, perhaps not *all* of them and admittedly not every person will have an up-to-date browser. But still, my point here is that there are an astonishing amount of people using the web, with more and more getting connected every day. Even if we just counted Firefox users, that's hundreds of millions of people (a lot). And Facebook users? That's well over 800 million people (more than a lot)!

How you distribute your game to all those people is another problem entirely, and one that I will touch on briefly further on in this chapter.

What is the current state of open web games?

The past few years have seen a massive improvement in browser platforms and the adoption of technologies required to create open web games. This is coupled with the recent increase in the quantity of open web games that are being distributed on app stores and social networks, a number that is increasing every day. Also, large game studios are beginning to take interest and the general quality of these games are improving at a noticeable rate.

However, I think what has been most key in the recent improvements in open web gaming is the unease surrounding the future of Flash on mobile and the web. What we have now with HTML5 and JavaScript is a platform that can no longer be simply cast aside as unviable—open web games are definitely here to stay.

Game-related browser technologies already exist

What I still find most fascinating with this area of the web are the technologies that already exist and that are arriving soon; things like the Gamepad API, Mouse Lock API, and Full Screen API, among many others. These simple technologies are the ones that will help demolish the idea that games on the web are small boxes played embedded within another web site. Instead, with the ability to connect gamepad controllers and allow HTML elements to run full screen, open web games will become much more immersive experiences, much like on consoles and the desktop.

The following are just a few examples of the technologies that are in browsers today or on their way very soon. I encourage you to look into them all in more detail to discover how simple they are to get started with. It's also worth mentioning that browser support for these technologies changes at a rapid pace. I would check out the web site When Can I Use... for up-to-date information (http://caniuse.com).

2D graphics with HTML5 canvas and SVG

Visual output is one of the core components of most games, so the ability to produce and manage 2D graphics within a browser is very important. This is where both HTML5 canvas and scalable vector graphics (SVG) come in.

HTML5 canvas (often referred to as simply "canvas") is a JavaScript API and corresponding HTML element that allows for bitmap graphics to be created and edited within the browser. The plus points of canvas are that it's speedy and that can produce pin-point pixel graphics without relative ease. The negative aspects to canvas are that performance varies across platforms and animation functionality isn't built in.

On the other hand, SVG is another 2D solution that uses the document object model (DOM) to produce and manage vector graphics. The plus points of SVG are that it's accessible (in that the graphics are described with DOM elements), has animation ability built in, and that the vector approach means that graphics can be scaled easily to accommodate various devices and screen sizes. The negative aspects of SVG are that it isn't as popular as canvas and that it doesn't cope as well with pixel-perfect precision.

3D graphics with WebGL

If you're looking for 3D graphics for your game, then the WebGL JavaScript API is exactly what you need. It's based on OpenGL ES 2.0 and provides all the functionality required to produce some pretty spectacular effects.

The plus points of WebGL are that it's hardware accelerated (fast) and allows for some pretty complex visual effects. The negative aspects are that it is complicated to learn and isn't supported by Internet Explorer (IE) yet. The factor of it being complicated can by mitigated by using frameworks such as three.js (`https://github.com/mrdoob/three.js/`).

Better animation performance with requestAnimationFrame

Most animation within open web games is created by repeatedly changing what's on the screen with what's known as a loop, and if you do this fast enough, the updating graphics appear to move smoothly.

Until now the easiest way to do this has been with the JavaScript `setTimeout` or `setInterval` methods. However, the problem with this is that they run constantly and can cause all sorts of performance issues. They also don't stop running when a game is left open in an inactive tab or when the browser is minimized, which isn't ideal.

To solve this, the `requestAnimationFrame` JavaScript method has been introduced. The purpose of this method is to give control of the animation loop to the browser so that it can be performed in the most optimal way possible. This often increases performance and prevents those nasty situations where a 30-millisecond loop is running continuously in an inactive tab or hidden browser window. With the new method, the animation loop is drastically slowed down or even stopped, which can have a positive effect on things like battery life on mobile devices.

Music and sound with HTML5 audio and the audio data APIs

Another fundamental aspect to most games is audio, something that until recently would have been difficult to implement and would likely have used Flash. The HTML5 audio element has removed this need and provides a pluginless method of playing audio within the browser.

The limitation of the HTML5 audio element is that its purpose is really to play single audio files, like background music within a game. It isn't suitable for sound effects, particularly if they are fast paced and if there are many of them to play at once.

To solve this, the Audio Data API (Mozilla) and Web Audio API (Chrome) have been introduced to allow for much more fine-grained audio functionality. With these data APIs, you can create sounds from JavaScript, you can edit audio on the fly, you can play more than one channel of audio at a time, and you can retrieve data about the audio in real-time as it plays.

Unfortunately, the audio data APIs solutions aren't yet housed within a single specification, and as such, you need to accommodate both slightly different Mozilla and Chrome proposals. My hope is that in the near future common ground will be found for a single audio data API to be born from.

Real-time multiplayer gameplay with WebSockets

If you're thinking of creating a multiplayer game, then before now you would either have put up with the latency involved in constant AJAX requests, or you would have moved to Flash. Neither option is ideal. What's cool is that since 2011, this is no longer the case, WebSockets have now arrived in all the major browsers (yes, including IE10) to allow for real-time *bi-directional* communication between the browser and a server.

But why is bi-directional real-time communication important for games? Well, this means that you can now literally *stream* data to and from a player's browser in real time. One obvious benefit to this is that it saves bandwidth by not requiring constant AJAX requests to check for new data. Instead, the WebSocket connection is left open and data is instantly pushed to the player or server as soon as it is needed. This is perfect for fast-paced games that require an update every few milliseconds. On top of this, the bi-directional nature of WebSockets means that data can be instantly sent both from the server to the player and from the player to the server *at the same time*.

Store data locally with IndexedDB, Local Storage, and other APIs

Many games require data to be stored on the player's machine so that it can be retrieved at a later date—things like save-game data or cached graphical assets. Until recently, the only way to do this has been to store data on a web server and put up with the latency, or to use things like cookies and only store very small pieces of data.

Fortunately, there are now a variety of solutions that solve various aspects of this problem. The most common are IndexedDB, Local Storage, as well as the various File and FileSystem APIs. The first two allow large quantities of data to be stored in a structural way within a player's browser, with IndexedDB even allowing files to be stored. The File and FileSystem APIs allow a game to access the player's OS file system using JavaScript, letting you save and retrieve files much larger than would be permitted in any other solution.

Play games offline with the application cache

Creating games on the web is all well and good, but what about if you want to play that game offline? Or, what if the player's internet connection drops out half way through an epic gaming session? Most open web games today would, at worst, simply stop working as soon as an internet connection failed, and, at best, they would stop sending data to your server and saving player data. When your player refreshes the page that the game is on, they'll just see a blank page and all their hard work achieved while offline will have been lost. That probably won't make your players very happy, and unhappy players are not ideal.

There are a few solutions available today that can help solve these issues. The first is the application cache, which allows you to use a cache manifest to declare particular assets (like HTML, CSS, images, and JavaScript) that you would like the browser to cache for offline use. Not only that, the browser uses the cached versions of the files when online to speed up the loading process.

Another technique that you can use is to store a player's game data locally and periodically sync it with the game server. Normally you wouldn't be able to store enough data in the browser to achieve this (like with cookies), but with Local Storage and IndexedDB you can now store many megabytes of data in a structured way.

You can also add functionality to your game so that it is alerted when a player's internet connection goes offline. The navigator.onLine property allows you to use JavaScript to see if your player is currently online or not. You can also use the offline and online events to trigger automatic behavior in your game when a change in connection occurs, like stopping all WebSockets communication and caching player data locally until the connection is back.

Immersive gameplay with the FullScreen API

Something that prevents current games on the web from feeling immersive is that they look like they're just tiny boxes embedded into another web site. Why do they feel like that? Well, because they *are* just tiny boxes embedded into other web sites. The odd five-minute puzzle game during your lunch hour might feel OK in a tiny box surrounded by browser UI and other distractions, but a first-person shooter or driving game certainly wouldn't.

Fortunately, the FullScreen API has arrived to solve this problem. It allows you to make any DOM element fill the player's entire screen, something normally only considered for videos. Using this in a game can make the difference between five minutes of relative fun and hours of immersive delight.

Tame the mouse with the Mouse Lock API

An issue related to input in games is that of misbehaving cursors, where the mouse is used to rotate a player around a fixed point (like moving the viewpoint in a 3D first-person shooter) or rotating the player in a top-down 2D game.

In both of these situations, the mouse cursor is visible at all times, which is generally annoying and ruins the experience. However, the most debilitating problem is that all movement stops when the mouse cursor leaves the browser window. This same behavior occurs in full-screen mode when the mouse cursor hits the edge of the screen. It's a horribly simple problem for a player that completely ruins the experience.

The good news is that the Mouse Lock API has been created to solve this problem, and it just landed in experimental builds of Firefox Nightly and will soon land in Chrome (it is likely that the support will be in public builds of these browsers by the time you read this). Its sole purpose is to tame the mouse by hiding the cursor and locking it in place so that it doesn't hit the edges of the screen. This means that instead of relying on x and y coordinate values for mouse position in related to the top-left corner of the browser, you instead rely on x and y distance values from the position that the mouse was locked to.

Console-like experience with the Gamepad API

Another input-related improvement that is coming to the web is that of the GamepadAPI. No longer are the keyboard and mouse the only options available for your players to engage with your game. The GamepadAPI now allows for all sorts of gamepads to be accessed via JavaScript. This even includes some of the console controllers like those on the Xbox 360 and PlayStation 3 (with third-party drivers)!

Like the Mouse Lock API, the GamepadAPI has just landed in experimental builds of Firefox Nightly and Chrome—and it's nice and simple to use (again, it is likely that the support will be in public builds of these browsers by the time you read this). Coupled with the Full Screen API, gamepad support can really change the experience of your game from that of a game within a web site to that of a desktop game or console.

Identify players with services like BrowserID

Just like how iOS has services like OpenFeint and the Apple Game Center, games on the web need open and reliable methods of identifying players. BrowserID is one of Mozilla's solutions to this problem, which allows players to log into your game using their existing e-mail address and without needing a password.

Identifying players in this way is just the first step in providing all sorts of functionality with your game, like friends lists, leader boards, chat, and multiplayer.

Create native OS applications with environments like WebRT

One of the more profound initiatives within Mozilla is the integration of a web run-time (WebRT). It allows players to install your game "natively" on their chosen operating system (Windows, Mac, and Android right now), with a launch icon just like standard OS applications.

WebRT also runs your game using an app-centric user agent (in contrast to browser-centric user agents like Firefox) and runs your game using a separate user profile and OS process to your player's normal Firefox that they use for browsing.

The ability of WebRT to break away into another process and remove all the browser UI makes the experience for gaming that much sweeter. There's something about having an icon in the dock on a Mac that launches your game in its own "native" window with no mention or feel that this is a browser.

As a developer, this is slightly magical. It allows you to break free from a game being a glorified web site and instead turning it into an application, an experience in its own right. Mark my words: this will be a turning point in the transition from five-minute puzzle games on the web to professional-grade games that have a console-like experience.

With much more on the way

These technologies are really just scratching the surface when it comes to creating games on the web using open technologies. Mozilla and other companies are working hard to bring you these APIs and services to help make the web a better place for games.

There are plenty of good open web games out there

Although open web game development is still fairly new, there are already many great examples of games out there today. I'd like to briefly highlight just a few of them.

Bejeweled

Towards the end of 2011, PopCap released a HTML5 version of their massively popular *Bejeweled* game (see Figure 1-1). It uses WebGL to provide accelerated graphics, falling back to HTML5 canvas if WebGL is not supported. You can play this game by visiting `http://bejeweled.popcap.com/html5`.

Angry Birds

Arguably one of the most popular games around right now is *Angry Birds*, and earlier this year Rovio brought out an HTML5 version (see Figure 1-2). It uses WebGL for accelerated graphics. You can play this game by visiting `http://chrome.angrybirds.com`.

Robots Are People Too

Unique gameplay always stands out amongst the plethora of clones and ports from existing and popular games. *Robots Are People Too* (see Figure 1-3) requires two players to cooperate to survive, helped by the innovative split-screen mechanic within the game. It uses HTML5 canvas for the graphics. You can play this game by visiting `http://raptjs.com`.

Runfield

As part of the Firefox 4 release earlier in 2011, *Runfield* (see Figure 1-4) was created to show off some of the capabilities of the browser. It used HTML5 canvas for the graphics and HTML5 audio for the sound. You can play this game by visiting `https://developer.mozilla.org/en-US/demos/detail/runfield`.

TF2 WebGL demo

Arguably not a *real* game is the TF2 demo (see Figure 1-5) created by Brandon Jones. It's a tech demo that shows how Valve's Source maps can be rendered with high performance using WebGL graphics. You can find out more by visiting `http://blog.tojicode.com/2011/10/source-engine-levels-in-webgl-video.html`.

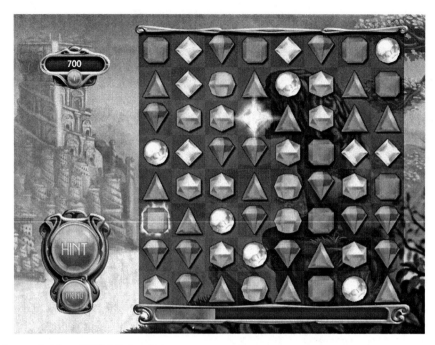

Figure 1-1. Screenshot from HTML5 *Bejeweled*

Figure 1-2. Screenshot from HTML5 *Angry Birds*

Figure 1-3. Screenshot of the *Robots Are People Too* web site

Figure 1-4. Screenshot from *Runfield*

Figure 1-5. Screenshot from Brandon Jones's TF2 WebGL demo

Distribution and monetization options already exist

Something that I touched on earlier in this chapter is the ability to distribute your games and make money from them, something that is necessary for the web to become a viable platform for games. The good news is that there are plenty of services and platforms around to do this, with even more coming in the near future. I'd like to highlight a few of the available options.

Mozilla Labs Apps project

Currently, most app platforms are closed ecosystems that prevent apps and games from being used on all platforms and devices, which threatens the freedom of your users. Mozilla believes that the current app platforms can be improved upon through the creation of an open ecosystem, one that gives developers the ability to distribute their apps and games with as much freedom and choice as possible. Right now this project is called the Mozilla Labs Apps project and much more information can be found out about it online at https://apps.mozillalabs.com.

For the Mozilla app marketplace, the payment provider of choice is PayPal. All you need do is set a price on the store and the rest will happen automatically; as people start paying for your game, you'll start receiving money in your PayPal account. In the future, you'll be able to provide your game on your own web site or another store and charge for it there, too. This means you'll be able to use your own payment provider.

Chrome Web Store

Google's vision of an app platform is the Chrome Web Store. Although closed, the applications on the Chrome Web Store are likely to work on browsers other than Google Chrome; however, they currently can't be installed in those other browsers directly from the store. You can find out more online at http://code.google.com/chrome/apps/.

The Chrome Web Store uses Google Checkout as the payment provider and they will take 5 percent of each transaction, which is significantly less than the rates on platforms like iOS.

Facebook

With over 800 million users, it made a lot of sense for Facebook to get into app distribution. The applications and games provided on Facebook can be installed by any user, with the added draw that you can tap in to the user's social graph of friends. You can find out more online at https://developers.facebook.com/docs/guides/canvas/.

Facebook uses a system called Facebook Credits for in-app and in-game payments and is effectively a proxy on top of a huge selection of standard methods of payments like major credit cards and PayPal.

iOS App Store

Although a closed platform, the App Store is a viable option for open web games that are ported to iOS applications through technologies like PhoneGap (http://phonegap.com). You can find more about distribution via iOS online at http://developer.apple.com/programs/ios/distribute.html.

The iOS App Store uses Apple's own payment gateway and they will take 30 percent of each transaction.

Many more

These three examples are just the tip of the iceberg and it is fair to say that many other companies are exploring the concept of app platforms to help developers distribute and sell their games. It will be interesting to see which solutions have proven the most popular in a few years.

The not-so-good side to open web games

Now, it's very easy to write a chapter like this and focus only on the positive aspects to open web game development. I've tried to present an unbiased view and I believe it is important to highlight some of the non-so-good aspects of the web as a platform for game development (fortunately there aren't many).

The first is that there are varying levels of performance across platforms and devices, which is expected due to hardware, but flies in the face of "write one, use anywhere." Because of this, it is important to research the platforms you are targeting your game towards and make sure that the functionality is supported at a level that will allow your game to be a fun and playable experience.

The second issue is that the support of the gaming-related technologies is inconsistent across the various browsers. For example, the GamepadAPI is only supported in Firefox and Chrome, and there is currently no word on whether the other browsers will adopt it. The same can be said for the Mouse Lock API and a few others. Another example is that Internet Explorer doesn't support WebGL and is unlikely to support it in the near future, at least until they stop developing Silverlight.

The final issue is that the open nature of game development on the web is just not feasible for some people right now, perhaps due to legal requirements. As I've mentioned previously, it is highly unlikely that the open foundation of the web will change enough to accommodate DRM and compiled code across all browsers. If the open nature really is not an option to you, then perhaps open web gaming is not something to consider until you can justify the pros and cons that come with it as a platform.

However, all of this doesn't necessarily mean other platforms are more viable. For example, Flash isn't developed for mobile devices any longer and other technologies like Google's Native Client don't work in all browsers. No single platform is perfect, and no single platform will rule them all. It is important not to pit the platforms as equals and to treat them as individuals; that way, you will pick the right one for your needs.

What does the future hold and what still needs to be done?

I hope it is obvious by now that we're living in a massively exciting time for open web game development. I also hope it's obvious that open web gaming isn't a magic bullet that solves the problems of all the other platforms out there. In fact, this is categorically untrue and it won't be a viable platform for all games and developers. Just because there is an open web game development platform, it doesn't mean that everyone should be using it.

Aside from that, it is clear that open web game development is something to celebrate. It is a platform that is improving each and every day, but to do that, there are a few key events that need to occur.

The first is that browsers need to consistently adopt the necessary technologies for open web games, specifically in order to stop the platform battles we're seeing with the current influx of WebKit-only games that target the Chrome Web Store. Prominent examples of areas to improve are the audio data APIs, WebGL, the Gamepad API, and the Mouse Lock API.

Second, more methods of distribution and monetization are needed. We need solutions that are cross-browser and distributed in themselves, like the Mozilla Labs Apps project. After all, there is no point in web games if they can't be used and installed from all browsers and platforms.

Third, we need proven and easy-to-use systems for monetizing games, both through initial unit sales and through further in-game purchases. PayPal and Google Checkout are great, but this is the web and we need to allow developers to choose their own payment systems and be given the freedom that the web allows.

We also need more documentation and shared code to help novices and proprietary game developers get started. The beauty of the open web games community is that it can thrive off the sharing of techniques and code to help others create games, just as web developers share code and techniques for building web sites. We also need more specific documentation on areas that are less about making a fun game and more about making a living from your work and marketing your game effectively.

And finally, we need a success story like the *Angry Birds* or *Minecraft* of open web games. We need this to validate the open web as a platform for games and show that money can be made. I think this will be a pre-cursor for the influx of large-game studios and investment funds getting involved in a significant way.

Perhaps you will be the spark that helps propel the open web as a viable and stable platform for game development. I sure hope so.

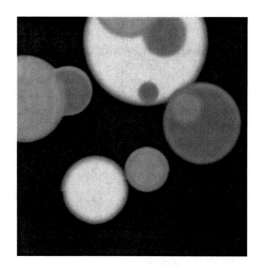

Chapter 2

Complexity from Simplicity

This chapter will take a look at game design to see how you can make a game fun at its most basic level. A case study of a game called "A to B" will be used to highlight some of the essential theories of design implementation. This chapter will also discuss the use of the JavaScript library, Processing.js in the implementation of A to B. We will go over some advantages and disadvantages of building your game with this framework.

By the end of this chapter, you will have a better understanding of the following:

- Game design fundamentals
- Workflow
- Processing.js
- How to use Processing.js for HTML5 games

Who am I?

As of this writing, I am working towards a graduate degree in media art at Emerson College in Boston, Massachusetts. The beginning of my academic career was centrally focused on computer science. As I advanced, however, I found myself less interested in algorithms and efficiency and more interested in graphics. This sparked an exploration into the fine arts. At the end of my undergraduate studies, I found that the overlap of the two fields was what really inspired me. Since then, I've been exploring the hybrid art of programming and visuals. This has manifested in the form of data visualizations, interactive installations, and most recently, gaming.

Game design background

Unlike many game designers, I have never been obsessed with gaming. As a child, I was not allowed to own a gaming console (PC not included) until I was in high school. However, like most game enthusiasts, I can recall the first moment games became an important part of my life. For me, it was when my babysitter brought me a floppy disk (remember those?) with the classic Atari games. I can't even begin to imagine how many hours I logged playing *Asteroids* and *Battlezone*. From then on, I have been in and out of the game world. Occasionally, I find a great game that captivates me for a couple weeks, but I am not a gamer.

More recently, my work began to take on some game-like qualities. It started with an experimental game called "The Sea," which was an attempt to bring Brian Eno's theory of ambient music into the realm of gaming. While it wasn't well-received by my peers (mainly due to the fact that it was a game without input), it got me in the game mindset. The timing was just right for me to get into games. I was not only reading some wonderful theories on gaming, but HTML5 was hitting the web. As a freelance web designer, naturally this was on my radar. It was at that time that I realized I needed to make a game for the web.

A to B

For my first HTML5 game, I created a simple puzzle game called A to B (check it out at http://russellgoldenberg.com/atob). Like the title states, the goal of the game is to get a ball from point A to point B (see Figure 2-1). Before the game even starts, the player is greeted with an old-school, high-score list, much like old arcades. The game environment is an empty two-dimensional space. At the beginning of each level, the ball is placed (frozen) at a pre-determined point A on the screen. There is a point B that refers to the target, and a set of modifiers on the bottom.

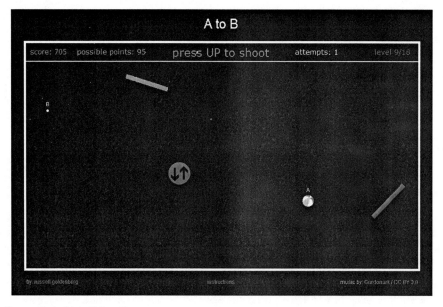

Figure 2-1. Screenshot of A to B in action

When the player presses Go, the ball is launched (at the same angle and velocity every time), and then is subjected to gravity. If the ball hits point B, the player receives points and moves on to the next level. If the ball goes off screen, the ball is returned to its original resting position and is allowed to go again until the player hits point B. In order for the ball to get to point B, the player must position a set of modifiers to guide the ball there. The possible modifiers include a wall, a bouncy wall, a speed booster, a speed reducer, and a gravity flipper. Each level has between one and five modifiers. The ball *must* interact with each modifier in order to pass the level. Additionally, a modifier becomes invisible or non-interactive once it has been used.

There are 18 levels in all. The levels start out with only one modifier and eventually progress up to a set of five. The player can obtain a maximum of 100 points each level. The way the scoring system works is that a player starts with 100 potential points. With each failed attempt, the points available decrease by five. Essentially, if a player wants to score any points at all, he must get the ball to point B in less than 20 attempts.

Influence and inspiration

A to B is actually derived from a piece I created a year earlier called "Infinite Loop" (see Figure 2-2), which was essentially a criticism of certain online games. The entire "game" consisted of a ball that you need to drop through a loop to hit a target. Every time you hit the target, you would get a point. The game would continue forever until the player quit. The experiment was to see how long people would actually repeat the boring task simply to receive points.

Figure 2-2. Screenshot from the game Infinite Loop

At its core, A to B is influenced by the Atari classics that I mentioned earlier. At the start, I recognized that since I am new to gaming, I needed to keep it simple. *Asteroids* was in black and white and the player controlled a triangle, yet somehow it was one of the most compelling games I ever played. I decided that in order to enter into the world of gaming, I needed to understand fundamentally why games are fun. Without going into the detail, I will strongly recommend reading a copy of Ralph Koster's *A Theory of Fun for Game Design* (Paraglyph Press, 2004). This text was an extremely insightful look into what makes games fun. Inspired by his discussion and my appreciation of some of the originals, I set out with a strong vision for A to B.

Brainstorming phase

All the details and many alterations of A to B were conceived during brainstorming sessions. I find that a very informal and unplanned brainstorming process works best. This produces the most natural flow of ideas and information. For me, this amounted to a pretty simple loop. One day when thinking about the game (usually on the train to school or while exercising), I would have an idea for how something should function. I would then sketch out my vision and present it to a friend. The process of clearly explaining my idea was not only good for the friend to see what I was seeing, but it also provided an indirect way to stumble upon more issues and possibilities. In particular, I found that almost all the good "what-ifs" came from conversations with my friends. Having active conversations was the best way to get the creative juices flowing and to consider other viewpoints, eventually resulting in the best possible implementation.

Pre-production

Once the idea was officially cemented, it was time to plan out the development. The first thing I determined was the technology. Having decided the game was going to be exclusively HTML5, I knew I was going to be using the newly-implemented canvas and audio tags. I also realized that I wanted a high-score table, both for the retro-arcade feel and as a secondary motivational factor in the game itself.

In order to make the high-score table, I needed to utilize an online database, so I went with MySQL and PHP to make that happen. In terms of the actual scripting for the game, I decided to use the Processing.js (PJS) library. PJS is a JavaScript port of Processing, a popular creative coding language geared towards artists and beginner programmers. It has become a cornerstone in the programming world because it is both accessible for new users and powerful to handle advanced ideas and implementation. PJS allows the developer to write in the original Processing syntax, which is then automatically converted to the canvas element. This was a major factor in the timeline for the A to B project because I am an avid Processing user. PJS enabled me to handle the bulk of the coding and debugging within the familiar Processing environment before making it internet-ready.

This brings me to another lesson that I learned; which is as long as the job gets finished, who cares what you used to do it? People are often too concerned with keeping up with the latest and greatest technology. If the end product is what matters, then it shouldn't matter how you get there, as long as you do.

In addition to learning a bit of PHP and MySQL, I had to touch up on my jQuery skills. jQuery proved to be very helpful with the high-score table. Since JavaScript is a client-side language, I needed a way to read and write to my database from the JavaScript, which is where jQuery came in handy.

Once I established the technology, I set up a list of deliverables and deadlines. Planning out a timeline for this is useful for project organization and motivation. Having certain deliverables due at a certain time not only made me stay on schedule, but prevented me from getting sidetracked. My initial goal was to finish the entire project in four weeks and be able to submit it to a few different game festivals. By planning out due dates, I was able to realize these goals.

Production

The development of A to B followed a pretty standard loop, which looked like Figure 2-3.

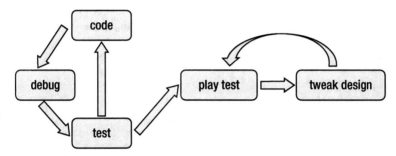

Figure 2-3. Stages of development of the game

While it is generally good practice to plan the entire system before one begins development, I followed a looser approach. Since I knew the game wasn't going be a large scale software project, I knew I could get away with a more unscripted design. Essentially, this resulted in less efficient and less modular code. There are many people (like me), however, that believe that as long as you get the job done effectively, it doesn't matter how you get there. As you can see in Figure 2-3, I always started by coding something. Usually, I would break down my code sessions to set up and accomplish small achievements. For example, one session revolved around getting a ball to adhere to "real" physics.

Instead of building the system with breadth and no depth, I approached a specific topic and went all the way down. Although this was less modular in terms of focus and learning, it proved to be a more effective approach. I would immerse myself in a single issue and not stop until it was resolved. This allowed me to not have a bunch of loose ends to tie up at the end.

The next layer of production after coding, debugging, and testing, was play testing. Play testing is one of the most helpful areas of the development process. During play testing two major things occur: bugs and what-ifs. When coding, you often lose sight of the bigger picture. You know exactly how you want things to function, but you don't see it from a different perspective. Having other people who aren't familiar with the operations of the code play test for you is like stepping back from the painting. In doing so, they may approach the same problem from a different angle. This can reveal inconsistencies or bugs in your code. It is much like pouring water in a bucket. If there are tiny holes, it will be obvious where they are.

Additionally, and possibly more importantly, you will begin pondering the what-ifs. What-ifs are an extension of the brainstorming phase. As you're watching the tester play, you immediately see something that could be changed, enhanced, or removed that will make the game better. To help manifest this activity, you should inform your players to use the "think aloud" method. This is a common practice in user interface prototyping. You instruct players to verbalize all of the decisions and thoughts that are going through their minds as best they can. This gives you insight into what everything in your game is triggering in players' minds. If a player sees a red object and is thinking it means danger (but it doesn't), then maybe you need to change the color. Small details of what the mind is actively doing can expose flaws and/or things that are successfully working in your game.

Once the game engine was in place, it was time to sugarcoat it. Since A to B is minimalist at its core, the graphics needed to represent that. I chose to stick with few effects and basic graphics to embody this theme. I believe this emphasized the point of the game, which was built on the basic concept of getting the ball from one point to another. To make the game a little more alive, I added a soundtrack. I chose to utilize the web resource ccmixter.org. This web site provides Creative Commons licensed music. Each song on the site specifically covers how the song may be used; be it commercial or personal use, it is very explicit. I found a fun and simple song called "Kindergarten" by a user named Gurdonark.

Post-production and release

Once the site was up and running, submissions to festivals and a little promotion was in order. Being a novice game developer, I was unfamiliar with many of the available festivals. In the end, I only ended up submitting it to two competitions: the IGF Student Showcase and Mozilla's Game On competition. I did a small bit of social network promotion to get some foundational users as well. A few posts to both Facebook and Twitter got friends and some random people involved. There are many other ways to promote your game, but I was relying on the power of word of mouth to carry this project.

Reception

As of this writing, the high score on A to B is 1795 (see Figure 2-4). Sadly, I do not possess the high score; although I am on the list with 1665. A perfect game would be an 1800. I still have not figured out how the highest score was even possibly obtained.

In Mozilla's HTML5 game competition, A to B was a finalist. The game has also been featured on a few blogs and HTML5 game sites, and reviewed on playthisthing.com. Within the first three months of the release, it received over 10,000 plays. To date, 274 people have beaten the entire game.

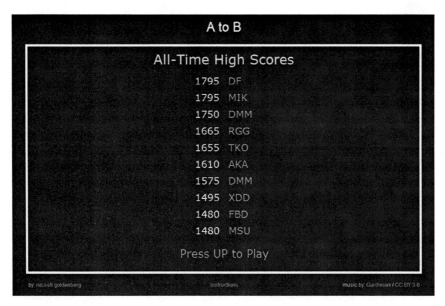

Figure 2-4. A to B high-score list

Rules of simplicity

A to B helped me learn a few valuable lessons for making a simple, yet compelling, game.

- *Focus on the core mechanics.* By keeping A to B stripped down and transparent, the player is able to participate directly with the core mechanics of the game. While I'm not saying that every game should do this, it does prove a valuable lesson: the core mechanics are what ultimately drive the game. In A to B, there is no story involved or other components to get distracted by. The game's title even reflects this transparent nature of the mechanism. Despite the lack of substance or depth, however, the game is still fun and played by many people. That is because as a designer, I only worry about the game's mechanics. The object of the game is clear, and the player's role is also clear: move the modifiers so that the ball hits them and gets to point B. By focusing my attention on how that simple process would work, as well as continually tweaking everything based on that idea, the game became a success.

- *Aesthetics are secondary.* This is basically a sub-section of rule number one. Like the story, the aesthetics are mostly fluff. Aesthetics can play a major role in the game, but I feel that it is secondary. Aesthetics are what initially intrigue players; mechanics are what make them continue playing. There is no doubt that aesthetic choices can have a major impact on the game, but they are like a magic spell that eventually wears off. If the visuals and audio are amazing but the game play is boring, a player will stop playing. The substance of the game is the mechanics, so don't invest too much effort into the aesthetics unless it plays an integral role in the core of the game.

- *Be explicit with instructions.* Since there are hundreds of thousands of games available, a player won't give a game much of a chance to let it make its point. Therefore, it needs to be clear and not frustrating to learn how to play the game. It is important to immediately provide the tools for or instruction on how to play your game. Players should be able to participate and understand how the mechanics work right off the bat. This does not imply, however, teaching players how to solve the problems. You want to leave that to them, because that is the point of the game.

- *Don't reveal everything.* Although we want the player to immediately understand how the mechanics work, you don't want to give away everything. The element of positive surprise is a very powerful tool in games. Players enjoy discovering something unexpected. Therefore, it is wise to keep some things hidden. Even in a simple game like A to B, I was able to withhold some key information and let the players discover it on their own. I utilized the fact that players didn't necessarily realize that they could make a ball go in the opposite direction. More astute players discovered this right away, while others came to realize it down the road—creating an "Aha!" moment.

- *Patterns are good.* The final rule of simplicity is about creating patterns. Patterns allow you, as a developer, to recycle code and mechanics. This makes it super-easy to create new levels and experiences without having to do much work. In order for this to work from a player's perspective, you must continue to feed them new content. While they will enjoy recognizing the patterns, they need something fresh to apply them to. For example, in A to B, when a player realizes that a good combo is to use a speed reducer immediately followed by a bouncy wall, he discovers a re-usable pattern. By changing up the locations of points A and B, however, and adding additional modifiers, the player is presented with a new situation to apply what they've learned. This is an effective method to keep the player in a state of flow. This means the challenge is the perfect balance between difficult and easy. By slowly compounding more and more of the skills they have developed, you can maintain this flow state and progress from easy to difficult levels quite smoothly.

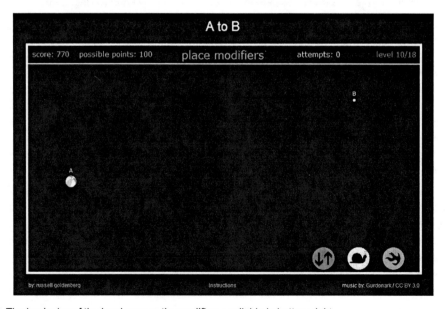

Figure 2-5. The beginning of the level screen, the modifiers available in bottom right

Why A to B works

Whether or not you care for the simple graphics, game play in A to B just works. This can be attributed to much of the theory that I read surrounding game development. First and foremost was Jesse Schell's *Art of Game Design: A Book of Lenses* (Morgan Kaufmann, 2008). This book did a fantastic job breaking down game design. Everything from inspiration to execution was covered in detailed and easily digestible checklists and methods. In the book, Schell claims that the mechanics are the foundation of the game, so most of your attention needs to be focused on it. For me, this was the most important piece of information in the book, and became the basis for my first rule of simplicity.

Another helpful idea was from the seminal work on the concept of flow by Mihaly Csikszentmihalyi. Flow is the idea that a perfect state of mind is achieved through the balance of skill and challenge. Too much challenge causes anxiety, too little causes boredom. There are number of other resulting emotions, but flow occurs when everything is just right. This idea was instrumental in the process of level design. Between fine-tuning the positions of A and B, along with carefully selecting the number and set of modifiers, I hoped to provide the perfect balance. This is essential in almost any type of game. If the game starts out and is too challenging, the player will quit. If it takes too long to become challenging, the player will quit. The level of skill involved in the challenges provided another key component. In a game like A to B that relies on precision and repetition, everything needed to be entirely skill-based. Leaving anything up to chance would simply frustrate the player. However, there are certain games where chance and uncertainty play an important role in the game. It is crucial to analyze your exact circumstances to decide how much skill vs. chance should be involved.

One of the most important elements to the success of the game was the balance of risk vs. reward. Similar to skill and chance, there needs to be an appropriate balance between the two, or else a game will feel "off." With A to B, reward always came in the form of more points. Risk is a little more difficult to identify, but was equally as critical. For example, if a player has laid a certain path of modifiers and is struggling to get to point B, there are two options. The first and safer method is to continue to tweak the current setup slightly until the ball reaches point B. The riskier, but potentially more rewarding option is to totally rearrange the modifiers to create a different strategy. While this might pay off big-time, the player might also end up back-tracking and have to do many more minor tweaks. This example illustrates how you can provide subtle design elements to make for a more compelling game.

Processing.js

While Processing has been around since 2004 and has grown into a powerful tool, Processing.js is in its infancy. There are a few distinctions between Processing and its JavaScript brother. Processing has more than 100 libraries. This is a central attraction to using Processing because it greatly expands its functionality. The libraries include everything from physics simulation to camera and face detection. The first downside of the JavaScript version is that there is no ability to import and utilize these libraries. Essentially, you only have access to the core functionality of Processing. That being said, there are people out there who are attempting to port some of the popular libraries to JavaScript to allow for some more expanded integration.

Additionally, Processing.js lacks power. In the original version, you can draw thousands of objects to the screen without sacrificing frame rate. With the JavaScript port, however, there is a significant disparity between the two. This is largely due to the constraints of using the HTML5 canvas; but with each browser update, we are seeing increased rendering speeds on the side of the canvas.

How does Processing.js work?

Although Processing.js can be viewed as a "lite" version of Processing, it is still an exceptional tool considering that it runs on the web. The way it works from a user perspective is quite simple. All you have to do is code as you would in Processing. Then, when you want to make the project web-ready, you follow some simple instructions to connect it to the canvas. The way Processing.js works is that it simply converts what you've written and applies it to the HTML5 element, the canvas tag. It makes life easier for the coder because instead of learning a new technology, you can simply apply what you already know and instantly make Processing sketches deployable on the web.

> **Note** In Processing, a sketch is simply the resulting visual application that runs once your code has been compiled.

Who should use Processing.js?

New coders would benefit from using Processing.js. Since the library revolves around the creation of visuals, it is a very intuitive way for beginners to learn and understand the concepts of programming. You don't even need to download any software to get started. If you check out the Resources section of this chapter, you will find a few different online editors that make working with Processing.js hassle-free.

Web designers who want to add some interactivity or dynamic elements to their web sites can also benefit from using it.

Game developers are another group that should utilize Processing.js for the ease of creating graphics and visuals, and the power of flexibility. Not only do I find working with Processing.js more intuitive than JavaScript and the canvas API, but you are able to intertwine the two.

In short, Processing makes programming accessible. It enables people with little to no coding knowledge an easy transition to powerful tools. It also provides experienced programmers with dozens of libraries geared towards coding visuals to accommodate a nearly infinite array of ideas.

What are its strengths and weaknesses?

The two major players in the creative, coding-specific software industry are Processing and openFrameworks. The major difference between the two is that openFrameworks is based on C++ while Processing is based on Java. All in all, they are very similar in terms of functionality and capability, much like Coke and Pepsi. While other creative coding software exists (Cinder, VVVV, and nodeBox, to name a few), Processing and openFrameworks are the most popular.

In regards to the JavaScript version of Processing, the following is a rundown of the strengths and weaknesses of Processing.js:

Strengths

- Excellent graphics library
- Don't need to learn JavaScript
- Great forum and community
- Cross-browser compatibility
- Can write stand-alone or JavaScript integrated code
- It's free!

Weaknesses

- Limited functionality (missing a few core libraries, such as video and audio support)
- Limited access to Processing libraries
- Difficult to debug
- Significantly less powerful than the offline version

Is it a good fit for games?

The short answer: yes.

Certain types of games will lend themselves better to using Processing.js. Puzzle-based games like mine that are less reliant upon stunning visuals are the perfect form for Processing.js. With fewer on-screen objects to be rendered, the canvas has no issue. A full-on, simulation-based soccer game or a multi-player shooter, on the other hand, is best left to the more sophisticated engines like Unity, which has a far more powerful graphics-rendering engine that can handle a large amount of objects. Unity is, at heart, a game engine; so it has built-in game functionality that relieves you from making code.

I believe that the aesthetic is what draws you in to a game, while the game play is what keeps you there. If you design with this in mind, Processing.js can be the perfect solution—not only to prototype a game, but to create a final product.

Examples and integration of Processing.js

With all of this talk about Processing.js, it is time to take a look at how easy it is to put into action. This section will take a look at the basics of getting started with Processing.js. I will provide a few examples with code on how to get started. We will also take a look at a few of the tricks that I learned to make some of the more important features happen.

Basic Processing syntax

If you are familiar with Processing or Java, this bit will look familiar to you.

```
void setup(){
size(400,200);
}
void draw(){
background(0);
fill(255,0,0);
ellipse(mouseX,mouseY,50,50);
}
```

This is a very basic example of the Processing syntax. This code will create a canvas that is 400 × 200 pixels. It will then repeatedly draw an ellipse at the x and y positions from the mouse's current location for width and a height of 50 pixels. The color will be red. As mentioned earlier, Processing is basically a wrapper for Java. With Processing, there is a setup function that is run only once on the start; then the draw loop runs repeatedly until the program exits. Also, creating any sort of graphic is as simple as entering the parameters into the function.

Embedding a sketch

Now that we've had a glimpse of what Processing looks like, we will now take a look at how you embed it into your HTML to get it up and running with the canvas tag. Let's say you have written the program in the previous section (called a "sketch" in Processing lingo). The sketch will have a file name ending with the extension .pde. The following shows how to embed our example.pde sketch into HTML5.

```
<html>
<head>
<title>Processing with HTML5 </title>
<script type="text/javascript" src="processing.js"></script>
</head>
<body>
<canvas id="processingCanvas" data-processing-sources="example.pde"/>
</canvas>
</body>
</html>
```

You only need two things to get your first sketch up and running online: your processing sketch and the processing.js file, which can be downloaded at Processing.js.org/download. Simply download the latest stable version of the processing-x.x.x.js file, and you are ready to go. All you have to do is define the canvas, tell it to load your sketch, and voila, you have Processing on the web. In the upcoming release of Processing (2.0), you can actually click a button to switch into JavaScript mode. This means you don't even have to download a library because when you export your sketch, it will create the web page and include the JS library by default.

In-line processing

For people like me, you may want more access to the code than this. Processing.js allows you to write your Processing code directly in the script tag. The processing.js file will automatically convert what you write into Processing. The following is what the same sketch would look like using this method.

```
<html>
        <head>
                <title>Processing in HTML5</title>
                <script type="text/javascript" src="processing.js"></script>

        </head>
        <body>
                <script type="application/processing" >
                void setup() {
                size(400,200);
                }
                void draw() {
                background(0);
                fill(255,0,0);
                ellipse(mouseX,mouseY,50,50);
                }


                </script>
                <canvas id="processingCanvas"></canvas>
        </body>
        </html>
```

Notice that instead of the standard type="text/javascript" we have replaced that with "application/processing". This lets the compiler know that we are including Processing in here, not just JavaScript.

Integrating JavaScript

So why do this over the embed version? Because now you are able to combine JavaScript and Processing code in the same space. The compiler will be able to differentiate between the two. This means you can use a hybrid style of coding that gives you access to functions of Processing and traditional JavaScript. Let's say we have a simple ellipse that is growing in size. If we want to alert the user once it has hit a certain size, we can tap into the JavaScript functionality right inside the Processing code.

```
<html>
        <head>
                <title>Processing in HTML5</title>
                <script type="text/javascript" src="processing.js"></script>

        </head>
        <body>
                <script type="application/processing" >
                int ellipseSize = 5;
                void setup() {
```

```
size(400,200);
}
void draw() {
background(0);
fill(250);
ellipse(mouseX,mouseY,ellipseSize,ellipseSize);
ellipseSize++;
if(ellipseSize==100){
alert("the ellipse is 100!");
}
}


</script>

<canvas id="processingCanvas"></canvas>
</body>
</html>
```

Switching between the JavaScript and Processing code couldn't be easier. You can also pass variables and values from JavaScript into the Processing code. This functionality makes Processing.js a great choice for people who already know JavaScript. You get a very powerful graphics library that plays nicely with the canvas tag.

Using audio

Audio is another feature that nearly anyone making a game will need. In A to B, I made use of both background music and small audio bits throughout the game. To incorporate audio into your HTML game, you must make use of another new feature of HTML5, the audio tag.

First, you must create your audio tags, which is done in the body of your HTML. By default, the audio tags will create mini audio players that will appear on screen. You can turn these off in your stylesheet.

```
<audio id="sound1"><source src="boom.mp3"></audio>
```

This is a basic audio tag. However, there are a few properties that you can define within the tag that are really helpful. For example, I wanted my background soundtrack to loop repeatedly throughout the game and play automatically once it loaded.

```
<audio id="soundtrack" autoplay loop><source src="snowfall.mp3"></audio>
```

Once you have created your audio object, you are ready to insert it into your Processing code. You can place this anywhere, just make sure you use the proper variable names.

```
document.getElementById("sound1").play();
```

Since different browsers utilize different audio codecs, it is important to have multiple types of audio files to ensure cross-browser compatibility. Use a free application like Audacity to convert your audio file to other formats. For example, if you wanted to have an MP3 version and a WAV version, it would look like this:

```
<audio id="sound1"><source src="boom.mp3"><source src="boom.wav"></audio>
```

The browser will choose whichever audio file that it supports to load.

Importing and loading images

For anyone out there that wants to make a game, it is quite likely that you will want to have some sort of images involved. In order to incorporate them in your Processing.js code, it is handled a bit differently than with building web sites. The following is a sample code that will import two images and then display them on the screen. Also, two slashes (//) means a comment in Processing. I will use the comments in line to describe what is going on.

```
<script type="application/processing">
//first we have to preload the images from the directory, assuming they are in the root
folder
/* @pjs preload="snow.png , squiggle.png"; */

//next, we must make some variables that will reference these images

PImage theSnow, theSquig;


void setup(){
size(400,200);

//in Processing, you must load the images inside of the setup function

theSnow = loadImage("snow.png");
theSquig = loadImage("squiggle.png");

}
void draw(){
background(255);
//displaying the images simply pass the function the variable and a location

image(theSnow,0,0);
image(theSquig,mouseX,mouseY);

}
</script>
```

One thing to note is that when you preload and load the images, you must make sure to include the proper path to the file. For example, if the picture is in a sub-folder called `pictures`, in both places it would look like `"/pictures/theBall.jpg"`.

High-score list with jQuery

In order to implement a high-score list, you need to create a database. Once a database is created and you have written the PHP file that talks to the database, you can make calls to the database within the Processing code. Normally this would not work because PHP is a server-side language, while JavaScript is client-side; but thanks to the magic of jQuery, it is possible. Simply use the jQuery `$.post` function. The following is my code:

```
$.post("highscorelist.php",{score: theScore, name: playerName},function(data){
result = data;
}
```

As long as you can do some simple PHP communication, you can easily implement any sort of data storage that you can envision.

Summary

By now you have hopefully witnessed the power of Processing.js and the benefits of keeping things simple. While games are becoming more graphically and technologically advanced, a good game must always adhere to some core principles. The cliché expression "the simplest idea is often the best" couldn't be more true when it comes to online games. Players have extremely short attention spans, so it pays to concentrate on the heart of the experience to make it come across.

Resources

To learn more about Processing, check out some of the following web sites:

- `processing.org`: download processing; check out the forum, examples, and reference docs

- `Processingjs.org`: the JavaScript port of Processing

- `sketchpad.cc`: an online editor to write and save Processing.js sketches

- `openprocessing.org`: share and explore sketches

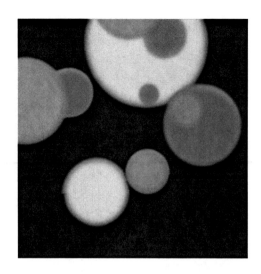

Chapter 3

How to Make Multi-Platform HTML5 Games from Scratch

Introduction

Today, applications like Twitter, or games like *Angry Birds*, are available on many platforms. The number of different instances of an application can become huge.

Such an application can target the number of platforms (mobile, tablet, desktop), the number of operating systems (iOS, Android, webOS, etc.) and the number of application versions (free and full versions, for instance). Hence, there are potentially **P*O*V** applications to develop.

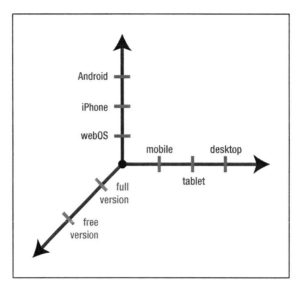

Figure 3-1. Various platform directions

It's almost unfeasible to develop so many instances and maintain them yourself. You want to fix bugs and add features once—and only once.

Hence, what's required is a common language to describe an application for multiple instances—and that's exactly what the web proposes. We don't need to learn new, device-specific languages, and API—the web is our strong, high-level, common language.

Recent years have seen a powerful rise of web technologies, including the advancement of rendering engines (WebKit, Gecko, etc.), the considerable improvement of JavaScript engines (V8, SpiderMonkey, etc.), and the emergence of new HTML5 API and CSS3 support (Animations, Transitions, etc.). It's highly likely that these standard technologies will replace RIA (Rich Internet Application) browser plugins like Flash or Silverlight.

> **Note** WebKit is an open-source layout engine that is broadly used across multiple platforms, such as desktop browsers like Chrome and Safari; Android smartphones and the iPhone; the Android tablet and the iPad; and "smart" TV (for example, France's Freebox 6 browser). Future devices will probably continue using WebKit, benefitting from its experience and performance.

Having this portable technology, we must now find an easy way to integrate our application to any app store (Android Market, Apple Store, Chrome Web Store). We also want to keep a single code source to write and maintain. This will be done through the use of frameworks. We'll talk about PhoneGap, which provides a skeleton required for packaging an application for an OS and the PhoneGap JavaScript library, which exposes an API to exploit full functionality of the device.

Throughout this chapter, we will examine the case study of *Same Game Gravity* (a game available on six platforms: iPad, iPhone, Android, web, Chrome Store, and Facebook; see http://github.com/gre/chess-game) and look at how we can apply these lessons to our own projects.

Same Game Gravity is a mind-bending, ball removal puzzle game where you try to remove all of the balls from a board. Balls can only be removed when they are grouped with others of the same color. The balls are influenced by gravity. On mobile, you influence gravity by rotating your device, and on the desktop you have arrow keys.

The *Same* game is not new, but the gravity principle gives it a unique twist. You can rotate the game board through 360 degrees to change the gravity of the game and consequently, the balls' positions.

The first challenge in the game development was to maintain most of common source code while adapting it to the device. For instance, the game's gravity is handled by the accelerometer for mobile and tablet versions, but just the mouse/keyboard for the web version.

The second challenge was to reduce maintenance cycles (bug fixes, features add) and game instance "deployment." Reducing the number of steps to move from a **n** to a **n+1** version on different markets is very important, so we need tools to easily build game packages (in fact, PhoneGap build is a new web service that satisfies this need).

For *Same Game Gravity*, I developed and used a micro framework I called "WebAppBuilder," which is a mashup of tools to perform different game instances "compilation."

Once we've covered the basics, we will then apply this knowledge to creating a multi-platform chess game that will run on desktops and smartphones.

The web offers an interesting architecture for making dynamic applications. Web development is usually split in three parts: HTML, CSS and JavaScript. Let's focus on and independently explain the power of each—then mix them together to bootstrap our multi-platform chess game from scratch.

Three-part code organization

Web client-side development is about HTML, CSS, and JavaScript. Basically, HTML helps us to describe **the content**, CSS describes **how that content is displayed**, and JavaScript describes **what the content does**.

It is essential to make the best use of each part and not to blend their goals. The source code separation is important because it adds modularity for the developer and allows us to be more productive: we only have to focus on one part at a time and our repository also becomes far more maintainable.

For now we will focus only on client-side parts of a game, but it is also possible to have a web server that receives, for instance, player scores via asynchronous requests (Asynchronous JavaScript and XML).

HTML, a content language

HTML (HyperText Markup Language) is the language that describes all the content of a web page. Like XML, it is a *markup language*, meaning it is structured as a tree of tags with content. The current range of available HTML elements is very rich. It links and structures different resources: images, videos, stylesheets, and JavaScript scripts (to learn more about all available elements, see the Other Resources section).

The most recently released version of the HTML specification is HTML4, but for several years the fifth version has been a work in progress and its release is imminent. But "HTML5" as a buzzword describes more than just the next version of HTML: it includes new HTML5 tags, new (JavaScript) APIs like canvas, video, audio, geolocation, drag and drop, and more.

Writing HTML5 is straightforward. All HTML source code should start with a doctype, a meta comment that describes the nature of a document. For HTML5, it's simply `<!DOCTYPE html>`.

This doctype must be followed by an `<html>` tag containing all the HTML content.

This tag will contain two tags:

- The `<head>` tag contains all the metadata and resources to load.
- The `<body>` tag contains the body of the page; in other words, the content to display.

Listing 3-1. Hello world in HTML

```
<!DOCTYPE html>
<html>
  <head>
    <title>My first page</title>
  </head>
  <body>
    <h1>Hello world!</h1>
  </body>
</html>
```

Bootstrapping our game

It is good practice is to keep HTML code simple, readable, semantic, and valid. Again, HTML should only focus on "the content." This will help to keep your application portable. A good reference for how to best control your HTML content to keep the code simple is *Pro HTML5 and CSS3 Design Patterns* by Michael Bowers, Dionysios Synodinos, and Victor Sumner (Apress, 2010). This book provides solid templates and guidelines to minimize verbosity in your HTML code.

Now let's analyze how a game is structured. You often have different pages, like the menu page, the settings page, the about page, the help page, the high score page, and the game page itself.

For our chess game, we'll just have a menu page, a game page, and a help page.

Listing 3-2. game.html

```
<!DOCTYPE html>
<html>
<head>
  <meta name="viewport" content="user-scalable=no, width=device-width, initial-scale=1, ↵
  maximum-scale=1, minimum-scale=1;" />
  <title>A Chess Game</title>
  <link href="game.css" rel="stylesheet">
```

```
  <script type="text/javascript" src="game.js"></script>
</head>
<body>
  <div id="pages">
    <section id="menu" class="current"></section>
    <section id="game"></section>
    <section id="help"></section>
  </div>
</body>
```

In the <head>

The `meta` viewport tag helps to display the game on smartphones and tablets, and avoids some default web page behaviors like zooming.

We link the CSS stylesheet with a `link` tag, and the actual game logic JavaScript script with a `script` tag. These two resources will be loaded and executed before the page displays.

In the <body>

Instead of having multiple content HTML files, we have chosen to represent each page of the game with an HTML5 section tag. This gives us a simple maintainable codebase. These sections are wrapped in a `<div id="pages">`. Defining an id for each section is important in order to be easily styled in CSS and accessed via JavaScript.

We must also identify which page is currently visible. This is the goal of the "current" class. And that's all for the moment; but in the coming sections, we are going to style the page in CSS and make a page router system in JavaScript.

> **Note**   An important convention we have taken is to order pages by navigation level. This means the menu page comes before the game page or the help page. This will help us in the next CSS section.

We can now focus on the content of each page. See Listing 3-3.

Listing 3-3. Menu Section

```
<section id="menu">
  <h1><img src="icon.png"/> Chess</h1>
  <ul>
    <li><a class="showOnlyIfContinuableGame" href="#!/game/continue">Continue
Game</a></li>
    <li><a href="#!/game/new">New Game</a></li>
    <li><a href="#!/help">Help</a></li>
  </ul>
</section>
```

The menu is simply a title followed by a list of links, where each link targets another page. We have chosen to start the `href` of pages with a "#!/". The JavaScript router explained in the JavaScript section will work with this convention.

CSS, a descriptive stylesheet language

CSS (Cascading Style Sheets) allows us to easily describe web application styles through a list of rules. CSS is often neglected or misunderstood in game development, but CSS—especially in its third version—is a very powerful tool that you should most certainly be interested in. With CSS, we can tersely describe styles and behaviors (like a mouse hover).

The cascading of CSS is a powerful "transversal" inherence system that allows us to easily redefine existing styles just by providing a more accurate CSS selector. The browser defines default styles that you can override. You can then express broad, general styles that "cascade" to many elements, and then override these for any specific elements, as necessary.

CSS also allows us to perform animated transitions, which is often a better alternative to JavaScript animation because it's hardware-accelerated by the render engine of the browser.

In our game, we will do exactly this, and use CSS Transitions for our page change animations.

CSS syntax

A CSS stylesheet is structured as a set of rules. A CSS rule has two main parts: a **selector** and one or more **declarations**. Each declaration is composed of a **property** and a **value,** as shown in Figure 3-2.

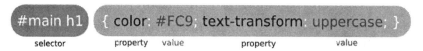

selector   property value   property   value

Figure 3-2. Selector and declarations

A CSS property is actually a style attribute. The set value will style all elements of the page that match the current selector in which the declaration is defined.

There are many CSS properties that you can use for different needs: font properties, color and background properties, text properties, "box" properties, transforms properties, transition properties, animation properties, and much, much more.

The property value is linked to the property itself. In other words, each property's value has its own syntax.

However, some domain values are defined, as follows:

- **Pixels**. For example: 45px

- **Colors**. For example: red, #F00, #FF000, rgb(255,0,0), rgba(255,0,0,1) and hsl(0,100%,50%) are different ways to obtain a red color

- **Percentages**. For example: 33%

- **Strings** in double quotes. For example: h1:before { content: ">"; }, which add a > character before all h1 headings.

And much, much more.

Some significant CSS properties

If you want to learn some basic CSS properties, we recommend you follow some of the resources listed at the end of this chapter. For now, we'll concentrate on some of the more advanced and indispensable features for games.

> **Note** *Some of the upcoming features we'll cover still need a vendor prefix to work properly in every browser. For some CSS properties, Firefox requires the -moz- prefix, Chrome and Safari requires the -webkit- prefix, and Opera requires the -o- prefix. These prefixes are temporarily required until the specification's final standardization.*

Web fonts

Web fonts are perhaps the most indispensable feature that you will need for your game. You can use your own fonts and attach a font file to improve text displays.

The @font-face rule allows for linking to fonts. To use it, you need to define a src property to link the related font resource. Typically for a link, you will use url().

Next, you have to assign some "character" to the font context; usually it is a font-family, but also a font-style, or a font-weight, and so forth. Then if you define these properties anywhere in your CSS code, the selected elements will have this font.

In our chess game, we will use a custom true type font, Chewy.ttf, which is placed in the same directory of our CSS file and linked to the "body" selector (see Listing 3-4). Hence, all our pages will use this font by default (because "body" is the highest selector, after html).

Listing 3-4. Using Chewy.ttf

```
/* Defining a "Chewy" font linked to Chewy.ttf */
@font-face {
  src: url(Chewy.ttf);
  font-family: Chewy;
}
/* Using the "Chewy" font */
body {
  font-family: Chewy, arial, serif;
}
```

> **Note** *Google Fonts is a cool tool that can help you to select the perfect font for your game; it's available at www.google.com/webfonts.*

Transitions

CSS Transitions are a way to easily add animations to a web page. Basically, it allows us to perform an animation between two given states. CSS properties will change CSS values, which will be animated smoothly over a specified duration.

To use CSS Transitions, like in a state machine, we first need to identify states and actions. *States* are CSS selectors and *actions* are changes made between these CSS selectors.

We'll describe the transition with the following four CSS Transitions properties:

> `transition-property`: describes properties to use for transitions (all by default)

> `transition-duration`: describes the duration of the transition

> `transition-delay`: describes the delay before starting the transition

> `transition-timing-function`: describes the speed variation of the transition

If you want to make an effect when hovering the mouse over an element, for example, you will use the `:hover` pseudo-class and your two selectors could be `#myel` and `#myel:hover`.

The following code makes a one-second color transition from red to green when the mouse is hovering.

```
#myel {
  transition-duration: 1s;
  color: red;
}
#myel:hover {
  color: green;
  /* transition-duration: 1s; is found through by inherence */
}
```

> **Tip** *The transition-duration property describes the transition time to enter to the related state. Hence, we can have different times for the two directions.*

You can also have different transitions for different properties by splitting values between commas. For instance, from #myel to #myel:hover, you can easily and simultaneously

- increase the padding from 0 to 10 pixels within 2 seconds

- change the color from red to green after a 1 second of delay

Listing 3-5. The code

```
#myel {
  transition-duration: 1s, 2s;
  transition-delay: 1s, 0s;
  transition-property: color, padding;
  color: red;
  padding: 0px;
}
```

```
#myel:hover {
  color: green;
  padding: 10px;
  /* transition-* are getted by inherence */
}
```

CSS Transitions allows us to make *degradable* games because CSS interpreters are nice; if they meet unknown properties, they simply ignore them and keep working. So if a browser doesn't support CSS Transitions, the state transition will still be executed—but without animation. Anyway, today's modern browsers are all supporting CSS Transitions (even Internet Explorer version 10).

CSS Animations is another way to animate page elements. CSS Animations is a more "global" animation concept for CSS, but currently it is only available on WebKit and the latest Firefox versions. It is a very powerful tool and you should think about it for your future games development.

Transforms

CSS Transitions become even more powerful using with CSS Transforms, which allows elements to be translated, rotated, scaled, and skewed in two-dimensional space. There is also a CSS 3D Transforms spec, but it hasn't yet been implemented everywhere.

We will focus on CSS 2D Transforms, which provides the following two properties:

- The transform-origin property helps you to define the center of the transformation.

- The transform property allows you to apply transformations to selected elements. Its value can take different transform functions at the same time. There are four significant transform functions: translate(x, y), scale(x) or scale(x, y), rotate(angle), and skew(angle).

For example, the following code will translate selected elements 10 pixels to the left, scale by 2 and rotate by 45 degrees:

```
transform: translate(10px, 0) scale(2) rotate(45deg);
```

Don't forget to provide vendor prefixes.

> **Tip** You can directly define a transform matrix with matrix(a,b,c,d,e,f) transform functions; see www.w3.org/TR/css3-2d-transforms/.

Fixing user interface for your needs

Web usage is huge, but creating dynamic and real-time games is not the primary purpose of the web. That's why some decisions made in terms of user interface design are not very relevant for games. However, web technologies are flexible enough to make changes and some CSS properties allow us to redefine how the user interface behaves for our games.

First of all, avoiding text selection in games is important. A visual selection on inconvenient elements (such as images, animated elements, transparent elements) can break the style and the professionalism of a game. It can occur when dragging and dropping the mouse or triggering some shortcut like Select All

(Ctrl+A). Moreover, on mobile and tablet, you usually want your application (your game) to look like a real native application. Imagine playing a real-time game and accidentally triggering the text select mobile user interface! It will rudely interrupt the game, most likely leading to a dead player and an angry user. Hence, you have to prevent the default behavior of text selection.

To do this, you have to use the user-select property, which can be set to none to disable the text selection feature on selected elements.

If you want to prevent all elements from user selection, use the following code:

```
* {
 user-select: none;
}
```

Let's now introduce two further properties that disable some unwanted default behaviors on smartphones and tablets:

- The -webkit-tap-highlight-color property, which allows us to set the color of the default highlight feature when you tap on some element (like a link, a canvas, etc.). Set it to a transparent color to disable it.

- The -webkit-touch-callout property, which when set to none, disables the default callout shown when you touch and hold an element.

```
* {
 -webkit-tap-highlight-color: rgba(0, 0, 0, 0);
 -webkit-touch-callout: none;
}
```

The cursor

To get closer to a desktop game experience, you usually want to change the mouse cursor when hovering over particular elements; you do this by using the cursor property. There are already default cursor changes on some elements like links and inputs, but you can override them.

The value can be taken in a set of specified cursors; the most used are as follows:

- move: usually used for draggable elements

- help: indicates that help is available

- pointer: the default cursor hover links

- text: the default cursor for inputs and texts

- crosshair

- wait

> **Tip** See the documentation on the cursor at www.w3.org/TR/css3-ui/#cursor for more details.

Stylesheet languages above CSS

SASS (or SCSS) and LESS are both stylesheet languages that simplify writing and maintaining CSS source codes. They are compiled into regular CSS.

We will use SASS in our examples (in fact, we're using the "old SASS style," which is just personal preference; both provide quite similar features).

The following is a list of the main advantages of such languages:

- **Nesting** selectors avoids repetition (don't repeat yourself)
- Defining your **variables** helps to define once and easily change shared assets
- Using elementary **operations** on pixels, colors, and so forth
- **Reusability** lets you define your own "mixins" to factorize your source code
- CSS **minification** and unification (with an include system)
- The syntax is simplified in CSS—no more brackets or semicolons—but indenting is essential

> **Tip** For more information on SASS and LESS, visit http://sass-lang.com and http://lesscss.org/.

Compass

Compass defines a set of ready-to-use SASS mixins. It helps to easily use CSS3 features. Moreover, it provides browser support for not-yet-standardized CSS properties.

We will now go deeper and see a real usage of Compass and SASS in the next section.

> **Tip** For more information on compass, visit http://compass-style.org.

Making our page transition effects

Today, navigation in games and applications is done with links and back/next buttons and, usually, some animated transitions between pages occur.

We will style the work made in the HTML section and make page transition effects. We will use CSS Transitions and CSS Transforms to perform them, as shown in Listing 3-6.

Listing 3-6. The CSS Transitions and Transforms

```
// page generic styles
#pages > section
  background: black url(background.jpg) no-repeat 50% 0%
  position: absolute
```

```
    top: 0
    left: 0
    width: 100%
    height: 100%
    +box-sizing(border-box)

#pages > section
  z-index: -1
  opacity: 0
  +translate3d(-100%, 0, 0)
  +transition-property((transform, opacity))
  +transition-duration((1s, 0s))
  +transition-delay((0s, 2s))
  &.current
    z-index: 0
    opacity: 1
    +translate3d(0%, 0, 0)
    +transition-delay((0s, 0s))
  &.current ~ section
    z-index: -1
    opacity: 0
    +translate3d(100%, 0, 0)
    +transition-delay((0s, 2s))
```

There are a few things to keep in mind about CSS selector operator and Compass mixins:

- The #pages > section selectors target the #pages direct section children.

- The section.current ~ section selectors target all sections that are after any section with a "current" class.

- The +translate3d($x, $y, $z) Compass mixin is equivalent to:

```
-webkit-transform: translate3d($x, $y, $z);
transform: translate3d($x, $y, $z);
```

A convention we described in the HTML section was to sort section by ascendant priority in order to know if a page has to transit to the left or to the right.

Because we have these two different possible directions, we have three states for a page, as follows:

- The page is the current visible page: #pages > section.current

- The page is before the current visible page: #pages > section

- The page is after the current visible page : #pages > section.current ~ section

As you can see, we have split transitions in two kinds: a transform transition and an opacity transition.

The transform transition will translate the page on the X axis. We have chosen to use 3D Transforms because they are better optimized on WebKit and especially because they are hardware-accelerated on Safari and iPhone. We could also have used a 2D Transforms for the desktop version. A current page is placed at the origin (x=0%). Pages before the current pages are stacked precisely to the left of the current page (x=-100%). Pages after the current pages are symmetrically placed on the right (x=100%).

This means that only the current page is in the viewport of the browser (and take the full space with the styles we defined), other pages are outside, so are effectively invisible. We define a 1-second transition duration to perform a smooth animation.

The opacity transition is indispensable: it prevents pages from showing up where they aren't wanted, especially sections that transit from state B to state C and vice versa.

This transition is a little special: there is no transition-duration, only transition-delay, which is used for the opacity property. Basically, if the page is current, it takes a full opacity (opacity set to 1), otherwise it is transparent (opacity set to 0). Just doing that, this will not work because transparency would occur before the page switch animation ends. To ensure this blink effect doesn't occur, we have set a transition delay to 2 seconds.

JavaScript, a high-level dynamic language

JavaScript is a dynamic and weakly-typed script language supporting imperative, functional, and oriented-object programming paradigms. It follows the ECMAScript standard.

HTML provides a JavaScript API called DOM (Document Object Model), which allows us to work with the document tree.

JavaScript libraries like jQuery (and its little brother, Zepto) help us work with the DOM, and provide full support of its features for whatever the browser used. We'll cover more on jQuery and Zepto a little further into the chapter.

Coding the game controller

Let's finish our page system by making a router and a controller for our game. The router is the entry point of a controller's action. It helps to bind a URL to an action: when the URL hash changes, the related action is called. This is done with the hashchange event.

We have made a scene function, which just moves the "current" class on the right page.

Listing 3-7. The Game Controller

```
ns.Controller = function(){
  var scene = function(id){
    $('#'+id).addClass('current').siblings().removeClass('current')
  }
  return {
    route: function(path) {
        callRouteChangeFunctions();
        if(path=="/") return this.index();
        if(path=="/menu") return this.menu();
        if(path=="/game/continue") return this.continueGame();
        if(path=="/game/new") return this.newGame();
        if(path=="/game") return this.game();
        if(path="/help") return this.help();
    },
    index: function(){ return this.menu(); },
    menu: function(){ /* ... */ scene('menu');  },
```

```
        continueGame: function(){ /* ... */ },
        newGame: function(){ /* ... */ scene('newgame'); },
        game: function(){ /* ... */ scene('game'); },
        help: function(){ /* ... */  scene('help'); }
    }
}();
```

Listing 3-8. Starting the Router Entry Point of the Game Controller

```
$(document).ready(function(){
    ns.Controller.init();
    $(window).bind("hashchange", function() {
        var uri = !location.hash ? '/' :location.hash.replace('#!','');
        ns.Controller.route(uri);
    }).trigger("hashchange");
});
```

Coding our Chess Game

After setting up some game pages, let's get to the heart of the matter. We will start by writing a quick specification of the game and then have a look at the main parts of the code.

Game specification

We will start by specifying the user interface. This means defining the HTML structure, the basic styles, states and properties that each element can have. Each state will be translated via a class, which will also help us to style the game with CSS.

The game chessboard is an 8 × 8 square board. We have chosen to represent it with a div#chessboard element (a div with the chessboard id) containing 64 div empty elements (created in JavaScript). Each of these elements represents a square ordered from left to right and from top to bottom.

> **Note** We could have used a table element, but our solution is still viable: CSS can help us to style a sequence of div elements like a table.

We define the states of the chessboard, the classes we are going to set on #chessboard:

> player-black | player-white means it's the black (or white) player's turn.

Let's now establish the states (and classes) that we are going to use on each square:

- A **square code** to identify a square in the chessboard and follow chess name conventions: (from a1 to h8)

- lighter indicates the square is lighter on the chessboard (1 out of 2 vertically and horizontally)

- piece indicates the square has a **piece**

- black | white indicates the **color** of the piece

- rook | knight | bishop | queen | king | pawn indicates the **type** of the piece
- current means the piece on the square is **selected** by the user
- playable means the square is **playable** for the selected piece

That's everything to make the user interface work. We can now style it in CSS and use it in JavaScript. As you can see, most of the work falls on the shoulders of CSS; hopefully, this gives you a small taste of its awesome power!

Game styles

We will now use SASS to describe the style of our game. Listing 3-9 is the complete code used to style our chessboard. It uses classes defined in the specification to style the game.

Listing 3-9. Code Used to Style Our Chessboard

```
$pieceSize: 40px // define $pieceSize somewhere
// Generate background image for all pieces
.piece
  @each $color in black, white
    &.#{$color}
      @each $type in rook, knight, bishop, queen, king, pawn
        &.#{$type}
          background-image: url("images/#{$color}_#{$type}.png")
// Styling the chessboard. pieceSize must be defined before
#chessboard
  width: 8*$pieceSize
  height: 8*$pieceSize
  &.player-white .piece.white, &.player-black .piece.black
    &:hover:not(.current)
      background-color: #cce // highlight pieces on hover
  > div
    padding: 0
    margin: 0
    width: $pieceSize
    height: $pieceSize
    display: block
    float: left
    background-size: 100% 100% // scale the bg image to the pieceSize
    background-color: #cba
    &.lighter
      background-color: #edb
    &.current, &.current.lighter
      background-color: #beb
    &.playable
      background-color: #bbe
      &.lighter
        background-color: #ccf
```

Note that the & character replaces the parent selector; for example, the following SASS code:

```
#chessboard > div
  &.current, &.current.lighter
    background-color: #beb
```

results in the following CSS:

```
#chessboard > div.current, #chessboard > div.current.lighter {
  background-color: #bbeebb;
}
```

Game logic

We will now implement the game logic in the game.js JavaScript file.

Before writing it, we need to know some best practices for good code organization, such as **scope** and **namespace**.

Scope and namespacing

Scope refers to where variables and functions are accessible, and in what context it is being executed. You have two kinds of scopes: the *global scope* (like window, document, etc.) and the local scope, which you can define. Any variables or functions put in the global scope can be accessed anywhere in the code. For instance the alert() function defined in window.alert is available anywhere. On the other hand, the *local scope* means some variables can only be accessed in a particular context; for instance, a variable defined in a function can only be accessed in this function.

On a browser, the default scope used is window (a global object representing the window itself). Hence, variables or functions you define without scoping are defined in this window object.

It's a bad (and old school) practice to define all your variables and functions in the window scope. It's a bit like defining all your C variables in the global scope. You should avoid polluting the global scope.

Hence, a good practice is to isolate the code from the window scope. You can put it in your own scope with a closure. However, you still need to access to some of your objects. Let's look at how to achieve it.

The following is a code skeleton to isolate some source code from a global scope:

```
(function(){
  // put your code here
}());
```

We just have defined an anonymous function that is instantly called.

Now let's look at the closure power, as follows:

```
(function(ns){
  // ...
  ns.Service = function(){
    var private = "something";
    // inaccessible code and scoped inside ns.Service
    return {
      publicFunctionGetter: function(){ return private; }
```

```
    }
  }();
  // ...
}(window));
```

Inside the first closure, we have defined a ns argument, which refers to the window variable because we pass it in argument at the end. This is how you can redefine an object access name.

This ns argument is used as the "root" of all services we want to expose outside. In this example, calling window.Service.publicFunctionGetter() will return "something".

We could use another argument instead of window, like window.Game:

```
(function(ns){
  // ...
}(window.Game={}));
```

We have set window.Game to the empty object. This assignment is optional if you have already done it elsewhere.

A real example for our chess game

In our game, we will use Zepto on mobile and tablet platforms, and jQuery for web browsers (see the Mobile Frameworks section). Both libraries provide almost the same API, but jQuery provides a better fallback and support for all browsers (from IE6). Zepto is lighter and convenient for WebKit browsers that are used by most of the smartphones and tablets today. To perform full support and have a generic code for both libraries in total transparency, we use the following code:

```
(function(ns, $){
  // ns namespace is defined in window.Game
  // jQuery OR Zepto are available by using $
}(window.Game={}, window.jQuery||window.Zepto));
```

The Game class

The Game class contains all the logic of the chess game. In Listing 3-10, notice the init method, which initializes piece positions in the game board.

Listing 3-10. init Method

```
ns.Game = function(o){
  var self = this;
  self.pieces = [];
  self.whiteEated = [];
  self.blackEated = [];
  self.currentPlayer = 'white';
  self.currentPiece = null;
  self.init = function(){ // Init the chessboard pieces
    var piece = function(c, t, p){ return { color: c, type: t, position: p } };
    var firstRowTypes = ['rook', 'knight', 'bishop', 'queen', 'king', 'bishop',↵
'knight', 'rook'];
    for(var i=0; i<=7; ++i) {
```

```
      var c = String.fromCharCode(i+97);
      self.pieces.push( piece('white', firstRowTypes[i], c+'1') );
      self.pieces.push( piece('white', 'pawn',           c+'2') );
      self.pieces.push( piece('black', 'pawn',           c+'7') );
      self.pieces.push( piece('black', firstRowTypes[i], c+'8') );
    }
  }
  // ... the rest of the game logic code ...
}
```

We can now focus on the game logic code independently of the content and the style.

The Renderer class

The Renderer class intends to bring the game logic (from the Game class) into the DOM. It helps the Game class development to focus only on the pure logic of the game; whereas the Renderer will connect it to the user interface. Following our game specification, all it will do is update classes on squares, as shown in Listing 3-11.

Listing 3-11. Renderer class

```
ns.Renderer = function(){
  var self = this;
  self.init = function(game){
    self.game = game;
    self.board = $('#chessboard').empty();
    forEachPosition(function(p){ /* init chessboard squares */ });
    self.render();
    self.game.bindChange(function(){ self.render() });
    return this;
  }
  self.render = function(){
    self.board[0].className = 'player-'+self.game.currentPlayer;
    forEachPosition(function(p, l, d){ // on each square p:
      // [code] Update the classes of p for the current game state
    });
    // [code] update black eated div
    // [code] update white eated div
  }
}
```

The Storage class

We will use Local Storage, an HTML5 feature that allows us to persist data on the client side.

The localStorage variable has three main methods:

- A setter setItem(key, text)

- A getter getItem(key)

- and a "remover" removeItem(key)

We want to be able to save a game, as shown in Listing 3-12, so that we can retrieve it between interruptions.

Listing 3-12. Saving Game

```
ns.Storage = function() {
  var gameKey = 'chessdemo_game';
  return {
    saveGame: function(game) {
      localStorage.setItem(gameKey, JSON.stringify(game));
    },
    retrieveGame: function() {
      return JSON.parse(localStorage.getItem(gameKey));
    },
    emptyGame: function() {
      localStorage.removeItem(gameKey);
    }
  }
}();
```

Implementing our controller

Let's implement the actions of the controller made previously. You will see the entry point of the game initialization in these actions. We are going to use all classes defined before, as shown in Listing 3-13.

Listing 3-13. Insert Listing Caption Here.

```
// ...
continueGame: function(){
    if(!ns.currentGame && ns.Storage.hasGameSaved()) {
      ns.currentGame = new ns.Game( ns.Storage.retrieveGame() );
    }
    return this.game();
  },
  newGame: function(){
    ns.Storage.emptyGame();
    ns.currentGame = null;
    return this.game();
  },
  game: function(){
    var renderer = new ns.Renderer();
    if(!ns.currentGame)
      ns.currentGame = new ns.Game().init();
    var game = ns.currentGame;
    renderer.init(game);
    game.bindChange(function(){
      ns.Storage.saveGame( game.export() );
      if( game.isFinished() ) {
        alert("CheckMate!"); // TODO: render a finish page instead
        ns.currentGame = null;
        history.back();
      }
    })
    scene('game');
  }, // ...
```

The result

Figures 3-3 and 3-4 show how the chess game should appear.

Figure 3-3. Menu display

Figure 3-4. chessboard

Mobile frameworks

jQuery and Zepto

jQuery is an awesome, widely-used JavaScript library that makes working with the DOM easier and offers an abstraction to support all browsers. Zepto is an alternative to jQuery that only targets WebKit browsers. Its usage is perfect for mobile and tablet platforms because they mostly use a WebKit browser.

To summarize, take jQuery, clean it from all hacks, polyfill, and fallback aimed to support old browsers, and you get Zepto—a lightweight and efficient library.

> **Tip** To learn more about the jQuery API, visit http://jquery.com.

PhoneGap

PhoneGap is a convenient library for deploying web applications to most of the smartphone and tablet platforms. The PhoneGap JavaScript library enhances the HTML5 API to gain access to *native device features* in JavaScript. For instance, if you have permission, you can theoretically access phone contacts, access the accelerometer (used in *Same Game Gravity*), shoot a photo, get a geolocation, get the network state, and so forth.

Some of these features (like geolocation) are available in HTML5 specs and are already implemented in browsers. Globally, most of these features will be implemented. PhoneGap is just a polyfill, a shell that guarantees the support of a feature.

It also provides app skeletons that help you to build packages for app stores.

Figure 3-5. Supported platforms

PhoneGap Build

PhoneGap Build is a web service that helps you to build your web application for different platform packages (Android *apk*, iOS *ipa*, Symbian *wgz*, Blackberry *ota*, webOS *ipk*). You just upload your zip application or link to a Git repository to get these different packages. That's revolutionary because you no longer require thousands of frameworks to build your application for each platform, and it's much, much faster.

The application configuration is described in a config.xml manifest, which is an abstraction of platform-related manifests.

The first limitation of PhoneGap Build is the security/privacy: will a company trust this cloud system and accept its certificates? The second limitation is, in my opinion, the coverage of the config.xml: will this manifest cover all the needs and possibilities a platform provides?

Configuration of our chess game

Listing 3-14 shows the `config.xml` we used to make our chess game:

Listing 3-14. `config.xml`

```xml
<?xml version="1.0" encoding="UTF-8"?>
<widget xmlns="http://www.w3.org/ns/widgets" xmlns:gap="http://phonegap.com/ns/1.0"
        id="fr.gaetanrenaudeau.chess" version="1.0.0">
  <name>Chess</name>
  <description>A Chess Game demo</description>
  <author href="http://greweb.fr" email="renaudeau.gaetan@gmail.com">
    Gaetan Renaudeau
  </author>
  <icon src="icon.png" gap:role="default" />
  <feature name="http://api.phonegap.com/1.0/network"/>
  <preference name="orientation" value="portrait" />
</widget>
```

Figure 3-6. Simple interface of PhoneGap build

WebAppBuilder

This tool was created during the *Same Game Gravity* development—and does not claim to be a solution to all problems of the world! It was born with the objective of automating a number of commands needed to create multiple instances of an application. It's actually a mashup of many tools.

We could simply have the exact same source code inside all application instances (in assets/ for Android; www/ for iOS; and / for the web versions) and it works in most simple cases, but you can also have very specific code, which would not be used in other instances. You could also use different libraries for different platforms like we did with jQuery and Zepto.

Moreover, we need tools to make game development and maintenance easier. In fact, this tool quickly becomes essential to quickly spread (you can almost even say "compile") the changes we made on a single source to different instances of the application.

WebAppBuilder is just a configurable Makefile, which targets call some scripts to perform some code transformation and build an application instance.

You can extend WebAppBuilder, adding other tools to fit your needs. The following is a partial list of features:

- Easy templating of your HTML files with Mustache
- Copy, concatenate, and minimize JavaScript the way that you want
- Retrieve JavaScript files from URLs (useful for libraries)
- Compile SASS files into CSS files (and possible usage of the Compass framework)
- Merge your CSS files
- Copy and optionally rename resources that you want to include (images, fonts, sounds, etc.)
- Error handling and atomicity: if one operation fails, the make fails (JavaScript syntax error, SASS syntax error, etc.)

Makefile for of our chess game

We have used WebAppBuilder for making our chess game. We currently target only two versions, but it can easily evolve. Targets are stored in android/ and desktop/. We bootstrapped the android/ directory with a PhoneGap Android skeleton. Some modifications have to first be performed on this skeleton to make it ready for deployment.

All our application source code is stored in the src/ directory. Some of the source files used in our chess game include the following:

- common.sass: all stylesheets
- desktop.sass: defines some variables specific to desktop versions and imports common.sass
- mobile.sass: defines some variables specific to mobile versions and imports common.sass
- desktop.html: the wrapper page that embeds game.html in an iframe for desktop versions
- game.html: the game page
- game.js: the game logic
- jquery.min.js: the jQuery library; only used by the desktop
- zepto.min.js: the Zepto library (alternative to jQuery) for mobile versions
- underscore-min.js: provides some functional programming concept
- images/: contains all chess piece images

- `background.jpg`: the background of the game

- `icon.png`: the icon of the game

- `Chewy.ttf`: the font used

The following is an extract of an Android/Makefile:

```
SRC_DIR = ../src
DIST_DIR = assets
RESOURCES = images Chewy.ttf background.jpg icon.png
VIEWS = index.html=game.html:"{version:'1.0'}"
SCRIPTS = game.min.js=!game.js lib.min.js=underscore-min.js,zepto.min.js
STYLES = game.css=mobile.sass
# ...
```

The following is an extract of a desktop/Makefile:

```
SRC_DIR = ../src
DIST_DIR = assets
RESOURCES = images Chewy.ttf background.jpg icon.png
VIEWS = index.html=desktop.html game.html:"{version:'1.0'}"
SCRIPTS = game.min.js=!game.js lib.min.js=underscore-min.js,jquery.min.js
STYLES = game.css=desktop.sass
# ...
```

Figure 3-7 shows making the desktop instance:

```
[gre@gre-macbookpro:~/Dropbox/webappmaker/sample/chess/desktop]$ make
    Welcome to ~ Web App Builder ~ by @greweb

      VIEWS: assets/index.html <= desktop.html (without Mustache)
      VIEWS: assets/game.html <= game.html with {version:'1.0'}
    SCRIPTS: assets/game.min.js <= !game.js
    SCRIPTS: assets/lib.min.js <= underscore-min.js,jquery.min.js
     STYLES: assets/game.css <= desktop.sass
  RESOURCES: assets/images <= images
  RESOURCES: assets/Chewy.ttf <= Chewy.ttf
  RESOURCES: assets/background.jpg <= background.jpg
  RESOURCES: assets/icon.png <= icon.png
```

Figure 3-7. Desktop instance

Internationalization

Internationalizing your game is important because it can greatly expand your user base. An internationalization system is quite simple to make and has many possible implementations.

The internationalization of a word or a sentence in many languages is done with a key identifier to represent the text to translate. We want to both load translations on page load, and also to access a translation later.

To do this, we'll inject translations in the DOM on page load with JavaScript. Our convention to identify a translation key is to have a i18n-{key} class on the DOM tag to replace the translation where {key} is the key of the translation (the key should only contain alphanum and _ characters to be selected properly).

The example

Table 3-1 shows the English and French translations we used for the example.

Table 3-1. Example Translations in English and French

Key	i18n['en'][key]	i18n['fr'][key]
hello_world	Hello world	*Bonjour le monde*
gamegoal_1	In SAME, your goal is to remove all balls in the grid.	*Dans SAME, l'objectif est de retirer toutes les billes d'une grille.*

HTML code

```
<!doctype html>
<html>
  <head></head>
  <body>
    <div><span class="i18n-hello_world"></span>. bla bla bla</div>
    <div><span class="i18n-gamegoal_1"></span>. bla bla bla</div>
  </body>
</html>
```

JavaScript i18n basic code

Listing 3-15 is a simple internationalizer code using jQuery or Zepto.

Listing 3-15. Internationalizer Code

```
var Locale = { get: function(){ ... } };
var i18n = function() {
  var lang, defaultLang = "en";
  var dictionaries = {
    "en": { "hello_world": "Hello world", "gamegoal_1": "In SAME, your goal is to↵
remove all balls in the grid." },
    "fr": { "hello_world": "Bonjour le monde", "gamegoal_1": "Dans SAME, l'objectif↵
est de retirer toutes les billes d'une grille." }
  };
  var updateDOM = function() {
    var dict = dictionaries[lang] || dictionaries[defaultLang];
    for(var key in dict) $(".i18n-"+key).text(dict[key]);
  }
  return {
    init: function() {
      lang = Locale.get() || defaultLang;
```

```
      updateDOM();
    },
    get: function(key) {
        var dict = dictionaries[lang] || dictionaries[defaultLang];
        return ""+dict[key];
    },
    updateDOM: updateDOM
  }
}();
$(document).ready(i18n.init);
```

Pure DOM vs. canvas–based game

There are mainly two ways to develop a game.

The first solution, which we call "Pure DOM," is to decompose the game into multiple HTML elements (for each game atomic element) and to use the power of CSS to style this game. This is what we did with our chess game.

Another solution is to use a big canvas to run the game. Canvas allows you to manipulate bitmap pixels in JavaScript. It provides a low-level API with different draw methods and properties that we will explore.

Both solutions are viable, but do not cover the same needs. The solution depends on the game type.

Overview of the Canvas API

To manipulate the canvas API, you need to get a context. It can be "2d" for the Canvas 2D, "webgl" for WebGL, and so forth. For the Canvas 2D API, you retrieve it with

```
var ctx = document.getElementById("mycanvasid").getContext("2d");
```

You can now access to the full Canvas 2D API from the ctx variable.

Listing 3-16 is an example of the canvas code that I used in *Same Game Gravity*. It draws a piece of the game.

Listing 3-16. Canvas Code from Same Game Gravity

```
var canvas = document.getElementById("mycanvasid");
var ctx = canvas.getContext("2d");
function drawBrick = function(brick, size) {
  if(!size) size = 1;
  ctx.save(); // Save the current ctx state
  ctx.translate(brick.x, brick.y); // change origin and units
  ctx.scale(brick.w, brick.h);     // to work with easy values

  var gradient = ctx.createLinearGradient(0,0,0,1);
  gradient.addColorStop(0, brick.colorLighter);
  gradient.addColorStop(0.6, brick.color);
  ctx.fillStyle = gradient; // the fillStyle is a gradient

  ctx.clearRect(0,0,1,1); // empty the rect
```

```
    ctx.beginPath();
    ctx.arc(.5, .5, .4*size, 0, Math.PI*2, true);
    ctx.fill(); // fill a disc with gradient
    ctx.restore(); // restore the last ctx state saved
}
```

> **Tip** *There is much more to explore with canvas; see www.w3.org/TR/html5/the-canvas-element.html.*

Solutions comparison: Canvas

The problem with canvas-oriented applications is that you usually have stacks of JavaScript code that are probably far more complex. Choosing this solution means reducing the usage of CSS and HTML, so everything these technologies give us now has to be implemented in JavaScript. For instance, you have to handle "redrawing" yourself. If you are used to DOM development, then you will have to learn new concepts to deal with efficient re-drawing, layering, mouse selection, and so forth—all on your own. At best, you must use a library (sometimes heavily) to abstract these concepts. Another problem is that you can encounter cross-browser issues. For instance, I experienced an issue with the Android 2.1 browser; the drawImage method didn't work properly.

Although JavaScript performance has been remarkably improved, it is generally less efficient to make JavaScript animations than use CSS Transitions and Animations, which can be more easily optimized and hardware-accelerated. Anyway, it's a tricky claim since requestAnimationFrame, the JavaScript function designed to make animation loop, is implemented by browsers.

There are also some advantages with using canvas. The major advantage is that possibilities are clearly wider. Accessing the pixels array, you can do whatever you want. For instance, making a particle system should be done with canvas and especially using the powerful canvas blend mode (see www.mrspeaker.net/dev/parcycle).

Moreover, 3D has recently been introduced as a web specification. Supported by almost all recent desktop browsers, WebGL is a bridge to OpenGL. Hence, it allows us to create high-performance 3D with impressive graphic acceleration.

Solutions comparison: Pure DOM

For now, the Pure DOM approach is usually better because it takes more advantage of web technologies. First of all, it's generally more efficient and optimizable with the browser (if only to a certain extent; for instance, if you have a very large number of DOM elements, then the performance will suffer—especially for animations). Second, as we explained before, it's more maintainable and easy to split the content, the style, and the logic into separate and descriptive parts. CSS is a descriptive language, meaning you define how elements are styled. There are also some beneficial side effects, such easier debugging with a DOM inspector.

However, CSS is limited. With the new CSS3, browser display differences occur when a browser doesn't yet support a given CSS property. But the good news is, because the CSS is descriptive, there is usually an acceptable fallback: the application should work even if some effects don't occur (for instance, not supporting CSS Transitions will simply disable the transition animation). CSS transforms are very powerful and efficient (rotation, scale, skew, etc.) and are hard to make in canvas.

You can mix both

To summarize, canvas is awesome but should be used wisely. Otherwise, favor a DOM solution to your problem. Of course, we can compromise and mix both Pure DOM and canvas. It is not illegal to use some canvas in the Pure DOM solution! For instance, you could have a background canvas under the game to draw special effects.

While we're talking about mixing and matching, there is also a third solution to drawing game graphics—SVG usage. Libraries like Raphaël JS help to build SVG interfaces in JavaScript.

In our chess game, the pure DOM solution fits because there was no need for complex animations or effects.

However, *Same Game Gravity* uses canvas. This choice is mainly for the ball animation. On one hand, having elements influenced by gravity is not efficient when animating with CSS; but on the other hand, the balls must move at the same speed as they fall independently of the move offset. It's not something trivial to do in CSS. In the spirit of having "the right tool for the right job," however, some parts, like the time bar, are still made with CSS.

Conclusion

This chapter introduced you to some techniques for making HTML5 games from scratch.

The full code of the chess game we developed is available at http://github.com/gre/chess-game.

Keep in mind that HTML, CSS, and JavaScript are all important languages that help you make the work easier.

One thing that I really enjoy is working with the web's openness. If open, a web application is hackable—you can browse the source code of any web game and learn from it. Web developers are open-minded and have developed open-source libraries and frameworks all around the web.

In this chapter, we focused on just a small fraction of web technologies, in order to meet our given needs; but there is so much more to explore: web APIs, libraries, web services, and so forth. You should stay tuned to the important web actors (developers, designers, specification writers, etc.) to keep up-to-date on today's web evolution—because web technologies are moving extremely rapidly. For several years AJAX allowed you to make HTTP requests in JavaScript, but today we are able to keep a socket connection between a client (browser) and a server with WebSockets, which is a fantastic feature for making real-time games.

With every cool new feature—from WebSockets to WebGL—we see a new era dawning. It's up to us to take advantage of it to create awesome multi-platform games.

Other resources

The following web sites provide additional useful information on HTML5, the latest web technologies, and advanced JavaScript:

- www.w3.org: Web specifications are available at The World Wide Web Consortium (W3C), an international community that develops open standards to ensure the long-term growth of the web.

- https://developer.mozilla.org: The Mozilla Developer Network features documentation, links, and demos of the latest web technologies.

- http://diveintohtml5.info and www.html5rocks.com: The Dive into HTML5 and HMTL5 Rocks web sites contain well-written articles about HTML5.

- http://ejohn.org/apps/learn: "Learning Advanced JavaScript" by John Resig, jQuery's creator.

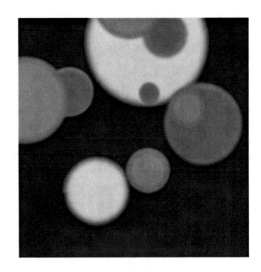

Chapter 4

Creating, Saving, and Loading Tracks

This chapter will explain a few of the basics on structuring games in JavaScript as well as game play in general. We will also cover a few JavaScript tips and tricks.

Who we are, what we will build, and why

We are two of the five creators of Marble Run (marblerun.at), a rather successful browser game. The team that created Marble Run consists of two designers (Matthias Hempt and Nicola Lister) and three developers (Eberhart Graether, David Strauss, and Mathias Paumgarten). David and Mathias are the authors of this chapter.

In this chapter, we will create a small application using both canvas and DOM elements. The app consists of a grid and a simple list (see Figure 4-1). The idea is that you will be able to build something, what we refer to as a track, and save it in a database-compatible format.

The idea is that you can reload the saved tracks onto your grid.

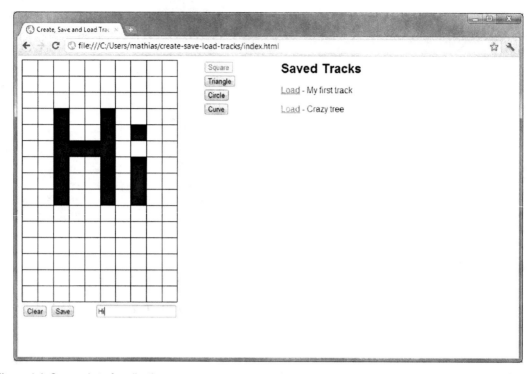

Figure 4-1. Screenshot of application

The application and the sense behind it

The goal of Marble Run is to build the longest marble run in the world. Every player can build his own little marble run, also called a "track." After saving this track, it will be appended to the existing tracks, forming a big, collaborative marble run.

A track is built with pre-defined bricks that the player can rotate and place freely on the grid. To get an idea of how it looks, see Figure 4-2.

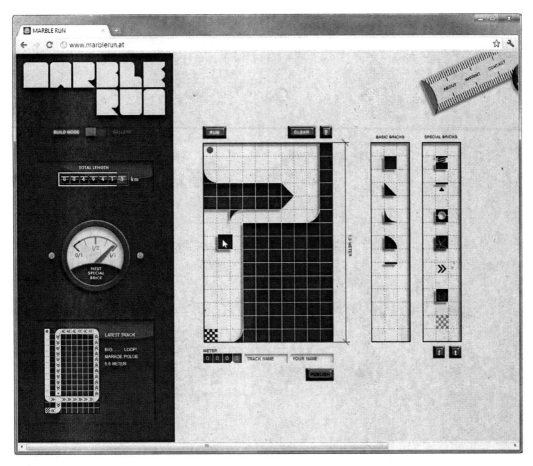

Figure 4-2. Screenshot of Marble Run

You see, Marble Run is very similar to what we plan to do in this chapter—and that's not by accident. We get a lot of questions about the way we do this and that in Marble Run. So, our little application makes a great example of how you can store certain user data (such as the tracks you create in this application) on the server side and how you parse the data to re-create the track.

We will also demonstrate certain practices on how to draw on the grid and when you should draw your game content. We would like to add at this point that we will not go into too much depth when it comes to performance optimization. We will, however, add a few notes here and there to explain possible optimization and go over a few thoughts on how to speed up an application that has a lot of interactive content on the canvas.

Why levels are important

We want to take a closer look at the different types of games and how they are built up. There are basically two kinds of game plays when it comes to browser games.

- The ones build on certain levels, created by the maker, such as all the jump-and-run games, or, for instance, *Angry Birds*.

- Then there is the kind with unlimited levels, such as *Doodle Jump*. The levels are either automatically generated by the machine or created by the user as part of the game play.

There are good reasons for each game play. Either way, when you think of a game for the browser there are two major things that you want to consider.

- You want the user to come back

- You want the user to spend as much time on the game as possible

With those two key values in mind, you can see why you might want to confront the user with different levels, which you have already created; that way the user has an ongoing challenge without having to come up with interesting tasks for himself. Most users return because they don't want to leave with unfinished business. But the obvious downside is that the levels will eventually run out—and you have to spend a significant amount of time to create those levels.

This means that once a user plays through all your levels, you have a very hard time keeping him interested in the game. So, the challenge is to find a way to keep the user interested. Games like *World of Warcraft* accomplish this by giving the player the chance to interact with other players. But that's a very hard thing to do in a browser game. You constantly need a lot of players playing the game at the same time.

Back to levels, you need a lot of interesting levels to keep the users happy. Since constantly creating good levels is not an option, we have to look for another solution. *Minecraft* is a very basic game out of the box, but it gives its players the option to be creative. Players can build stuff on their own; they can sort of make their dreams a reality. And that opportunity makes *Minecraft* such a great game; players can be creative on their own.

Allowing the user to be creative and to bring his own style into the game is the most valuable feature you can offer. Now, if you also let him or her share her work—you scored.

Let's take Marble Run as an example. We have many users who keep returning to our page and building tracks that are of no interest when it comes to length or trickiness. The tracks they have built are artistic pieces. Take a look at the screenshot in Figure 4-3 to see a wonderful artistic track.

Of course, that was in no way our intention when we built this game, but it was greatly appreciated. So, we basically gave the user opportunities to do what he wanted, and that made him stick around longer than simply challenging him with a certain number of levels.

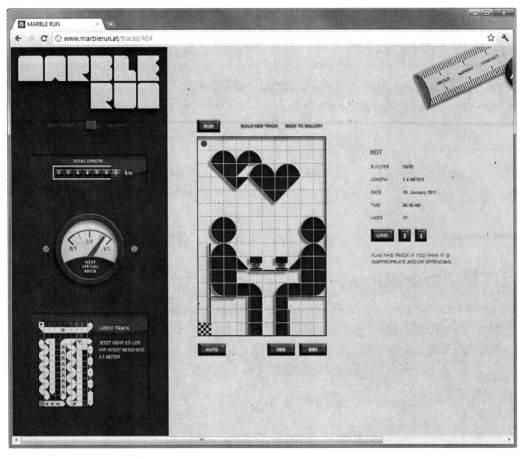

Figure 4-3. Screenshot of a creative track on marblerun.at

Split the big thing into small components

Now it's time to get back to our little app. The first step with every application is to make a basic plan of how it's going to be structured. Everything seems very easy at first, but it's for sure that it will turn into more code than you originally expected. Therefore, you always need a well thought-out base to build your application upon.

The good thing with HTML- and JavaScript-based applications is that the technology itself forces you into some kind of structure. With CSS files, the styling of the page is automatically separated from the content that is included in the HTML. So, the interactive user input and the game logic all takes place in JavaScript.

To get this started, we create a folder that will hold our application. Let's name that folder `create-save-load-tracks`. Inside that folder, we now create the basic structure. First of all, there is the HTML file `index.html`, which will hold our entire markup. Currently it's an empty file; we will go over the HTML markup itself a little later.

For the styling of the application, we need some CSS. So within the `create-save-load-tracks` folder, we create another folder named `stylesheets`. Now let's add an empty `style.css` file to that folder for our CSS. But as you probably have already figured out, that is not enough. When writing a browser game you typically have to expect lots of JavaScript. So, for the moment let's just create a folder called `javascripts`.

When we are finished with those first steps, we should have the structure shown in Figure 4-4 that we can build upon.

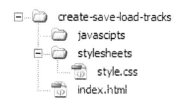

Figure 4-4. Folder structure

The HTML markup

As we create an application that uses the `<canvas>` tag, we will also use the HTML5 Doctype. So our `index.html` will start as follows:

```
<!DOCTYPE html>
<html>
 <head>
   <meta charset="utf-8">
   <title>Create, Save and Load Tracks</title>
 </head>

 <body></body>
</html>
```

As you can see in Figure 4-1, we have three different parts: the grid and the controls beneath to save or clear the current track; in the middle, the column of buttons for the different bricks; and, on the right, a list of all the previously saved tracks.

For every part, we use a separate `<section>` tag; so let's put the following three HTML markup snippets into the `<body>` tag of our `index.html` file.

The first section is the grid, for which we need a `<canvas>` element so that we can display the grid and all the bricks on it. Plus, we add a little form with two buttons and a text field. The first button is our Clear button, which helps us clear the entire grid if we have the urge to start from scratch. The second button allows us to save our track. Using the text field, we can give every track a name. We also add meaningful ids to the different HTML tags so that we can access them later via JavaScript.

```
<section id="grid-container">
 <canvas id="grid"></canvas>
 <form>
   <button id="clear-track">Clear</button>
   <button id="save-track">Save</button>
```

```
    <input id="track-name" type="text" placeholder="Track Name"/>
  </form>
</section>
```

The second section element holds a form with a lot of buttons, with each button representing a brick. Later these buttons will be used to select a specific brick type.

```
<section id="bricks-container">
  <form>
    <button id="square-brick">Square</button>
    <button id="triangle-brick">Triangle</button>
    <button id="circle-brick">Circle</button>
    <button id="curve-brick">Curve</button>
  </form>
</section>
```

And the last section will eventually hold all saved tracks.

```
<section id="tracks-container">
  <h1>Saved Tracks</h1>
</section>
```

When we are done with the first three steps, our index.html should look like the following:

```
<!DOCTYPE html>
<html>
  <head>
    <meta charset="utf-8">
    <title>Create, Save and Load Tracks</title>
  </head>

  <body>
    <section id="grid-container">
      <canvas id="grid"></canvas>
      <form>
        <button id="clear-track">Clear</button>
        <button id="save-track">Save</button>
        <input id="track-name" type="text" placeholder="Track Name"/>
      </form>
    </section>

    <section id="bricks-container">
      <form>
        <button id="square-brick">Square</button>
        <button id="triangle-brick">Triangle</button>
        <button id="circle-brick">Circle</button>
        <button id="curve-brick">Curve</button>
      </form>
    </section>

    <section id="tracks-container">
      <h1>Saved Tracks</h1>
    </section>
  </body>
</html>
```

Adding a little style

When you open the HTML file in a browser, you will notice that things look a little shaken up. What we need is a basic CSS stylesheet to get all the parts of our application into the right places. To accomplish this, we link to our previously created `style.css` file. After adding the stylesheet link, the `<head>` block of our HTML markup looks like the following:

```
<head>
  <meta charset="utf-8">
  <title>Create, Save and Load Tracks</title>
  <link rel="stylesheet" href="stylesheets/style.css">
</head>
```

Let's open the `style.css` file in your favorite text editor and start adding some CSS rules. For an easy start, we'll just change the font settings for the entire HTML document.

```
body {
    font-family: Helvetica, Arial, san-serif;
}
```

Now it gets a little trickier. We need to align all three sections next to each other. We give the two outer sections each a width of 300 pixels, whereas the center section is only 100 pixels wide. We add a margin of 50 pixels to the left and center sections so that it doesn't look too clustered. To get the sections next to each other, we float all three of them to the left. Everything put together gives us the following CSS rules:

```
section#grid-container {
    width: 300px;
    margin-right: 50px;
    float: left;
}

section#bricks-container {
    width: 100px;
    margin-right: 50px;
    float: left;
}

section#tracks-container {
    width: 300px;
    float: left;
}
```

To round off the appearance, we remove the margin from the saved tracks headline and float to the right the Save button and the text field for the track name. After adding those last two CSS rules, the finished `style.css` file looks like the following:

```
body {
    font-family: Helvetica, Arial, san-serif;
}

section#grid-container {
    width: 300px;
```

```css
    margin-right: 50px;
    float: left;
}

section#bricks-container {
    width: 100px;
    margin-right: 50px;
    float: left;
}

section#tracks-container {
    width: 300px;
    float: left;
}

button#save, input#track-name {
    float: right;
}

section#tracks-container h1 {
    margin: 0;
}
```

The JavaScript structure

After finishing the HTML markup and the CSS stylesheet, we can focus on the cool stuff: the JavaScript code. So, let's add some JavaScript `<script>` tags! Those go at the bottom, right before the `</body>` tag closes; that way we can make sure that the browser parses the DOM and creates all the elements before it starts interpreting the JavaScript. Browsers start working up the JavaScript as soon as they load it, whether the DOM is ready or not.

To start, we simply add two JavaScript `<script>` tags: one for jQuery and the other for our `application.js` file.

```html
...
<section id="tracks-container">
  <h1>Saved Tracks</h1>
</section>

<script src="javascripts/jquery.js"></script>
<script src="javascripts/application.js"></script>
</body>
</html>
```

> **Note** jQuery is only used for DOM manipulation. No in-depth knowledge of jQuery is required. We just want to keep things simple.

After adding those two lines to the markup, we switch into our `javascripts` folder and create an empty `application.js` file. In order to get jQuery, we go to the jQuery web site (`www.jquery.com`) and look for the

Download (jQuery); button. Found it? Click it! In case your web browser doesn't ask you where to save this page, right-click in the page and select "Save page." Save the page as `jquery.js` into our `javascripts` folder.

There are many ways to structure an application in JavaScript, but one rule always applies: make your code as modular as possible! In our application, we currently have only one file, the `application.js`. Here everything falls into place, so let's take a look at the following different components that we have:

- `application.js`: This file is the heart of our application; here we make use of all the other files and modules. It's also the place where we react upon user input, and where basic global variables are set.

- `store.js`: This module is a middle layer between the application and the database. In our case, we don't have a database powered back-end, but this file would be the place where the magic happens. For our purpose, the store module just stores your saved tracks in memory.

- `grid.js`: This module is responsible for drawing the grid and managing all bricks that are on it.

- Bricks: Each brick type will be a JavaScript file; only the brick class knows how it is correctly drawn. We will cover specific bricks later.

So, what do we do first? We will need a couple of variables and constants. The following code goes into the `application.js` file:

```
// Constants
var NUMBER_OF_COLUMNS = 10;
var NUMBER_OF_ROWS = 15;
var BRICK_SIZE = 30;

// Grid  variables
var gridWidth = NUMBER_OF_COLUMNS * BRICK_SIZE;
var gridHeight = NUMBER_OF_ROWS * BRICK_SIZE;

// Canvas variables
var canvas;
var context;
var canvasWidth = gridWidth + 1;
var canvasHeight = gridHeight + 1;

// Application variables
var store = null;
var grid = null;
var selectedBrickClass = null;
var currentButton = null;
```

What do we do here? First of all, we define three constants that will determine the size of our grid. The grid has 10 × 15 cells, where a cell or as we call it, a brick, is 30 pixels × 30 pixels in size. With those values, we can calculate the grid's width and height with ease.

For the canvas size, we add an additional pixel to the width and the height; we will explain the reason for that later. The canvas and context variable will reference to the canvas DOM element and to the drawing context of the canvas. The canvas element is an actual DOM element that is inserted in the DOM to declare a canvas with a certain height and width (just like you would insert a div into HTML code), while the context is more the API of the canvas to be used with JavaScript. We will explain how to get the context of a canvas element later.

In the last block, we declare four global variables. The store and grid are two instances of store.js and grid.js, the two modules that we talked about earlier. The two other variables are needed for the brick selection.

Now that we have declared all the global variables that we need, the next thing to do is kick off the application. jQuery provides us with a very handy function that is called once the browser is finished building the HTML document.

Once the browser is done, we can grab the canvas element and get the drawing context. Without the context we cannot draw anything on the canvas, so this step is important. When we have the context, we clear the canvas so that we can be sure nothing is painted on it. The jQuery function and our described code looks like this:

```
$(document).ready(function() {
  canvas = document.getElementById('grid');
  context = canvas.getContext('2d');

  clearCanvas();
});
```

> **Note** For the purpose of this chapter, we assume that there is a canvas element with the id 'grid' and that the browser supports the 2d context. Normally, you should check if that's really the case—and if not, react accordingly!

One thing is still missing. What does our little clearCanvas() function look like? It's pretty simple.

```
function clearCanvas() {
  canvas.width = canvasWidth;
  canvas.height = canvasHeight;
}
```

Why did we call it clearCanvas() if it's basically just setting the size of the canvas? It is because every time you change the size—or set either the width or the height—it will automatically swipe the entire content of the canvas; even if you set it to the same size it was before. So, we only use it initially to set the size, but further calls will actually clear the canvas—just like the name of the method. Why is everything erased on resize? Luckily, that is how the canvas is defined in the specs.

The drawing loop

As explained in the previous section, the canvas provides a pixel grid that can be freely manipulated. By default, the context of the canvas is blank—just like a blank sheet of paper before you set your pencil on it for the first time. That means that we have to draw all the elements with the functions that the canvas context provides. It actually works similar to how you draw with a pencil, but more on that later. It also means we have to be very aware of the order in which the elements are drawn onto the canvas. Once you draw something on it, you cannot draw underneath it.

First things first. In this case, we want to draw the grid before we draw any bricks. This is why we decided to have everything drawn in a recursive sort of way. The application contains a grid. The grid contains all the bricks. Therefore, the application is only responsible to draw the grid. The grid itself is responsible for drawing the bricks.

Before we start implementing the basic draw function in application.js, we need to set up a class for the grid. As it is somehow implied by the previous paragraph, the grid will be responsible for a few things! We need to add a grid.js to our JavaScript <script> tags in the index.html file, as follows:

```
<script src="javascripts/jquery.js"></script>
<script src="javascripts/grid.js"></script>
<script src="javascripts/application.js"></script>
```

The grid.js file will look like this:

```
var Grid = function(width, height, cellSize) {
  this.width = width;
  this.height = height;
  this.cellSize = cellSize;

  this.bricks = [];
}
```

So, it will basically hold the width and the height of the grid, as well as the brick size. As mentioned, it also has to manage the bricks, so we use a simple array to save all the bricks that are on the grid.

We will instantiate this class one time in our entry point of the application.js, as follows:

```
$(document).ready(function() {
  canvas = document.getElementById('grid');
  context = canvas.getContext('2d');

  grid = new Grid(gridWidth, gridHeight, BRICK_SIZE);

  clearCanvas();
});
```

Let's get back to the drawing cycle. The application.js gets a draw() function. This function should be capable of drawing the current state of the grid, no matter at what time it's called.

So instead of calling clearCanvas(), we go ahead and call draw() to draw the initial state of the application.

```
$(document).ready(function() {
  canvas = document.getElementById('grid');
  context = canvas.getContext('2d');

  grid = new Grid(gridWidth, gridHeight, BRICK_SIZE);

  draw();
});
```

Now, for the draw function.

```
function draw() {
  clearCanvas();

  context.translate(0.5, 0.5);

  grid.draw(context);
}
```

First we clear the canvas. The command `context.translate(0.5, 0.5);` moves the drawing context half a pixel to the right and bottom. We need this because we will draw a lot of 1-pixel lines and the computer screen will display 1-pixel lines as blurry 2-pixel lines. The reason for this is rather simple. When you draw a black vertical line beginning at coordinates (1, 0), the context will actually try drawing it in between pixel one and pixel two. Due to sub-pixel accuracy, instead of coloring both pixels black, it colors both half way, which means black with only 50 percent opacity. Therefore, it would look like one blurry line. Now, if we draw a vertical line at (0.5, 0), the computer draws it in the middle of one pixel and, therefore, it results in one accurate line.

As you can already imagine, all this is not necessary when you draw 2-pixel-wide lines.

The only thing left is to tell the grid to do its job; because the grid is responsible for all the bricks, we don't have to worry about anything else. We now need to implement the draw function on the grid. Even though we have the context on a global variable, we still pass it as a parameter to make the code easier to read.

```
Grid.prototype.draw = function(context) {

  this.drawGrid(context);

  for (var i = 0; i < this.bricks.length; i++) {
    this.bricks[i].draw(context);
  }
}
```

We have to draw the grid as the base, and on top of that we draw all the bricks. (A brick is supposed to know how to draw itself, so this makes the grid simple.)

We create an additional method in the grid class that will draw the grid onto a given context.

```
Grid.prototype.drawGrid = function(context) {

  context.strokeRect(0, 0, this.width, this.height);

  var numberOfColumns = this.width / this.cellSize;
  var numberOfRows = this.height / this.cellSize;

  context.beginPath();

  for (var column = 0; column < numberOfColumns; column++) {
    context.moveTo(column * this.cellSize, 0);
    context.lineTo(column * this.cellSize, gridHeight);
  }
```

```
    for (var row = 0; row < numberOfRows; row++) {
      context.moveTo(0, row * this.cellSize);
      context.lineTo(gridWidth, row * this.cellSize);
    }

    context.stroke();
  }
```

Wow! That is a really big chunk of code. So, what do we do here?

For the rectangle around the grid, we simply use the `context.strokeRect()` function. The rectangle starts in the upper-left corner of the canvas, which has the coordinates (0, 0). The width and height for the rectangle is the grid width and height.

For the grid itself, we need something more like a pencil; thankfully the drawing context API works a lot like guiding a pencil across a sheet. First we have to pick up the pencil, metaphorically speaking. We tell the context that we start our drawing with `context.beginPath()`. After this, we move the pencil to where we want to start drawing the line. We also keep in mind that `moveTo` will move the pencil to a point without drawing the line, and `lineTo` actually draws a line.

Now we still have to draw the grid. First, we will draw the columns. We calculate the number of columns by dividing the width of the grid, which we set when initializing the grid class, by the `cellSize`, which was also set at that point. The rest is pretty much just looping over the amount of columns that we have, and always moving the pencil to the top and drawing a line to the bottom.

We use the exact same principle for drawing the rows. You might want to go over the lines closely and think about all the parameters. We believe that it might be good to leave a little bit of the crunching up to you!

Now, what is `context.stroke()` for? Both methods, `lineTo()` and `moveTo()`, just push orders into a stack. Whenever those methods are called, they are not directly executed. So without the `context.stroke()`, nothing except the frame would appear because the `strokeRect()`method actually creates the path and draws it all in one method call.

This is why we also called `context.beginPath()`. This method lets us create a new path and also clears the stack. So when we call `context.stroke()`, we draw all the lines that we have created since `context.beginPath()`.

So, what do we have so far? We can now exchange the `clearCanvas()` in the ready function with a `draw()` and we will be able to see our grid when we open the `index.html` file in a browser, as shown in Figure 4-5.

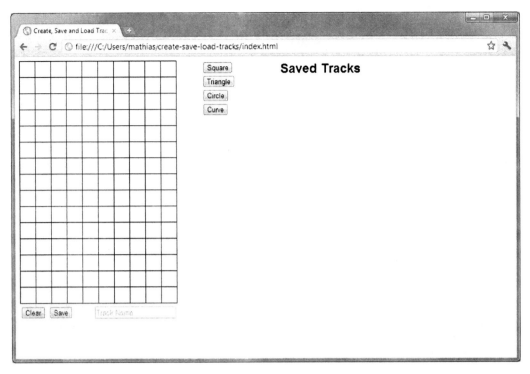

Figure 4-5. Screenshot of the application so far

The bricks

Now we get to a very interesting part: the first brick. First, we will have to create a new class in a new file. Since we are going to have a few different brick types, we might want to add a new folder, called bricks, in the javascripts folder (see Figure 4-6).

The first file we create is going to be the square.js. Let's not forget to add it to the JavaScript includes in the HTML. Add a <script> tag for the square.js file below the application.js <script> tag.

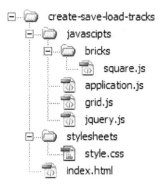

Figure 4-6. Folder structure

Square

The first brick that we go over is a simple rectangle.

```
var Square = function() {

this.row = 0;
  this.column = 0;
  this.type = "Square";
  this.rotation = 0;
}
```

We initialize the class with a row and a column attribute. We also need to know the type; that way we can easily find out what class it is. We'll explain later why that is important. We also have a rotation attribute. Although that is not really necessary on the square, we still want it to be compatible with the other brick types. More on that later, too.

As we saw in chapter: every brick class will need a draw method because it needs to draw itself onto the grid. We also know that it gets a context passed as an argument.

So it will look like the following:

```
Square.prototype.draw = function(context) {
}
```

So far, so good. Now we only need to draw it onto the grid.

```
Square.prototype.draw = function(context) {

  context.save();

  context.translate(this.column * BRICK_SIZE, this.row * BRICK_SIZE);
  context.fillColor = 0;
  context.fillRect(0, 0, BRICK_SIZE, BRICK_SIZE);

  context.restore();
}
```

To get our brick to the right position, we will translate the context to this point. `context.translate(x, y)` moves the coordinate system of the context by x and y. That means once you translated the context by (10, 10) you would start to draw at (10, 10), with a command like moveTo(0, 0). In our case, we move the coordinate system of the brick to the desired position of the brick. That means we multiply the column and row by the `BRICK_SIZE` and translate with those values. No problem so far. This would work perfectly fine for the first brick; but if the second brick would also translate the context, it would be translated to a wrong position since the first one already translated the context to its location. One solution is to translate the context back, but we would rather introduce you to a more powerful way of doing it.

With context.save() you can save the current status of the context. It actually puts the current status on a stack. If you then change the context and call context.restore() after that, you return to the same unchanged status. As mentioned, it actually puts the status on a stack so you can call save(), then change a few things, and call save() again. If you call restore() once you go on, step back to your last save() call. By calling restore again you'd be at the starting point.

So in between the save() and the restore() calls, we set our context to the right position. Then just set the fillColor to black and draw a rectangle. Easy, right?

After the drawing, we go back to the original status of the context by calling `context.restore()`. That way the next brick can do the same without knowing where the previous brick was placed.

Circle

Our next brick, the circle, is nearly as easy as the square. As with the square, we create a new `circle.js` file within our `javascripts/bricks` folder and add the `<script>` tag to our `index.html` file. The first few lines of code look very similar to the square code; we just change the type and variable name.

```
var Circle = function() {

    this.row = 0;
    this.column = 0;
    this.type = "Circle";
    this.rotation = 0;
}


Circle.prototype.draw = function(context) {
    var radius = BRICK_SIZE / 2;

    context.save();

    context.translate(this.column * BRICK_SIZE, this.row * BRICK_SIZE);
    context.fillColor = 0;

    context.beginPath();
    context.arc(radius, radius, radius, 0, Math.PI * 2);
    context.closePath();

    context.fill();
```

```
    context.restore();
}
```

The first difference is the radius in the draw function. We need to calculate it so we can draw a proper circle. The radius is half the brick size. After calculating, we do the same `context.save()`, `context.translate()`, and `context.restore()` magic we know from the square brick. Only this time, we use a path to draw the brick; so, the `context.beginPath()` and `context.closePath()` commands shouldn't catch you by surprise.

For the path itself, we use the `context.arc()` function to draw a circle. After closing the path, we fill it with the black fill color. And that's it. We are finished with our second brick, the circle!

Curve

The curve brick is our first asymmetric brick, so we must take the rotation into account when we draw the brick. But before we look into that issue, let's create a new `curve.js` file inside the `bricks` folder and add the proper `<script>` tag to our HTML. The following code is also nothing new to you:

```
var Curve = function() {
  this.row = 0;
  this.column = 0;
  this.type = "Curve";
  this.rotation = 0;
}
```

But now let's draw that little piece correctly on the canvas.

```
Curve.prototype.draw = function(context) {

  context.save();

  context.translate(this.column * BRICK_SIZE, this.row * BRICK_SIZE);

  context.translate(BRICK_SIZE / 2, BRICK_SIZE / 2);
  context.rotate(this.rotation * Math.PI / 180);
  context.translate(- BRICK_SIZE / 2, - BRICK_SIZE / 2);

  context.beginPath();

  context.fillColor = 0;
  context.moveTo(0, 0);
  context.bezierCurveTo(BRICK_SIZE / 2, 0,  BRICK_SIZE, BRICK_SIZE / 2, BRICK_SIZE,↵
BRICK_SIZE);
  context.lineTo(0, BRICK_SIZE);

  context.closePath();

  context.fill();

  context.restore();
}
```

The first special part is as follows:

```
context.translate(BRICK_SIZE / 2, BRICK_SIZE / 2);
context.rotate(this.rotation * Math.PI / 180);
context.translate(- BRICK_SIZE / 2, - BRICK_SIZE / 2);
```

What do we do here? We know that every brick saves its rotation in its this.rotation attribute. Before we draw anything, we must rotate the drawing context to the correct angle. The rotation won't affect any other bricks since the command happens between our context.save() and context.restore() pair. As we said earlier, this will undo anything we did to the context, so we have a clean start before we draw the next brick.

To be able to rotate the context correctly, we must translate it to the center of the rotation. The center is actually the center of the brick, so we translate by the half of the brick size in both directions. context.rotate() takes one argument, which tells it how far it should rotate the context in radians. Since this.rotation is a degree value, we must convert it from degrees to radians. We do this by multiplying the rotation with pi and dividing it by 180.

After finishing with the rotation, we translate by the negative half of a brick in both directions. This undoes our translate command before the rotation. Since we took the rotation into account, we can now focus on drawing the brick.

As with the circle, we start a new path and move to the coordinates (0, 0). Then we use the context.bezierCurveTo() function to draw a quarter circle from the top-left corner to the bottom-right one. From this corner, we draw a line to the bottom-left corner and are finished after closing the path. After calling context.fill(), we are finished and can move on to the next brick, the triangle!

Triangle

With the triangle brick, it's the same as with the others. The first few lines are not really surprising.

```
var Triangle = function() {
  this.row = 0;
  this.column = 0;
  this.type = "Triangle";
  this.rotation = 0;
}
```

The triangle is also an asymmetric brick, so we need to take the rotation into account in the same way we did with the curve brick. Nothing new here.

```
Triangle.prototype.draw = function(context) {

  context.save();

  context.translate(this.column * BRICK_SIZE, this.row * BRICK_SIZE);

  context.translate(BRICK_SIZE / 2, BRICK_SIZE / 2);
  context.rotate(this.rotation * Math.PI / 180);
  context.translate(- BRICK_SIZE / 2, - BRICK_SIZE / 2);
```

```
        context.beginPath();

        context.fillColor = 0;
        context.moveTo(0, 0);
        context.lineTo(BRICK_SIZE, BRICK_SIZE);
        context.lineTo(0, BRICK_SIZE);

        context.closePath();

        context.fill();

        context.restore();
    }
```

Drawing the triangle is also pretty easy. We move our imaginary pencil to the top-left corner after we started a new path. The next line goes straight to the bottom-right corner; after that, a line to the bottom-left corner. And after closing and filling the path, we are finished!

Adding bricks to the grid

Yes we know, after writing so much code for the different bricks, it's time to get them on the grid. We already have the drawing functionality implemented. So, what we still need to do is figure out in which cell on the grid the user has clicked. Let's walk through that process step by step.

First, we need a callback when the user clicks onto the grid so that we can react upon the click. Since we are going to have more user interaction and more buttons, we declare a function in the application.js that sets up all the click handlers. Let's call this function initUI(). It will be called in the ready function as follows:

```
$(document).ready(function() {
  canvas = document.getElementById('grid');
  context = canvas.getContext('2d');

  grid = new Grid(gridWidth, gridHeight, BRICK_SIZE);

  initUI();
  draw();
});
```

So, for the click callback we will use jQuery. It looks like this:

```
function initUI() {

  $(canvas).click(onGridClicked);

}
```

In the callback we call onGridClicked(), we first have to figure out where the user clicked, because so far, we only know that the user has clicked somewhere on the grid.

```
function onGridClicked(event) {

  var mouseX = event.offsetX || event.layerX;
```

```
    var mouseY = event.offsetY || event.layerY;

    var column = Math.floor(mouseX / BRICK_SIZE);
    var row = Math.floor(mouseY / BRICK_SIZE);
}
```

First we read the X and Y position relative to the top-left corner of the canvas element. Every mouse click triggers a certain event. This event contains a lot of information, including information on the position of the mouse while clicked. The only problem is that different browsers go by different naming conventions. WebKit browsers such as Chrome or Safari have an attribute called offsetX (or offsetY) and Firefox calls the same value layerX (or layerY).

For further details, you need to look up the specs of different browsers. But offsetX and layerX should cover most major browsers. So to get the mouseX value, we take the offsetX attribute; and if that is undefined, we take the layerX value. We do this in a one-liner using an OR.

> **Note** This method is not completely safe because the user might click on the very left top which would mean that the offsetX is 0 and, therefore, false when it comes to the OR. But that is a very unlikely case and, therefore, ignored in this simple demo.

After reading the exact mouse position, it's easy to get the cell the user clicked in. All we have to do is divide the value by the block size. But remember to round the value, or in this case to get more accurate values we use Math.floor. Why? Let's say the user clicks on a pixel left of the third brick in the first row. He is very close, but still on the second brick. So the value we would get after dividing the mouseX by the BRICK_SIZE would be something like 2.99. When we round that value, it is 3; but we still want it to be 2. Therefore, we always bring the value down to a round figure.

Now we need to create a brick on that cell. Let's call and create another function, createBrickAt(column, row).

The function will look something like this:

```
function createBrickAt(column, row) {

    var brick = new Square();
    brick.column = column;
    brick.row = row;

    grid.addBrick(brick, context);
}
```

A very straightforward function! First, we create a Square brick. (We'll differentiate between the different bricks later.) After that, we assign our row and column values to the brick and then we pass it to the grid, since the grid is supposed to manage all existing bricks. We also pass the context to the grid, so that it knows where the new bricks should be drawn.

So, what does the grid do with the brick? Thanks to the well-planned base we built, there is not much the grid has to do.

```
Grid.prototype.addBrick = function(brick, context) {
  this.bricks.push(brick);

  brick.draw(context);
}
```

It adds the brick to its container of bricks. And after that, we just have to draw the brick onto the grid. We don't have to trigger the big draw function in the application.js. This would be what we developers call overkill! There is no need to clear anything because we can add the new brick on top of the grid. So all we have to do is call the draw method of the brick.

Go ahead and try it! Open the index.html in the browser and add a few bricks to the grid. Fun, right?!

You are right! We still need to differentiate between different bricks. As you might remember, we already implemented the buttons in the HTML markup.

```
<section id="bricks-container">
  <form>
    <button id="square-brick">Square</button>
    <button id="triangle-brick">Triangle</button>
    <button id="circle-brick">Circle</button>
    <button id="curve-brick">Curve</button>
  </form>
</section>
```

First we will need to make those buttons react to something. We go back to our initUI() function and add a little more functionality.

```
$("#bricks-container button").click(function(event) {
  event.preventDefault();

  var id = $(this).attr("id");
  setBrick(id);
});
```

We add a click callback on every button. jQuery lets us do that with only one line, thanks to the incredible selector engine.

First we have to prevent the browser from reacting on the click with the normal behavior, such as linking to another page. Luckily, we can stop that by using the event object that we get sent with the click. This object offers information and functionality related with the click, such as preventDefault(). Calling this function stops the browser from doing what it would do; so we can implement the logic of the button ourselves.

Next, we have to find out which button was actually clicked. That is easy since the this within the click function is a reference to the button actually clicked. With a little help from jQuery, we get the id from the button because that lets us differentiate between the buttons easily. The id is just like every other attribute, therefore we can read it with jQuery's attr() function.

Now we want to set the brick type that should be used from now on when clicked on the grid. We create a function called setBrick and pass it the buttonID.

```
function setBrick(buttonID) {

  if (currentButton) {
    currentButton.removeAttr("disabled");
  }

  currentButton = $("#" + buttonID);
  currentButton.attr("disabled", "disabled");

  switch (buttonID) {

    case "square-brick":
      selectedBrickClass = Square;
    break;

    case "triangle-brick":
      selectedBrickClass = Triangle;
    break;

    case "circle-brick":
      selectedBrickClass = Circle;
    break;

    case "curve-brick":
      selectedBrickClass = Curve;
    break;
  }
}
```

Don't worry. That looks way more complicated than it actually is. At the top you see we use a global variable called currentButton. We added it in the beginning to our application.js.

This variable will hold a reference to the currently selected button. On the first click, no button will be referenced by currentButton, so the if statement is not executed.

After that, we use jQuery to add a disabled attribute to the button; because once you clicked it, you don't need to click it again. We can easily access the button because we know the id as it's passed via the function argument.

Now the if statement makes sense, too. When you click another button, you will have to re-enable the currentButton and disable the new one. Logic cycle, right?

Finally we use a switch statement to differentiate between the different behavior, depending on which button was clicked. Now we use another global variable we created at the beginning: selectedBrickClass. We always assign it with the right brick class, depending on the button.

We are almost good to go. Let's go to the createBrickAt(column, row) method and change just one little thing. Instead of creating a square brick every time, we create a selectedBrickClass because it is only a reference to the currently selected brick. It will look like this:

```
function createBrickAt(column, row) {
    if (!selectedBrickClass) return;
```

```
    var brick = new selectedBrickClass();
    brick.column = column;
    brick.row = row;

    grid.addBrick(brick, context);
}
```

And that was all you had to do for that!

> **Note** We also added a safety drop out of the function. If the user didn't select a brick type before clicking on the grid, the selectedBrickClass would be null; therefore, we just drop out of the function by use of the return statement.

Implement rotation

We have considered rotation on some of our bricks. How do we do that? For this example, we decided to let the bricks rotate whenever you click on them. That means we have to, once again, change our working code. In onGridClicked, the function that determines the cell that was clicked, we add functionality that determines whether a brick is already on the cell or not.

```
function onGridClicked(event) {

    var mouseX = event.offsetX || event.layerX;
    var mouseY = event.offsetY || event.layerY;

    var column = Math.floor(mouseX / BRICK_SIZE);
    var row = Math.floor(mouseY / BRICK_SIZE);

    var selectedBrick = grid.getBrickAt(column, row);

    if (selectedBrick) {
        selectedBrick.rotation += 90;

        draw();

    } else {
        createBrickAt(column, row);
    }
}
```

We call a function on the grid that returns the brick at a certain cell, and if there is none, it returns null. (We will go over Grid.prototype.getBrickAt in a bit. Right now, let's go further on this.)

If there is a brick, we increase the rotation of the brick by 90 degrees. After that, we redraw the entire scene. We already have that function all set up: draw()

If there is no brick at that cell, we continue with the procedure we have already built. Now before we are done, we still have to add a little function on the grid that returns a certain brick, if it exists.

```
Grid.prototype.getBrickAt = function(column, row) {
  for (var i = 0; i < this.bricks.length; i++) {
    if (this.bricks[i].column === column && this.bricks[i].row === row) {
      return this.bricks[i];
    }
  }
  return null;
}
```

Very simple! We just loop through all the bricks, and if the column and the row are the same as the arguments, we return that brick. If we can't find one, we return null. It's as easy as this!

Implement the Clear button

Adding bricks to the grid is pretty cool, but sometimes there are too many of them around and you wish you could start from scratch. So, guess what? We are going to now give you the magic Clear button! The button is already in the HTML markup, so let's add the click callback to our initUI() function so that we can react upon it.

```
$("#clear-track").click(function(event) {
  event.preventDefault();

  grid.clear();
  draw();
});
```

As with the brick buttons, the first thing we do is stop the browser from doing what it always does. The next step is calling the grid.clear() function, which removes all bricks from the grid. After that, we just need to call draw()—and we have a nice empty grid again, ready to build awesome stuff!

The grid.clear() function is a very easy one. We just re-initialize the bricks array as an empty array. That way, all bricks on the grid are gone.

```
Grid.prototype.clear = function() {
  this.bricks = [];
}
```

The Store

Let's get to a little more technical (with less HTML5) part of the application. We know this is only a small demo app, but when it comes to bigger games, there will always be a time when you want to save the user's work. This can sometimes be a little more complicated than expected, because when you work with JavaScript on the client side, but you have a MySQL database on the back-end, you cannot just send objects and arrays the way you have them in the browser.

Since this is only a small demo, we don't really have a back-end, but we will demonstrate how it could work. So what we want is a string-based data structure to store all the tracks. Instead of a database, we just have an array where every index stands for one line in a table in a MySQL database.

Saving tracks

Let's walk through this step-by-step. First, we create a Store class. We add another new file named `store.js` to our includes and start out with something like this:

```
var Store = function() {
  this.tracks = [];
}
```

The `tracks` array will resemble our database. That means we need a method that lets us add tracks to the array. What can we expect as an argument for this function? A track is basically just a collection of bricks, so it will be a method that expects an array of bricks. That also comes in handy because we happen to know that the grid always has an array of all the bricks on the grid. So it will look something like the following:

```
Store.prototype.saveTrack = function(brickArray) {

  var brickValues = brickArray.map(this.getDataForBrick);
  var trackJSON = JSON.stringify(brickArray);

  /*
    this would be where one could send the data to an actual
    database - in this example it's only saved array
  */
  this.tracks.push(trackJSON);

  return this.tracks.length - 1;
}
```

As mentioned, we get an array of bricks; but the thing is, we cannot work with the whole brick class, so we have to walk through the array and exchange every brick with a simple object that still holds all the necessary information. JavaScript comes with a very handy function on the Array class called `map()`, which loops over the array and calls a function, in our case `getDataForBrick`, with the current element of the array. It doesn't really work on the original array, though, but rather returns a new array with the changed values. So we now need to define a `getDataForBrick` function that returns a simple object for a brick class of some kind.

What does our `Store.getDataForBrick()` function look like? We know we must strip down a brick to its essentials. This means we must get all information we need to re-create the brick later, if needed.

```
Store.prototype.getDataForBrick = function(brick) {
  var values = {};

  values.column = brick.column;
  values.row = brick.row;
  values.type = brick.type;
  values.rotation = brick.rotation;

  return values;
}
```

The `Store.getDataForBrick()` function is called with a brick instance as argument. Before we can grab the interesting values, we create an empty object named `values`. Within that object, we will store the brick's information. So, what do we need for re-creation later? Obviously the position on the grid, so let's store the column and row properties in our values object. The brick.type property is also very important; without it we don't know what type of brick we are talking about, so let's save that too. The last important piece of information is the rotation; after storing that, we can return our filled values object.

So, what did we do here? We converted a big JavaScript object, the brick, into a little, handy, key-value object with only the interesting things we must know. We do this to save storage space and make things more simple and easy. This reduced data object is a lot easier to store.

Let's get back to the saveTrack method. We now have an array of simple objects called brickValues. But we are not done yet. As we mentioned before, we want a simple, string-based way to store the tracks. Luckily, JavaScript has another trick up its sleeve for us. It is called JSON. What is JSON? It stands for JavaScript Object Notation and as Wikipedia puts it very shortly: "a lightweight text-based open standard." That means it is a string representation of primitives such as numbers, booleans, etc. but also objects and arrays. That makes it exactly what we want. We have an array with objects that contain nothing but primitive values. That means with a little help of JSON, we can easily convert it into a string by doing that.

```
var trackJSON = JSON.stringify(brickArray);
```

Now that gives us exactly the string we want to save. If we had a back-end server, now would be the time when we want to send the newly-created string to the back-end. But for our application, it is OK if we just add that string to our array. We append it at the end with this.tracks.push(trackJSON); and return the index of where it was inserted, which is the very last position of the array. Indices start at 0, so length minus one will return that last position of the array. It was actually not so difficult to save a complex type such as a square brick and store it as a string.

But even more interesting: how can we get it back into an array of real bricks?

Retrieving tracks

We now know how to store a track. We can even get the id of our stored track. But how do we retrieve a track from the store? There's nothing easier than that. With the track id we can tell the store to get us a specific track, let's call this function getTrack.

```
Store.prototype.getTrack = function(id) {
    var trackJSON = this.tracks[id];
    var bricksValues = JSON.parse(trackJSON);

    return bricksValues.map(this.getBrickForData);
}
```

The first step is to get the stored JSON string representing our track; that's very easy since the track id is also the index within the tracks array.

> **Note** *This method is not secure! In a real project, you must check if the id is valid because a case that's not our getTrack method will fail. For the sake of simplicity, we assume we use the function only with valid ids.*

Once we have the JSON representing our track, we use the counter function to JSON.stringify, which is JSON.parse. This function will convert the argument string into a handy JavaScript object that we can work with. In our case, we get an array with all the brick value objects. This array now must somehow be converted into an array full of actual bricks.

We have to once again convert the objects, but this time it is the other way around. Now we have simple objects containing all the necessary information, but we want to have actual bricks.

Once again we use the map() function on our array full of brick value objects. We must supply it with the correct convert function. And since the map() function returns the new array, we can simply return the result and are finished. But what does the convert function look like?

The function actually looks very similar. We want to stick with the naming convention from before; therefore we call it getBrickForData.

```
Store.prototype.getBrickForData = function(brickData) {
    var brick = new window[brickData.type]();

    brick.column = brickData.column;
    brick.row = brickData.row;
    brick.rotation = brickData.rotation;

    return brick;
}
```

First, we have to create a new instance from the right brick kind. We know we have the brick type saved as a string in the brickData object. We also know that all the Brick classes are defined on the global window scope. Just as almost everything, the window scope behaves just like an object. That means using the square brackets, we can access all the variables and classes defined on that scope. Even though it is a funny looking syntax, the following line lets us create the instance we want:

```
var brick = new window[brickData.type]();
```

Now that we have the class, we have to assign the values we saved, such as the column, the row, and the rotation. And that is it.

So we have all the functionality the store needs. Where do we go from here?

Implement the Save button

Now that we have the store ready, we still need to instantiate it in our application. Let's create one more global variable called store and go back to the ready function to set it there.

```
$(document).ready(function() {
    canvas = document.getElementById('grid');
    context = canvas.getContext('2d');

    grid = new Grid(gridWidth, gridHeight, BRICK_SIZE);
    store = new Store();
```

```
initUI();
draw();
});
```

The next step is adding functionality to the Save button. So let's skip to the `iniUI()` function and add another click callback, as follows:

```
$("#save-track").click(function(event) {
  event.preventDefault();

  store.saveTrack(grid.bricks);
});
```

As you can see, this one is really easy. We basically have all we need implemented in the store and so the only thing left is grabbing the bricks array from the grid, which is exactly what we need, and pass it to the store. Done!

You are right. Saving the tracks is easy, but not very meaningful if you can't see or access what you saved.

Create the saved tracks list

When we started building this application, we set up all the markup necessary for a list of tracks.

So we need to start adding tracks to that list. Let's extend the save functionality just a little.

```
$("#save-track").click(function(event) {
  event.preventDefault();

  var trackID = store.saveTrack(grid.bricks);
  var trackName = $("#track-name").val();

  addTrackToList(trackID, trackName);
});
```

We keep the `trackID` that we get from the store and also read the value of the input field. We use this name as the track name.

Now let's create another function that adds certain elements to the DOM.

```
function addTrackToList(ID, name) {
  var entry = $("<p>");
  var link = $('<a href="">Load</a>');

  link.click(function(event) {
    event.preventDefault();
    loadTrack(ID);
  });

  entry.append(link).append(" - " + name);

  $("#tracks-container").append(entry);
}
```

This might look a little complicated, but it's actually very simple. First, we use jQuery to create an empty <p> tag and an <a> tag. We can leave the href of the <a> empty, but still set a href attribute. Why? That way the browser still marks it as a link. But we don't want it to behave as a regular link and, therefore, we once again overwrite the click functionality with jQuery's click function.

> **Note** Entry and link are already jQuery nodes, so we can use the jQuery API on them, including click, append, etc.

Whenever the user clicks on the link, it should trigger a function called `loadTrack()`. We will go over that one in just a minute.

Now we wrap it all up, putting it all together in the right way. We put the link into the <p> tag and add a little string that contains the name. So if the function would be called with a track name such as My Track, it would create the following DOM node structure:

```
<p id="tracks-container">
  <a href="">Saved Tracks</a> - My Track
</p>
```

Let's add this to our prepared container and we are good to go—almost! We still have one little thing to take care of. When the user clicks the "load" link, it will trigger a function called `loadTrack` with the ID of that track passed to it.

```
function loadTrack(ID) {
  grid.bricks = store.getTrack(ID);

  draw();
}
```

All we have to do is retrieve the right array of bricks from the store. We use the passed ID for that and it will give us an array in the exact structure we need. So we take that array and overwrite the bricks array on the grid with it.

If we redraw the scene, we have the load functionality completed.

Summary

Guess what? You are finished with our little demo application. Congratulations!

In modern software development, it's generally a good idea to look back at a project once it's done and reflect on how things went. Since this is a little hard to do in a book, we will focus on the things we think you have learned.

The most important thing is that you built something functional from scratch. You started with zero lines of code, HTML markup, and CSS rules. But you built, line by line, a really cool little application. Since the application is split into components, you also got a good sense of how this can be done in the other projects that you will hopefully tackle soon.

You can get the complete code for this project from GitHub; just head over to https://github.com/stravid/create-save-load-tracks and download everything. If you like, you can even press the Fork button and surprise us by adding other bricks to the application! How does a waveform brick sound? You get the idea, we are looking forward to your creativity!

Thanks for reading. We hope you enjoyed this chapter!

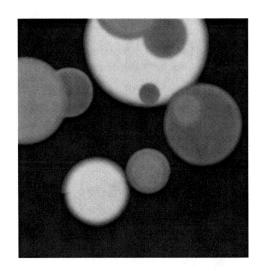

Chapter 5

3D CSS Tutorial
Harness the power of 3D CSS transformations to make a lightning-fast iPad game with creative JavaScript

Introduction

HTML5 canvas is, of course, brilliant. But it has to be said, its performance on iPads (and most other devices) leaves much to be desired. The GPU-accelerated canvas in iOS 5 is a definite improvement, but it's possible to create even smoother animated graphics with CSS manipulated in JavaScript, which runs lightning-fast—even on a first-generation iPad.

Using transformations, you can move HTML elements in 3D space (currently supported by most modern browsers, check caniuse.com for up-to-date browser support information). And when you transform HTML elements in 3D, they are automatically rendered by the GPU, which massively improves performance.

This works well on iOS, so read on to find out how to make a game that runs at a super-smooth 60 frames per second!

Overview of the elements

So here's our game. We have puffer fish rising up from the bottom of the sea—and when you touch them, they explode. It's a strange narrative, but *Angry Birds* is pretty strange, too, and it seems to be doing OK.

Our game has three main visual components: the puffer fish, the background layers, and the particles that occur when the fish explode (see Figure 5-1).

Every graphical object is a DOM element—in fact, they're all just divs with image backgrounds and I'm animating them by adjusting their CSS properties with JavaScript.

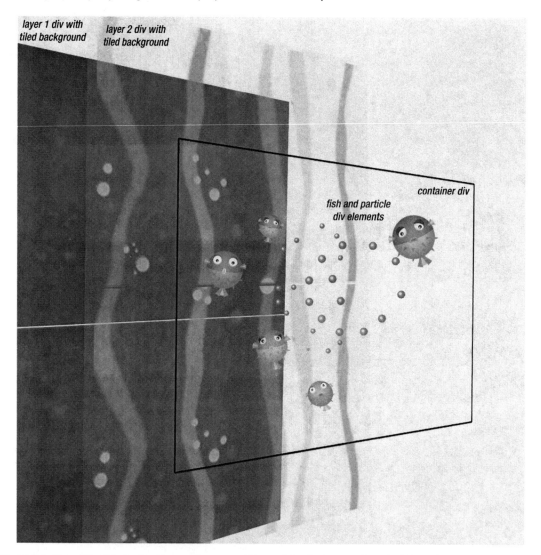

Figure 5-1. The puffer fish, the background layers, and the particles that occur when the fish explode

Game variables

The following shows the game variables.

```
// DOM elements
var container =    document.createElement('div'),

    layer1 = document.createElement('div'),
    layer2 = document.createElement('div'),

// screen size variables
    SCREEN_WIDTH = 1024,
    SCREEN_HEIGHT = 768,
    HALF_WIDTH = SCREEN_WIDTH / 2,
    HALF_HEIGHT = SCREEN_HEIGHT / 2,

// fish variables
    fishes = [],
    spareFishes = [],

    counter = 0,
    burstSound,

// the particle emitter
    emitter = new Emitter(container);
```

container is a div element that contains the fishes and particles; layer1 and layer2 are the two watery background divs.

We need to know half the width and height for working out the center of the screen. Fish objects are stored in the fishes array and spareFishes is used to store the fishes that we're not currently using.

counter is incremented every frame (more on that later) and burstSound is played when a fish explodes.

We also create a particle emitter, a custom object defined in particles.js that creates and updates our explosion particles.

The container's 3D properties

There are CSS styles at the top of the document as you would expect, but we're also setting some of them with JavaScript. Notice container.style.webkitPerspective, which specifies how extreme the 3D perspective is. This is like a field of view; in other words, how wide-angled our camera is. The webkitPerspectiveOrigin should be the middle of your game screen, otherwise things will disappear into the top left as they move into the distance.

```
// set up the CSS for the DOM elements
layer1.className = "parallax";
layer1.style.background = 'url(img/parallaxBack.jpg)';
document.body.appendChild(layer1);

layer2.className = "parallax";
```

```
layer2.style.background = 'url(img/parallaxFront.png) transparent';
document.body.appendChild(layer2);

container.className = "container";
container.style.webkitPerspective= "400";
container.style.webkitPerspectiveOrigin= HALF_WIDTH+"px "+HALF_HEIGHT+"px";
container.style.width = SCREEN_WIDTH;
container.style.height = SCREEN_HEIGHT;
```

Events and game loop timer

The following shows the events and game loop timer.

```
function init() {

    initMouseListeners();
    setInterval(gameLoop, 1000/60);
}
```

We use `setInterval` to call `gameLoop` 60 times a second. Because `setInterval` requires time in milliseconds, we need to know the number of mils there are per frame. To learn this, we first convert frames per second (fps) to seconds per frame by inverting, which gives us 1/60. Next, we convert seconds per frame to mils per frame by multiplying by 1000—which is 1000/60.

Did I just lose you? Don't worry, all you need to know is that to convert fps into mils per frame, simply divide 1000 by the frame rate.

> *requestAnimationFrame*
>
> *At the risk of getting even more complicated, modern browsers have started implementing requestAnimationFrame, which fires on a browser screen redraw. This has the benefit of syncing smoothly with the refresh cycle on your graphics card, which avoids screen tearing.*
>
> *But because you never know how frequently requestAnimationFrame will fire, ensuring that your game runs at the same speed across different computers and browsers is complicated. However, it's something to look out for in the future. Paul Irish has implemented a fallback that's worth looking at. For more information about this, see http://paulirish.com/2011/requestanimationframe-for-smart-animating/.*
>
> *The other benefit to requestAnimationFrame is that it stops firing when your browser tab is hidden, saving CPU and battery life. Chrome has implemented a throttle on setInterval so that it only fires once per second if the page isn't visible.*

Game loop overview

The following is the main game loop. The comments should explain enough about what's going on. We're adding more fish, updating the parallax layers, iterating through all the fish, and updating them all, then finally calling emitter.update(), which looks after the particles.

```
function gameLoop()
{

    // every 20 frames, make a new fish
    if(counter++%20==0)     makeFish();

    // update the parallax layers
    layer1.style.webkitTransform = "translate3d(0px, "+(-768 +((counter*5)%768))+"px, -
999px) scale(4)";
    layer2.style.webkitTransform  = "translate3d(0px, "+(-768 +((counter*10)%768))+"px, -
998px) scale(4)";

    // iteratate through each fish
    for (i=0; i<fishes.length; i++) {
            var fish = fishes[i];
            if(!fish.enabled) continue;

            // update the fishes position properties
            fish.update();

            // and then update the visible object for that fish
            fish.render();

            // if the fish is way off the top of the screen, then
            // remove it. For the finished game you would probably
            // add some kind of score penalty at this point.
            if(fish.posY <-200) removeFish(fish);

    }

    // then update all the particles.
    emitter.update();

}
```

Making new fish

Here's a trick I often like to use when things need to happen periodically. I'm using a counter variable that is incremented every frame. The % sign denotes *modulus*, which returns what is left when you divide the first value with the second. For example: 4 % 2 = 0, 5 % 2 = 1, 11 % 10 = 1, 345 % 10 = 5. So, counter%20 will be 0 every 20 frames.

Every 20 frames we'll make a new fish.

```
    // every 20 frames, make a new fish
    if(counter++%20==0)         makeFish();
```

Our Fish object handles the position, update, and appearance of our fish. The constructor parameters specify its 3D position, the image URL, and the image size. We're creating an HTML div element and setting its CSS properties so it has a fixed size, absolute position, and a background image.

```
function Fish(posx, posy, posz, imageSRC, imageWidth, imageHeight) {

    var TO_RADIANS = Math.PI/180;

    this.domElement = document.createElement('div');

    this.domElement.style.background = 'url('+imageSRC+') transparent';

    this.domElement.style.position = 'absolute';
    this.domElement.style.display = 'block';
    this.domElement.style.width = imageWidth+"px";
    this.domElement.style.height = imageHeight+"px";
    this.domElement.style.webkitTransformOrigin = (imageWidth/2)+"px
"+(imageHeight/2)+"px";
    this.domElement.style.pointerEvents="auto";

    // the position of the fish
    this.posX = posx;
    this.posY = posy;
    this.posZ = posz;

    // the velocity
    this.velX = 0;
    this.velY = 0;
    this.velZ = 0;

    this.size = 1;
    this.enabled = true;
    // add this to the yVel every frame to simulate gravity
    this.gravity = 0;
    var counter = 0;

    this.update = function() {

            // add gravity force to the y velocity
            this.velY += this.gravity;

            // and the velocity to the position
            this.posX += this.velX;
            this.posY += this.velY;
            this.posZ += this.velZ;

            //rotate pos and vel around the centre
            counter++;
            this.rotate(2);

    };

    this.render = function() {
            var dom = this.domElement,
```

```
                styleStr,
                sx = Math.sin(counter*0.4)*0.04 + this.size,
                sy = Math.sin(Math.PI + counter*0.4)*0.04 + this.size;

        dom.style.webkitTransform = "translate3d("+this.posX+"px, "+this.posY+"px,
"+this.posZ+"px) scale("+sx+","+sy+") rotate("+Math.sin(counter*0.05)*20+"deg)";

    };

    this.rotate = function(angle, useRadians) {

            // trig that rotates around the y axis (affecting x and z)
            var cosRY = Math.cos(angle * (useRadians ? 1 : TO_RADIANS));
            var sinRY = Math.sin(angle * (useRadians ? 1 : TO_RADIANS));

            var tempx = this.posX- HALF_WIDTH;
            this.posX= (tempx*cosRY)-(this.posZ*sinRY) +HALF_WIDTH;
            this.posZ= (tempx*sinRY)+(this.posZ*cosRY);

            tempx = this.velX;
            this.velX= (tempx*cosRY)-(this.velZ*sinRY);
            this.velZ= (tempx*sinRY)+(this.velZ*cosRY);

    };

}
```

div or img?

We're using divs with a background image for all our game objects, but we could just use normal image objects. However, if we wanted to create animations, it'd be easier with divs. Using a spritesheet image like Figure 5-2 allows you to switch "frames" by adjusting the div's background offset. This is how we created the animated characters on the iPad-optimized platform game Infector! *at Plug-in Media. More information is available at http://seb.ly/html5javascript-platform-game/.*

Figure 5-2. An example spritesheet from the Infector! game by Plug-in Media.

Fish update

Here's the Fish.update function.

```
this.update = function() {

    // add gravity force to the y velocity
```

```
        this.velY += this.gravity;

        // and the velocity to the position
        this.posX += this.velX;
        this.posY += this.velY;
        this.posZ += this.velZ;

        //rotate pos and vel around the centre
        counter++;
        this.rotate(2);

    };
```

As well as x, y, and z position, we also have an x, y, and z velocity. Velocity is how much it moves in each direction every frame.

First we add gravity to velY (the y velocity). This is part of the simple physics system, and in most circumstances gravity would be a positive number that gets added to velocity making things fall down. In our case we're subverting this system by giving gravity a negative value! This makes our fish accelerate upwards, which makes our game a little harder.

Fish render

This is a pretty scary-looking function, but it's quite simple at its core: it updates the DOM element's style properties to move, scale, and rotate the fish. It only looks complex because we have to make the strings that adjust these properties.

```
        this.render = function() {
            var dom = this.domElement,
                    styleStr,
                    sx = Math.sin(counter*0.4)*0.04 + this.size,
                    sy = Math.sin(Math.PI + counter*0.4)*0.04 + this.size;

            dom.style.webkitTransform = "translate3d("+this.posX+"px, "+this.posY+"px,
        "+this.posZ+"px) scale("+sx+","+sy+") rotate("+Math.sin(counter*0.05)*20+"deg)";

        };
```

The weird looking Math.sin function uses a sine wave to affect the fishes' x and y scale. This makes the fish wobble and look kinda squishy, like it's swimming through water.

The last line sets the CSS property webkitTransform, and we're adjusting translate3d, which is the 3D transformation. Then it's scaled in both x and y axis (the wobble). And finally it's rotated in 2D using another sine value that causes the fish's left and right oscillating rotation.

Making fish

Here's the first part of the makeFish(…) function. First, we check to see if there are any fishes for reuse (more on this in the "Recycling the fish" section), and if not, we create a new one. Notice that we're using the modulus (%) operator to make sure the fish image number is never higher than the number of fish images we have.

Then we're adding touchstart and mouseover events for the fish's DOM element, so that we know when the fish have been hit. If you're playing it on your desktop, you only have to move your mouse over the fish to burst them!

```
// create a new fish in the bottom middle of the stage
if(spareFishes.length&gt;0) {
    // if one is already in the spare array, recycle it
    fish = spareFishes.pop();
    fish.enabled = true;
    fish.domElement.style.visibility = "visible";
} else {
    // otherwise make a new one
    // Work out the fishimage URL
    var fishImageURL = "img/orangefish0"+((fishes.length % 4) + 1)+".png";
    // and then make a new fish object
    fish = new Fish(0, 0, 0, fishImageURL, 128, 128);
    // add it into the array of fishes
```

```
    fishes.push(fish);

    // then add touch and mouseover events to the fish.
    fish.domElement.addEventListener("mouseover", fishMouseOver, true);
    fish.domElement.addEventListener("touchstart", fishTouched, true);

    container.appendChild(fish.domElement);

}
```

Setting the fish properties

This is where we set each fish's position to be in the middle bottom of the screen, plus a random x and z offset between -250 and 250. We also give it a slightly random velocity and give it a gravity of -0.05, which is the negative gravity value I mentioned earlier that makes the game a little more fun—the longer it takes to hit the fish, the faster they move up.

```
    fish.posX = HALF_WIDTH + randomRange(-250,250);
    fish.posY = SCREEN_HEIGHT+100;
    fish.posZ = randomRange(-250,250);

    // give it a random x and y velocity
    fish.velX = randomRange(-1,1);
    fish.velY = randomRange(-1,-2);
    fish.velZ = randomRange(-1,1);

    fish.size = 1;
    fish.gravity = -0.05;
```

Recycling the fish

We have to get rid of a fish when it explodes or goes off the screen. We could just take it out of the array and forget about it, but this is bad for memory management. Even if a fish is cleared out of memory with the garbage collector, it still takes CPU to constantly create new DOM elements and JavaScript objects.

```
    function removeFish(fish) {

        fish.enabled = false;

        fish.domElement.style.visibility = "hidden";
        spareFishes.push(fish);
    }
```

So we've made a simple pooling system, when we've finished with a fish, we disable it (by setting its enabled property to false) and add it into the spareFishes array. We leave its DOM element in our document, but we set its visibility to "hidden".

In the makeFish function, we check if there are any fish objects in this spareFishes array to reuse before we make a new one.

Exploding the fish

The following are the listeners that are called when you touch or mouse-over a fish. In either case, we need to find the fish object for the DOM element that fired the event. Note that the touchstart event has an array of touch objects; it may well be that you touched down with multiple fingers at once.

```
function fishMouseOver(event) {
    event.preventDefault();
    var fish = getFishFromElement(event.target);
    if(fish) explodeFish(fish);
}

function fishTouched(event) {
    event.preventDefault();
    for(var j=0; j<event.changedTouches.length; j++) {
        var fish = getFishFromElement(event.target);
        if(fish) explodeFish(fish);
    }
}

function getFishFromElement(domElement) {
    for(var i=0; i<fishes.length;i++) {
        if(fishes[i].domElement == domElement) return fishes[i];
    }
    return false;
}
```

When we find the fish that was touched (or moused-over), we call explodeFish(…), which plays the explosion sound, calls makeExplosion(…) on the particle emitter (creating a burst of little particles), and finally calls the removeFish(…) function.

Sound

It's improving all the time, but sound in HTML/JavaScript is a bit broken at the moment. It's fine if you want to play some music, but if you're triggering sounds as you play a game, it's patchy. Dominic Szablewski, the guy behind impact.js, has a slightly ranty but informative blog post about this at www.phoboslab.org/log/2011/03/the-state-of-html5-audio. A slightly less ranty post is at www.phoboslab.org/log/2011/03/multiple-channels-for-html5-audio.

In iOS it's even worse. It seems as if you can play only one sound at a time, but it sometimes just doesn't play at all. Remy Sharp fixed some of these issues with his "audio sprite" (http://remysharp.com/2010/12/23/audio-sprites/), and if you use AIF format rather than MP3, it seems marginally more reliable. I found that it also helps if you use very short sounds (like in the Burst game).

If you're working across browsers, you'll need several audio file formats. You can test for a specific format playback capabilities using Audio.canPlayType (although, astonishingly, this gives the somewhat woolly responses of "probably" or "maybe"!) There's more information about HTML5 audio at the HTML5 Doctor (http://html5doctor.com/native-audio-in-the-browser/).

Particles

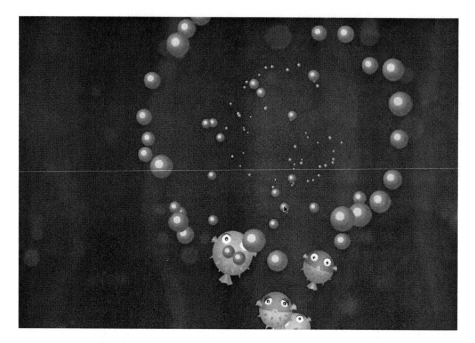

Figure 5-3. Image of exploding fish particles

We don't have room in this tutorial to look at the particle system in detail, but rest assured that it's a very similar system to the way that we manage the fish. The particle emitter has its own update loop, and each particle has a DOM element, position, and velocity. It just uses a slightly different physics model that includes drag and a *shrink* factor that causes the particles to get smaller.

Have a look through the Particles.js file to see if you can work out how it works. All the code is commented throughout.

For more information about particle systems, see the Seb Lee-Delisle tutorials at `http://seb.ly/tutorials`.

Parallax layers

I've implemented a parallax layer system with two background layers moving at different speeds to give the impression of 3D depth. Each one is a div that is twice the height of its image, and I move each y position relative to a counter.

```
// update the parallax layers
layer1.style.webkitTransform = "translate3d(0px, "+(-768 +((counter*5)%768))+"px, -999px)
scale(4)";
layer2.style.webkitTransform  = "translate3d(0px, "+(-768 +((counter*10)%768))+"px, -
998px) scale(4)";
```

The layer behind moves slower than the layer in front; in the following code, look where I'm multiplying counter by five for the back layer's y position. Remember that counter increments every frame, so our back layer will move down five pixels per frame.

The front layer moves twice as fast. We use the modulus of the screen height to ensure that when the position gets too high, it's reset down again. The div images tile vertically, so you don't notice this reset.

This method of moving the front layer faster than the back one gives the illusion of 3D depth, which is known as *parallax scrolling*.

I tried several different ways of implementing this (including adjusting the background image offset of a static div), but this method seems the best. Notice that I'm setting the translateZ CSS property to 0 in order to enable 3D rendering, which triggers GPU acceleration, even though I'm not actually moving it in 3D!

Disabling default touch/mouse behavior

Default actions happen on touch events—if you touch and drag, you scroll the web page. On some devices, a menu appears on a long touch. We need to disable these default actions by calling event.preventDefault().

```
function fishTouched(event) {
    event.preventDefault();
```

For a production-ready game, we should probably also listen to orientation change events and rescale our game accordingly, but I wanted to keep this tutorial code as simple as possible.

> *Getting it on the iPad*
>
> *It's easy to deploy this game on the web—just stick it on a server and open it on your iPad browser. You can even use the little forward button in mobile Safari to save it to your home screen, then it's just like any other app. There's even a meta tag you can add to your HTML that will make it run in full screen:*
>
> `<meta name="apple-mobile-web-app-capable" content="yes" />`
>
> *This is all cool, of course, but sometimes you want a proper app from the App Store—all official like! Good news—you can wrap up HTML/JS files into apps with PhoneGap (www.phonegap.com) and Titanium Mobile (www.appcelerator.com/products/titanium-mobile-application-development).*

Conclusion

As programmers, playability and responsiveness lies squarely on our shoulders—so making a game playable and responsive are skills that we need to acquire. Anyone can program a character that runs along a platform, but it's harder to adjust its speed, gravity, and control—to make it part of a game that feels fun. This is a creative skill that requires practice and a process of constant iterations.

The following are some exercises to expand the game and for you to get a feel for creating something special:

- Experiment with the speed and frequency of the fish to see how this affects gameplay.

- Use the core code to make a different game that moves sideways. Naturally, you'll want to use your own graphics and particle images.

- Add a screen orientation change listener so that the game works in portrait and landscape.

- Add an intro screen, a scoring mechanism, and a Game Over. Of course, you'll need to figure out what constitutes a game over. Perhaps there's a time limit? Perhaps you have to blow up all the fish?

Let me know what you come up with. Share your results here or with the #CreativeJS hashtag on Twitter.

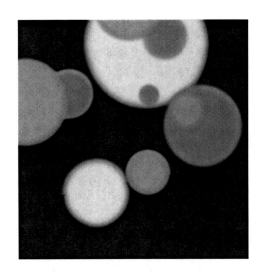

Chapter 6

Particle Systems

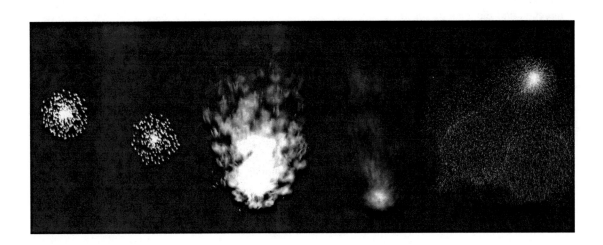

Introduction

Particle systems are used to create many different special effects like fire, rain, and smoke. They are used in virtually all video games, as well as in a lot of movie special effects. But what is a particle? In essence, a particle is something represented by a point in space, a dot. In practice, particles are often useful for simulating effects that consist of many small objects. Now "small" really depends on the context. If you are planning to simulate a galaxy, you will need to treat stars, or even clusters of stars as particles. If you are simulating rain, your particles will be individual raindrops.

In this chapter, I will show you how to design and implement your own particle effects using HTML5 canvas. We will gradually build up the code by adding the features we need to implement and improve the effects.

Please note that the code in this chapter is optimized to be simple and easy to understand. It should serve as an example of the mechanisms involved in a particle system. It does not always reflect best practices for production code. For example, the code does not use any namespaces or a module system, which is a must for any complex application. The examples shown are very high-fidelity and may need to be scaled-down to fit into the resource budget of a game.

Math

To create a particle system, you will need some basic math. The good thing about coding creative systems, however, is that you can't go wrong. **If it looks good, it is good.** So feel free to try out all your crazy ideas, even if they are "wrong," they might end up looking surprisingly good.

Vectors

To animate particles, some simple linear algebra is required. The most important concept for that is clearly the vector. A vector can describe a point in space, like the location of our particle. But it can also describe a direction and distance in space; for example, the speed and direction of a particle. If you are already familiar with vectors, you can safely skip this section.

A vector is defined by an n-tuple of numbers. As we will be operating in 2D space, our vector will have two components: x and y.

We will use the default coordinate system of canvas. So for a point, x denotes the distance from the left in pixels; and y is the distance from the top. For a velocity, x is the number of pixels the point will travel to the right in one second; and y denotes the number of pixels it will move down.

If you are building a game, it often makes sense to use SI units. For simplicity, we will stick to pixels and seconds as the units in this chapter.

```
function Vec2(x, y){
        this.x = x;
        thix.y = y;
}
```

We can now use Vec2 to define a basic particle.

```
function Particle(position, velocity){
        this.position = position;
        this.velocity = velocity;
}
```

Let's go through an example to see how those vectors work in practice:

```
    // The particle distance is 120 pixels from the left and 70 pixels
    // from the top
var position = new Vec2(120, 70),
    // and in one second the particle moves
    // 10 pixels to the right and -5 pixels down (5 pixels up).
    velocity = new Vec2(10, -5),
    particle = new Particle(position, velocity);

// 60 times per second
window.setInterval(function(){
    var time_passed = 1.0/60,
        movement_right = particle.velocity.x * time_passed,
        movement_down = particle.velocity.y * time_passed;
    particle.position.x += movement_right;
    particle.position.y += movement_down;
}, 1000/60);
```

> **Note** *I use setInterval for simplicity, in practice using requestAnimationFrame is a better idea.*

This code moves the particle velocity.x pixels per second to the right and velocity.y pixels per second downwards. As you can see, writing code like that is quite tedious. By adding some operations—like addition and multiplication—to the vector, we can make this code a lot simpler.

```
Vec2.prototype = {
    muls: function(n) { return new Vec2(this.x*n, this.y*n); },
    imuls: function(n) { this.x *= n; this.y *= n; return this; },

    mul: function(v) { return new Vec2(this.x*v.x, this.y*v.y); },
    imul: function(v) { this.x *= v.x; this.y *= v.y; return this; },

    divs: function(n) { return new Vec2(this.x/n, this.y/n); },
    div: function(v) { return new Vec2(this.x/v.x, this.y/v.y); },

    adds: function(n) { return new Vec2(this.x+n, this.y+n); },
    iadds: function(s) { this.x+=s; this.y+=s; return this; },

    add: function(v) { return new Vec2(this.x+v.x, this.y+v.y); },
    iadd: function(v) { this.x+=v.x; this.y+=v.y; return this;},

    subs: function(n) { return new Vec2(this.x-n, this.y-n); },
    isubs: function(s) { this.x-=s; this.y-=s; return this;},

    sub: function(v) { return new Vec2(this.x-v.x, this.y-v.y); },
    isub: function(v) { this.x-=v.x; this.y-=v.y; return this;},

    set: function(x, y) {this.x = x; this.y = y;}
};
```

The updated example now looks like this:

```
// 60 times per second
window.setInterval (function(){
    var td = 1.0/60;
    particle.position.iadd(particle.velocity.muls(td));
}, 1000/60);
```

Adding checks

In JavaScript, numeric errors lead to a special *NaN* (not a number) value. All operations done with a NaN as operand will result in another NaN. This can make it very difficult to track down the source of errors. In the following example, all the variables will become NaN:

```
// note the missing arguments to Vec2()
var v = new Vec2(),
    v2 = v.muls(2)
    v3 = v2.add(new Vec2(1, 2)),
    v4 = v3.subs(0.5);
// NaN, NaN
console.log(v4.x, v4.y);
```

In bigger applications, it can become very hard to find the origin of the NaN values. There are several solutions to this problem. You could simply not make any mistakes or you could add assertions to all operations. Adding assertions everywhere has its drawbacks: it's error prone, slows down, your code and increases its size. We can, however, write a helper, as follows, that will make sure that some properties will never become NaN by throwing an exception when they do so:

```
function notNaN(obj, name){
    var key = '__' + name;
    obj.__defineGetter__(name, function(){
        return this[key];
    });
    obj.__defineSetter__(name, function(v) {
        // you can also check for isFinite() in here if you'd like to
        if(typeof v !== 'number' || isNaN(v)){
            throw new TypeError(name + ' isNaN');
        }
        this[key] = v;
    });
}
```

notNaN can be used on both instances and prototypes. In our case, we will apply it to the prototype of Vec2. When we run the following example again with notNaN in place, we will get an exception on the first line—making it clear where the NaN values come from:

```
// Throw an exception if x or y of any Vec2 are set to NaN
notNaN(Vec2.prototype, 'x');
notNaN(Vec2.prototype, 'y');
```

There are drawbacks to using notNaN in production code, however. First, it doesn't work in IE8 or older. Second, it makes your code slow. Luckily, you can simply disable it for use in production.

```
var DEBUG = true;
...
if(DEBUG) {
    notNaN(Vec2.prototype, 'x');
    notNaN(Vec2.prototype, 'y');
}
```

Random values

To create varying particle effects, we are going to need random numbers. JavaScript only provides a very simple way to get random numbers, namely Math.random(), which returns a value between 0 and 1. For our particle engine, we will need random numbers in the form of 63 +/- 9.

```
function fuzzy(range, base){
    return (base||0) + (Math.random()-0.5)*range*2
}

// a random value from -10 to 10
fuzzy(10);
// a random value of 63 +/- 9.
fuzzy(9, 63);
```

We will also need to randomly choose an item from a list; for example, a texture. The following is a very simple function that will help us do just that:

```
function choice(array) {
    return array[Math.floor(Math.random()*array.length)];
}
```

Components

Our particle system consists of a few different components that work together to create many different effects. The design focuses on efficiency and simplicity. It makes heavy use of JavaScript features like first-class functions and closures. We start with a very simple, but flexible, base and add functionality as needed.

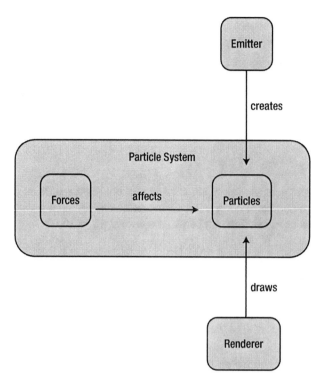

Figure 6-1. Component overview

Particles

Every particle in the system needs to have at least a position and a velocity. Other properties can be added as needed; and may include, for example, the following:

- color
- image
- alpha
- age
- mass

The update method of the particle updates its values for a single time step.

```
function Particle(position){
    this.position = position;
    this.velocity = new Vec2(0.0, 0.0);
}
Particle.prototype = {
    update: function(td) {
```

```
        this.position.iadd(this.velocity.muls(td));
    }
}
```

Emitters

Nothing comes from nothing. Unlike virtual particles in physics, our particles don't pop into existence spontaneously; they are created by the emitter. The emitter gives particles their initial attributes, including their position. Note that the emitter is a purely abstract concept and can be implemented in many different ways.

The following are examples of emitters:

- onclick emitter

- one time emitter

- constant emitter

Forces

After particles have been created by the emitters, they will be affected by the forces of the particle system. It's important that those forces are very different from the concept of a force in Newtonian physics. The interface for a force is as follows:

```
function force(particle, td){
}
```

td is the time that has passed since the last update.

A simple example of this is gravity:

```
function gravity(particle, td){
    particle.velocity.y += 50*td;
}
```

The following are other examples of forces:

- acceleration

- damping

- wind

- attraction

- repulsion

I will cover a more abstract way to create forces in the next section.

Renderer

The job of the renderer is to visualize all the particles in a system. There can be different renderers for different targets and rendering techniques. The following are examples of rendering targets:

- canvas image

- canvas pixel

- WebGL

- HTML

Different particles might require different renderer implementations to handle additional properties, like rotation or alpha values. The following is an example of a very simple renderer is the canvas image renderer:

```
function renderCanvasImage(ctx, particles, fade){
    for(var i = 0; i < particles.length; i++) {
        var particle = particles[i];
        ctx.save();
        ctx.translate(particle.position.x, particle.position.y);
        ctx.drawImage(particle.image, -particle.image.width/2, -particle.image.height/2);
        ctx.restore();
    }
}
```

System

The ParticleSystem contains all the particles and the forces acting on them. The emitter and renderer are not part of the ParticleSystem because they are often more tightly-integrated into other parts of the applications. Particles are often emitted as a result of events in the application. Also, most games already have some kind of rendering system that can be used. This makes the code for the particle system very simple, as follows:

```
function ParticleSystem(){
    this.particles = [];
    this.forces = [];
}
ParticleSystem.prototype = {
    update: function(td) {
        var alive = [];
        for(var i = 0; i < this.particles.length; i++) {
            var particle = this.particles[i];
            for(var j = 0; j < this.forces.length; j++) {
                var force = this.forces[j];
                force(particle, td);
            }
            if(particle.update(td)){
                alive.push(particle);
            }
        }
```

```
          this.particles = alive;
      }
};
```

Hello fireworks

We have now covered all the basics necessary to create different particle systems. Now it's time to get started with a simple example. Fireworks are definitely the "hello world" of particle systems. They look great, illustrate the concept well, and are fairly easy to create (see Figure 6-2). So let's create some fireworks.

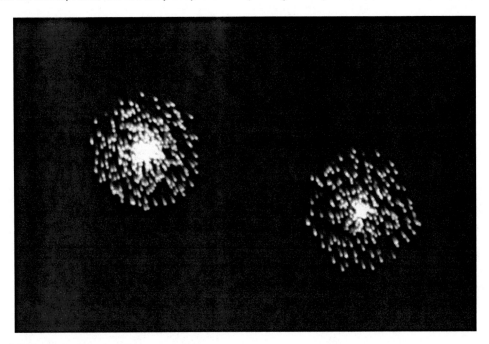

Figure 6-2. Fireworks demo in action

Designing the spark

The first step to create our fireworks is to design an image that we can use as a single particle (see Figure 6-3). I choose a simple eight by eight pixel radial gradient for this.

Figure 6-3. An individual spark

It is important that no component of the color used for the spark is 0. If one component is zero it will not get brighter when additively blended. That's because 0 * anything === 0 (except if anything is NaN!).

Implementing the main loop

The main loop for this example is very simple. For every frame, we update the particle system and draw all the sparks. There is a 1 in 100 chance that we emit a new burst of particles.

```
function main(){
    var canvas = document.getElementById('c'),
        ctx = canvas.getContext('2d'),
        system = new ParticleSystem();

    emit(system, canvas.width, canvas.height);

    window.setInterval(function() {
        if(Math.random() < 0.01){
            emit(system, canvas.width, canvas.height);
        }
        system.update(1/30);
        ctx.fillRect(0, 0, canvas.width, canvas.height);
        renderCanvasImage(ctx, system.particles);
    }, 1000/30);
}
var spark = new Image();
spark.onload = main;
spark.src = 'spark.png';
```

Implementing the emitter

For our fireworks emitter, we want to pick a random point on the canvas. We then spawn 100 particles at that point and give them random velocities. This will make them fly off into different directions.

```
function emit(system, width, height){
    var position =  new Vec2(Math.random()*width, Math.random()*height);
    for(var i = 0; i < 100; i++) {
        var particle = new Particle(position.copy());
        particle.velocity.x = fuzzy(100);
        particle.velocity.y = fuzzy(100);
        particle.image = spark;
        system.particles.push(particle);
    }
}
```

You can view the result of this in fireworks.0.html. As you can see, the pattern generated by the sparks looks a bit square. This is because we initialized the velocities independently. We can simply adjust this to create circles or spheres.

```
var particle = new Particle(position.copy()),
    alpha = fuzzy(Math.PI),
    radius = Math.random()*100;
particle.velocity.x = Math.cos(alpha)*radius;
particle.velocity.y = Math.sin(alpha)*radius;
particle.image = spark;
```

When the radius is randomized, you will get a sphere-like shape; when it is constant (radius = 50, for example), you will get a circle. Note that to get an even distribution, you would need to use the square root of the radius but, in my opinion, it *looks* better without it. You can see this in fireworks.1.html. Try to find other creative shapes on your own!

Forces

Right now, our fireworks look like they are in a vacuum and not affected by gravity or air. We can easily change this by adding some forces to the simulation.

A simple way to define gravity would be like this:

```
function gravity(particle, td){
    particle.velocity.y += td*10;
}
```

This is very specific, however. Often it makes sense to define forces in a more general way. Gravity, for example, is nothing but constant acceleration.

```
function accelerationf(force){
    return function(particle, td){
        particle.velocity.iadd(force.muls(td));
    };
}

var gravity = accelerationf(new Vec2(0, 50));
```

In addition to gravity, we also want to simulate the air the fireworks are in. There are two interesting forces to do this: drag (air resistance) and wind.

```
function dampingf(damping){
    return function(particle, td){
        particle.velocity.imuls(damping);
    };
}

var drag = dampingf(0.97);

function wind(particle, td){
    particle.velocity.x += td*Math.random()*50;
}
```

Again, drag is derived from a simpler damping function. With all the forces defined, we can now add them to our simulation.

```
system = new ParticleSystem();

system.forces.push(gravity);
system.forces.push(wind);
system.forces.push(drag);

emit(system, canvas.width, canvas.height);
```

As you can see in fireworks.2.html, our effect already looks more realistic.

Life and death

Nothing lasts forever, except for our fireworks. That's bad. For one, it looks very wrong, but it is also resulting in a memory leak because particles are never, ever removed from the system. To fix this, we need to add an age to our particles and remove them when they have exceeded that age.

We can implement this with two simple changes to our particle engine. We add an age property to our particle instances and we define a maxAge of Infinity on the prototype. In the update function, we update the age and return whether the particle is still alive. The updated particle will look like this:

```
function Particle(position) {
    this.position = position;
    this.velocity = new Vec2(0, 0);
    this.age = 0;
}
Particle.prototype = {
    maxAge: Infinity,
    update: function(td) {
        this.age += td;
        this.position.iadd(this.velocity.muls(td));
        return this.age < this.maxAge;
    }
}
```

We also need to add some code to the ParticleSystem to prune old particles. We will do this in a very simple way by using a new array for the particles that are still alive. This is not very efficient (it produces quite a bit of garbage), but it is very easy to implement and often good enough. The updated update() function will look like this:

```
ParticleSystem.prototype = {
    update: function(td) {
        var alive = [];
        for(var i = 0; i < this.particles.length; i++) {
            var particle = this.particles[i];
            for(var j = 0; j < this.forces.length; j++) {
                var force = this.forces[j];
                force(particle, td);
            }
            if(particle.update(td)){
                alive.push(particle);
            }
        }
        this.particles = alive;
    }
};
```

The last step is simply to define a maxAge for our firework particles. As always, making the value a bit fuzzy will make it look much more realistic.

```
particle.velocity.x = Math.cos(alpha)*radius;
particle.velocity.y = Math.sin(alpha)*radius;
particle.image = spark;
particle.maxAge = fuzzy(0.5, 2);
```

Rendering

Our fireworks now behave quite realistically. But they still don't look very good. Luckily, we can change this with a few little tweaks.

Our firework particles are emitting light; because of this, we should change the blend mode to be additive, so two lights on top of each other will be brighter than one alone. When using the canvas tag, we can do additive blending by setting the globalCompositeOperation to lighter. The globalCompositeOperation is very similar to layer modes in image editing software. It's important that we reset the globalCompositeOperation back to its default value of 'source-over' after drawing the particles to avoid side effects.

```
ctx.globalCompositeOperation = 'lighter';
renderCanvasImage(ctx, system.particles);
ctx.globalCompositeOperation = 'source-over';
```

Moving bright lights on a dark background usually leaves a trail because of motion blur. We can emulate this effect by changing the alpha of the background value that we use to clear the frame.

```
system.update(1/30);
ctx.fillStyle = 'rgba(0, 0, 0, 0.4)';
ctx.fillRect(0, 0, canvas.width, canvas.height);
```

With those changes in place, our fireworks look quite decent. Now it's your turn to play with the code and make them even better looking. You could, for example, add more colors or shapes to make the fireworks more varied.

Fire

Another classic particle effect is fire. In this section, we will implement a big, hot fire using a lot of particles (see Figure 6-4). So let's get started.

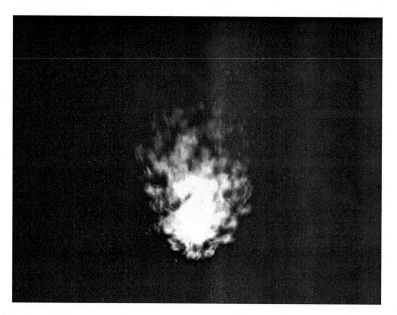

Figure 6-4. Fire demo in action

Creating the textures

Our fire will be created out of four different fire textures, plus one little spark that's just a scaled-down version of the spark we used to create the fireworks. As you can see in Figure 6-5, the flame textures are basically just flame-like shapes that have been blurred and colored. The first one is a bit sharper and has a more intense color; this is necessary to give the flame some edges. The second and the last one also have some noise added to provide some more detail. All of the textures are 32 × 32 pixels except for the last one, which is 64 × 64 in order to cover a bigger area. When colorizing the textures, it is again very important that no channel ends up at zero—or it will look wrong.

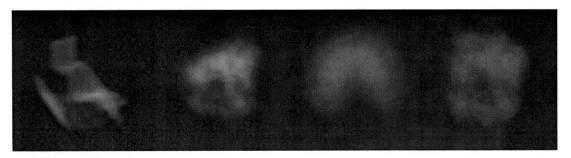

Figure 6-5. Individual flame textures

Loading the textures

In this example, we will need multiple images. In most cases, your application will already have a way of loading resources and you should use that one. For our examples, a very simple function will do. It takes an array of URLs and loads them as images. Once the images are all loaded, it will invoke the callback with an array of images.

Note that in production code, you will need to add error handling to this loader function.

```
function loadImages(srcs, callback){
    var loaded = 0,
        imgs;
    function onload() { if(++loaded == srcs.length) callback(images);}
    for(var i = 0; i < srcs.length; i++) {
        var src = srcs[i],
            img = new Image();
        imgs.push(img);
        img.onload = onload;
        img.src = src;
    }
}
```

Implementing the emitter

Our fire emitter should emit flame particles around a point similar to the fireworks. But whereas the firework emitter emitted bursts of particles, we need to emit particles continuously to create a fire (otherwise, you will get an explosion!). We don't want to spawn all the particles at the exact same location either, but with some random variation.

```
function emit(system, images, width, height){
    // emit the particle at the center of the canvas with some random
    // variation

    var position = new Vec2(width/2+fuzzy(5), height/2+fuzzy(5)+height/4),
        particle = new Particle(position),
        alpha = fuzzy(Math.PI),
        // note that here we use a proper linear distribution unlike in the
```

```
    // fireworks example. Again, just because I find it looks better that way.
    radius = Math.sqrt(Math.random()+0.1)*100;

// choose a random texture
particle.image = choose(images);
// make speed dependent on image size so the small spark will be faster
// and the big filling texture slower
radius *= 32/Math.max(25, particle.image.width);

particle.velocity.x = Math.cos(alpha)*radius;
particle.velocity.y = Math.sin(alpha)*radius-4;

particle.maxAge = 5;
system.particles.push(particle);
}
```

Implementing the forces

We will also need to adjust the forces a bit to create fire. We will turn gravity into anti-gravity to simulate the lift created by the hot fire, and make the wind a bit more extreme.

```
var drag = dampingf(0.975);,
    lift = accelerationf(new Vec2(0, -50));

function wind(particle, td){
    particle.velocity.x += td*fuzzy(50);
}
```

Implementing the main loop

The main loop we use to create fire is very similar to the one we used to create fireworks. The main difference is that we emit a new particle in every frame.

```
function main(images){
    var canvas = document.getElementById('c'),
        ctx = canvas.getContext('2d'),
        system = new ParticleSystem();

    system.forces.push(lift);
    system.forces.push(wind);
    system.forces.push(drag);

    ctx.fillRect(0, 0, canvas.width, canvas.height);


    window.setInterval(function() {
        while(Math.random()<0.80){
            emit(system, images, canvas.width, canvas.height);
        }
        system.update(1/30);
        ctx.fillStyle = 'rgba(0, 0, 0, 0.3)';
        ctx.fillRect(0, 0, canvas.width, canvas.height);
        ctx.globalCompositeOperation = 'lighter';
```

```
            ctx.globalAlpha = 0.6;
            renderCanvasImage(ctx, system.particles, 5);
            ctx.globalAlpha = 1.0;
            ctx.globalCompositeOperation = 'source-over';
        }, 1000/30);
    }
```

You can see the complete example in fire.0.html. It does already look like a fire, but something is still missing. It looks kind of blocky and inorganic. We can change this by introducing rotation.

Rotation

To add rotation, we need to extend our particle system a little bit. We will introduce an angle and angularVelocity to the particles. The angle is the rotation of the particle in radians. The angularVelocity is the change to that value in one second. Both default to zero in the prototype.

```
function Particle(position) {
    this.position = position;
    this.velocity = new Vec2(0, 0);
    this.angle = 0;
    this.angularVelocity = 0;
    this.age = 0;
}
Particle.prototype = {
    maxAge: Infinity,
    update: function(td) {
        this.age += td;
        this.position.iadd(this.velocity.muls(td));
        this.angle += this.angularVelocity*td;
        return this.age < this.maxAge;
    }
}
```

The render function also needs an update to deal with the rotation:

```
function renderCanvasImage(ctx, particles, fade){
    for(var i = 0; i < particles.length; i++) {
        var particle = particles[i];
        ctx.save();
        ctx.translate(particle.position.x, particle.position.y);
        ctx.rotate(particle.angle);
        ctx.drawImage(particle.image, -particle.image.width/2, -particle.image.height/2);
        ctx.restore();
    }
}
```

Now we can initialize the angle and angularVelocity in the emitter.

```
particle.angularVelocity = fuzzy(1.5);
particle.angle = fuzzy(Math.PI);
```

You can see the result of this change in fire.1.html. It is already looking much better. There is still a noticeable popping of the flames as they reach their end of life. We can improve this by slowly fading them out.

Fading out of existence

To make the particles fade out smoothly, we will increase their transparency as they get older. To do this, we add an optional parameter called fade to the renderer. The value of the fade parameter is the time it takes to fade out the particles. Usually this is equal to maxAge.

```
function renderCanvasImage(ctx, particles, fade){
    for(var i = 0; i < particles.length; i++) {
        var particle = particles[i];
        ctx.save();
        if(fade){
            ctx.globalAlpha *= (fade-particle.age)/fade;
        }
        ctx.translate(particle.position.x, particle.position.y);
        ctx.rotate(particle.angle);
        ctx.drawImage(particle.image, -particle.image.width/2, -particle.image.height/2);
        ctx.restore();
    }
}
```

When we now define the fade parameter in our fire main loop, we will get a nice and cosy fire.

```
renderCanvasImage(ctx, system.particles, 5);
```

You can see, the final result in fire.2.html. Now it's your turn to tweak the fire. How about changing the color of the flames or creating a fireball by removing the lift? Note that the fire effect we have created in this section is very high fidelity. It could make a nice prop for a menu screen or a demo but it would probably use up too much of the precious computing and drawing resources in a real game. You can scale this fire down for a game by using fewer and smaller particles.

Smoke

Smoke is very similar to fire. In fact, the forces we use to simulate smoke are the same. We just need to tweak the values a bit and create some new textures (see Figure 6-6). To make this a bit more interesting, we will emit the smoke at the cursor location.

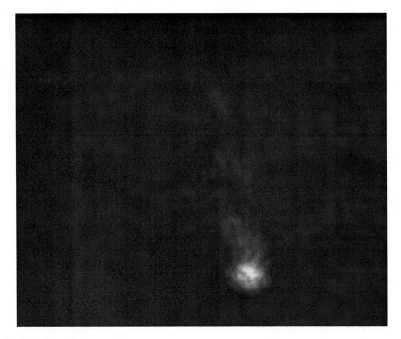

Figure 6-6. Smoke demo in action

Creating the textures

To create the 64 × 64 textures for the smoke particles, I have simply used some noise with a radial gradient as layer mask. The result is shown in Figure 6-7.

Figure 6-7. Individual smoke sprites

Implementing the emitter

The emitter for smoke is very similar to the one we used to create the fire effect. This makes a lot of sense because they are both simulating hot gas! To make the smoke a bit more interesting, we will emit it from the cursor. So our emitter will get the x, y coordinates of the mouse rather than the dimensions of the canvas we used in the fire emitter. As all the textures now have the same size, the code to make smaller particles faster is no longer needed. I increased the `angularVelocity` and `maxAge` a bit to match the behavior of smoke a bit better. The new emitter looks like this:

```
function emit(system, images, x, y){
    // emit the particle at the center of the canvas with some random
    // variation

    var position = new Vec2(x+fuzzy(5), y+fuzzy(5)),
        particle = new Particle(position),
        alpha = fuzzy(Math.PI),
        radius = Math.sqrt(Math.random()+0.1)*35;

    particle.image = choose(images);
    particle.velocity.x = Math.cos(alpha)*radius;
    particle.velocity.y = Math.sin(alpha)*radius;
    particle.angularVelocity = fuzzy(2.0);
    particle.angle = fuzzy(Math.PI);
    // choose a random texture

    particle.maxAge = 6;
    system.particles.push(particle);
}
```

Implementing the main loop

The main change to the main loop is the addition of the input handler to get the mouse position. I have also greatly reduced the alpha values used for clearing and drawing to make the smoke look more smooth and fluid.

For the fire, we emitted random amounts of particles from the main loop to get a flickering effect. Smoke is far more continuous than fire in that regard, so we emit it at a constant rate of 10 particles per second in an external callback. The updated code looks like this:

```
function main(images){
    var canvas = document.getElementById('c'),
        controls = new window.input.Handler(canvas),
        ctx = canvas.getContext('2d'),
        system = new ParticleSystem();

    system.forces.push(lift);
    system.forces.push(wind);
    system.forces.push(drag);

    ctx.fillRect(0, 0, canvas.width, canvas.height);

    window.setInterval(function() {
        system.update(1/30);
        ctx.fillStyle = 'rgba(0, 0, 0, 0.2)';
        ctx.fillRect(0, 0, canvas.width, canvas.height);
        ctx.globalCompositeOperation = 'lighter';
        ctx.globalAlpha = 0.1;
        renderCanvasImage(ctx, system.particles, 6);
```

```
        ctx.globalAlpha = 1.0;
        ctx.globalCompositeOperation = 'source-over';
    }, 1000/30);
    window.setInterval(function() {
        if(controls.hasFocus) {
            emit(system, images, controls.mouse.x, controls.mouse.y);
        }
    }, 1000/10);
}
loadImages('smoke.0.png smoke.1.png smoke.2.png smoke.3.png smoke.4.png'.split(' '),
main);
```

The forces acting on the smoke and fire are exactly the same. You can play with the result of this in smoke.0.html.

Optimizations

Our current particle system performs quite well for a relatively low (~1000) number of particles. If we need more particles than that, we need to write more optimized code. This will allow us to have tens of thousands of particles. To demonstrate how to do this, we will re-implement the fireworks demo in a more optimized fashion (see Figure 6-8).

Figure 6-8. High-performance fireworks in action

Please note that performance optimizations depend on the runtime environment. Optimizations that have a positive impact today can become useless, or even harmful, tomorrow. They will also severely impact the maintainability and readability of your code.

Single particles

If we want more particles, we will need to make the particles smaller to make them look right. If we restrict ourselves to single-pixel particles, we can gain a lot of performance by manipulating the image data directly.

The 2D context of the canvas element allows this by using the get/putImageData() methods. Note that calls to get/putImageData are quite expensive. They are only worth their cost when rendering a lot of particles (~1000), otherwise falling back to fillRect/drawImage is faster.

Typed arrays

Another performance bottleneck is the use of objects for each particle and vector.

We can do this much more efficiently by using a large array. When we use a single array and inline all operations, we gain a lot of performance. Some of the benefits of this approach are:

- No more function call overhead

- No more memory allocation (per particle) / garbage collection overhead

- Less time spent dereferencing properties

- Reduced memory usage

WebGL introduced typed arrays to JavaScript. Typed arrays are arrays that only accept a single type. Because of this, they can be stored and accessed in a more efficient manner. Their interface is mostly backwards compatible with the array interface. We can use this to fall back to normal arrays if the browser does not support typed arrays. The code for this can be as simple as this:

```
Var Float32Array = window.Float32Array || Array;
```

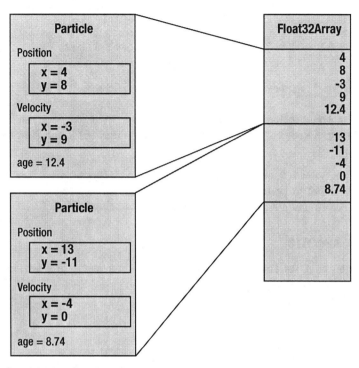

Figure 6-9. Nesting of particles in a flat array. All the particles are packed into a single array.

Removing particles from the middle of an array is very expensive. This is why we will leave dead particles (age > MAX_AGE) in the array and just skip them when drawing. While this makes the system a lot slower when there is only one particle, it won't affect the performance when reaching the maximal number of particles. Because the size of our array is finite, we will simply override the oldest particle when spawning a new one. To do this, we use our array like a ring buffer. The code for this is very simple:

```
particles_i = (particles_i+NFIELDS) % PARTICLES_LENGTH;
```

where particles_i is the position of the first field of the particle, NFIELDS is the number of fields (5), and PARTICLES_LENGTH is the total size of the array (the total number of particles times the number of fields per particle).

requestAnimationFrame

window.setInterval is not ideal for animations. The most obvious reason for this is that it is still called when the page is not visible. Another reason is synchronization with screen refreshes. If the screen is updated at regular intervals, you really want your updates to be aligned with those to get a smooth result. The solution to this problem is to use requestAnimationFrame(). As the specification is still a draft, you will have to use the prefixed versions for each browser; if it is not supported, you should fall back to setInterval or setTimeout. requestAnimationFrame is currently supported by Firefox, Chrome, and IE10. You can do the following simple snippet of code:

```
var requestAnimationFrame = window.requestAnimationFrame ||↪
  window.webkitRequestAnimationFrame || wi    ndow.mozRequestAnimationFrame ||↪
  window.msRequestAnimationFrame || function(f){window.setTimeout(f, 5); }
```

Micro optimizations

We can gain some additional performance by tweaking details in the code. Very often, this means trading readability for a little more speed. This is usually a very bad idea, but it can help to make inner loops significantly faster.

Micro optimizations are heavily dependent on the browser, so always time them to make sure they are actually faster. A good tool to perform this is found at jsfiddle.net. The more advanced JavaScript engines become, the less important these micro optimizations will become.

Chaining expressions

Looking up the value of a variable costs time. We can save some property lookups by chaining expressions. Thus,

```
vy += gravity*td;
y += vy;
```

can be rewritten as

```
y += (vy += gravity*td);
```

Rounding

The bitwise complement operator is used to round numbers. As it is a bitwise operator, it will convert the float value of the number into an integer and then flip all of its bits. By doing this twice, we can round a number. So instead of:

```
drawImage(img, Math.floor(x), Math.floor(y));
```

you can simply write:

```
drawImage(img, ~~x, ~~y);
```

Optimized fireworks

By putting together all those optimizations, we can handle a lot of particles.

```
(function(){

// fall back to normal arrays if the browser does not support
// float 32 arrays
var MAX_PARTICLES = 100000,
    NFIELDS = 5, // x, y, vx, vy, age,
    // size of the array
```

```
    PARTICLES_LENGTH = MAX_PARTICLES * NFIELDS,

    // compatibility with legacy browsers
    Float32Array = window.Float32Array || Array,
    requestAnimationFrame = window.requestAnimationFrame ||↪
window.webkitRequestAnimationFrame || window.mozRequestAnimationFrame ||↪
window.msRequestAnimationFrame || function(f){window.setTimeout(f, 5); },

    canvas = document.getElementById('c'),
    ctx = canvas.getContext('2d'),
    controls = new window.input.Handler(canvas),
    particles = new Float32Array(PARTICLES_LENGTH),
    // position to insert the next particle
    particles_i = 0,
    // time in ms
    t0 = new Date()*1,
    // some shortcuts, they don't seem to make to code faster
    PI = Math.PI,
    random = Math.random,
    cos = Math.cos,
    sin = Math.sin;

function emit(x, y) {
    for(var i = 0; i < 250; i++) {
        particles_i = (particles_i+NFIELDS) % PARTICLES_LENGTH;
        particles[particles_i] = x;
        particles[particles_i+1] = y;
        var alpha = fuzzy(PI),
            radius = random()*100,
            vx = cos(alpha)*radius,
            vy = sin(alpha)*radius,
            age = random();
        particles[particles_i+2] = vx;
        particles[particles_i+3] = vy;
        particles[particles_i+4] = age;
    }
}

function draw(){
    var t1 = new Date()*1,
        // time delta in seconds
        td = (t1-t0)/1000,
        MAX_AGE = 5,
        width = canvas.width,
        height = canvas.height,
        gravity = 50,
        drag = 0.999,
        // color
        r = 120,
        g = 55,
        b = 10;
    t0 = t1;

    // emit particles only when we have focus
    // if we don't have focus the coordinates are off anyway
```

```
    if(controls.hasFocus) {
        emit(controls.mouse.x, controls.mouse.y);
    }

    ctx.fillStyle = 'rgba(0, 0, 0, 0.4)';
    ctx.fillRect(0, 0, width, height);
    var imgdata = ctx.getImageData(0, 0, width, height),
        data = imgdata.data;

    for(var i = 0; i < PARTICLES_LENGTH; i+= NFIELDS) {

        // check age
        if((particles[i+4] += td) > MAX_AGE) continue;

        // ~~ = double bitwise inversion = Math.ceil
        var x = ~~(particles[i] = (particles[i] +
                (particles[i+2] *= drag)*td)),
            y = ~~(particles[i+1] = (particles[i+1] +
                (particles[i+3] = (particles[i+3] + gravity*td)*drag)*td));

        // check bounds
        if(x < 0 || x >= width || y < 0 || y >= height)
            continue;

        // calculate offset
        var offset = (x+y*width)*4;

        // set pixel
        data[offset] += r;
        data[offset+1] += g;
        data[offset+2] += b;
        // dont touch alpha
    }

    ctx.putImageData(imgdata, 0, 0);

    requestAnimationFrame(draw, canvas);
}
requestAnimationFrame(draw, canvas);

})();
```

You can find this example in `fastfireworks.html`. Play with it and see how crazy you can get.

Conclusion

In this chapter, I introduced you to particle systems and the basic math required to create them. I showed you how to create fireworks, fire, and smoke. I taught you to create a high-performance particle system that can deal with tens of thousands of particles. But all this is only the beginning. Play with all the examples in this chapter to get a feeling for what the individual parameters and forces do. Try to create your own particle effects based on the ones that I have shown you, or create your own from scratch. You might not always get what you expected, but more often than not, the result will be awesome!

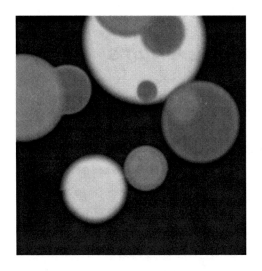

Chapter 7

Beginning WebGL

WebGL (Web-based Graphics Language) is a very exciting new technology that leverages the power of the Graphics Processing Unit (GPU) within the browser.

In this chapter, we will discuss the history and capabilities of WebGL. As a prerequisite to programming games with WebGL, we need to cover the following:

- checking for WebGL support
- working within a 3D coordinate system
- the WebGL graphics pipeline and GLSL (GL Shading Language) basics
- using buffers and drawing basic shapes
- setting up world view and projection matrices
- animating a 3D object
- enabling depth testing
- using a texture

Near the end of the chapter, we will present a simple game of darts. The techniques covered in this chapter will also enable us to progress to the more advanced topics covered in the *Cycleblob* games chapter. There is a lot to cover in one chapter, so let's get started!

WebGL Origins

Version 1.0 of the WebGL specification was completed in March 2011 by the Khronos Group. WebGL is based on OpenGL Embedded Systems (ES) 2.0, which, in turn, is derived from OpenGL.

In 1992, version 1.0 of OpenGL was released as a non-proprietary alternative to Silicon Graphics' Iris GL. The GL Shading Language (GLSL) was introduced in 2004 when version 2.0 of OpenGL was released. GLSL is a C-like language that lets you control the vertex and fragment shaders of the imaging pipeline. This pipeline will be discussed later in the chapter. As of this writing, the current version of OpenGL is 4.2.

OpenGL ES is a subset of OpenGL and is built for use in embedded devices like mobile phones, which have lower processing power and fewer capabilities than a desktop computer. OpenGL sometimes has multiple ways of performing the same task; for example, to draw vertices, you can use both a glBegin...glEnd section or vertex buffer objects (VBOs). OpenGL ES only uses VBOs, which are the most performance-friendly option. While more restrictive, having a cleaner API path can provide a more straightforward development direction to follow. Most things that can be done in OpenGL can be done in OpenGL ES (a notable exception is that there is no 3D texture support).

OpenGL ES 1.0 is based on OpenGL 1.5. OpenGL ES 2.0 is based on OpenGL 2.0 and so supports GLSL. In following with being a trimmed language, OpenGL ES 2.0 no longer offers fixed functionality. Having to use the GLSL does increase the learning curve of WebGL; however, you can set minimal shaders, which can then be incrementally enhanced.

How does WebGL work?

WebGL is a JavaScript API binding to the GPU of a computer's graphics card. WebGL is rendered within the HTML 5 <canvas> element and requires no browser plug-in. C style shaders (GLSL) are compiled at run time.

To use WebGL you need a browser that supports WebGL and a graphics card and operating system (OS) that are new enough to support OpenGL. We will discuss these requirements in more depth later on in the chapter.

Uses and limitations

Unlike some other HTML graphics APIs, obtaining a WebGL rendering environment does require quite a bit of work. This is because we have to set up the WebGL context, view matrices, and shaders. The payoff is the ability to draw rich 3D environs. As your skill level improves, you will find that moving more functionality to the shader can improve performance and offer a wide range of cool effects and realism.

If you are developing a 2D game with no textures or lighting, then WebGL is probably overkill, and using the "2D" canvas context could be better.

Demonstrations

There are many wonderful applications that show the power of WebGL. One of the best-known demos was Google Body, which is now at www.zygotebody.com. This demo displays an interactive 3D model of human anatomy. Another site with impressive applications is www.chromeexperiments.com/webgl and two of my favorites are a realistic water pool demo (http://madebyevan.com/webgl-water/) and a jellyfish demo at (http://aleksandarrodic.com/p/jellyfish/).

The webglsamples site (http://code.google.com/p/webglsamples/) shows various WebGL samples.

And existing games, such as *Quake II*, have been ported to WebGL.

OS, graphics card, and browser support

WebGL is a very new emerging technology. As such, unfortunately, not every computer supports it. In order to view a WebGL program, you need a new browser, a newer graphics card, and Operating System.

The following browsers support WebGL:

- Firefox 4+

- Safari 5+

- Chrome 10+

- Opera 11.1+

Support by these browsers is somewhat expected when you consider that Mozilla, Apple, Google, and Opera all belong to the working group of WebGL under Khronos. Microsoft, which produces DirectX, does not currently belong to the group or officially support WebGL within Internet Explorer (IE). However, workarounds, such as ChromeFrame and IEWebGL, do exist for IE. For more information, visit the following web site:

http://iewebgl.com/ and http://code.google.com/chrome/chromeframe/.

Furthermore, because of the potential for severe system crashes related to WebGL when running Windows XP, Chrome has opted to blacklist WebGL on the Windows XP operating system. According to Google Chrome Help (www.google.com/support/chrome/bin/answer.py?answer=1220892), Chrome supports WebGL on the following operating systems:

- Windows Vista and Windows 7 (recommended)

- Mac OS 10.5 and Mac OS 10.6 (recommended)

- Linux

This web page also lists some graphics cards that are not supported. It is recommended that you update your graphics card drivers for optimal WebGL support. If your graphics card does not support OpenGL 2.0, (which, as you may recall, is what OpenGL ES 2.0 is based on) then WebGL will not work with WebGL on Mac and Linux.

Ironically, Microsoft can help some old video cards work with WebGL on Windows machines. The ANGLE (Almost Native Graphics Layer Engine) project translates OpenGL ES 2.0 API calls to DirectX 9 API calls. The result is that graphics cards that only support OpenGL 1.5 (OpenGL ES 1.0) can still run WebGL.

Testing for WebGL support

There are several sites to test your browser's support of WebGL. Two of these are http://doesmybrowsersupportwebgl.com, which on success displays the attributes of your browser and its maximum WebGL capabilities, and http://get.webgl.org, which displays a spinning cube if your browser supports WebGL. We can also programmatically check for WebGL support using modernizr (www.modernizr.com).

Listing 7-1 shows a simple script that will alert you if WebGL is not initialized properly.

Listing 7-1. Testing for WebGL Support

```html
<!DOCTYPE html>
<html>
    <head>
        <style>
            body{   background: gray; }
            canvas{ background: white; }
        </style>
    </head>
    <body>
        <canvas id="canvas"></canvas>
        <script type="text/javascript">
            var canvas = document.getElementById("canvas");
            var gl;
            try {
                gl = canvas.getContext("experimental-webgl");
            } catch (e) {
                alert(e);
            }
            if (!gl) {
                alert("Error trying to initialise WebGL. Try get.webgl.org");
            } else {
            gl.clearColor(0.0, 0.7, 0.0, 1.0);
                gl.clear(gl.COLOR_BUFFER_BIT);
            }
        </script>
    </body>
</html>
```

> **Note** Once the WebGL specification is finalized, the canvas context will be "webgl" instead of "experimental-webgl".

When support for WebGL is not found, then we should fall back to a different technology if possible (such as a '2D' canvas context, a static image, etc.) and/or display an appropriate error message to the user.

Libraries

Rather than reinvent functionality, there are several excellent matrix libraries available for use with WebGL. There are also many higher-level graphics engines and APIs available.

Matrix libraries

Matrix operations—addition, multiplication, inverse, and so forth— are essential in 3D graphics for calculating transforms. They are also used in image processing as convolution masks and filters. Some existing JavaScript matrix libraries include the following:

- *CanvasMatrix.js*: `http://code.google.com/p/webglsamples/source/browse/collectibles/script/CanvasMatrix.js`

- *glMatrix*: `https://github.com/toji/gl-matrix`

- *Sylvester*: `http://sylvester.jcoglan.com/`

- *webgl-mjs*: `http://code.google.com/p/webgl-mjs/`

Of these, glMatrix claims to be the fastest and offers some benchmarks at `http://glmatrix.googlecode.com/hg/benchmark/matrix_benchmark.html`.

Higher-level APIs

This chapter will focus on explaining how to set up a basic scene and will not use a higher-level API. Frameworks can abstract basic scene set up and functionality, increasing productivity. Learning WebGL without a higher-level library can help you appreciate using one later on. Knowing the lower-level functions can also aid in understanding and increase performance.

For completeness, we will list some existing frameworks. At the time of writing, there are over twenty well-used frameworks, which have varying purposes. A complete list is available at

`www.khronos.org/webgl/wiki/User_Contributions.`

The following highlights some popular libraries that have distinct uses:

- *GLGE* (`www.glge.org`): Described as "WebGL for the lazy" its web site reads "The aim of GLGE is to mask the involved nature of WebGL from the web developer, who can then spend his/her time creating richer content for the web."

- *O3D* (`http://code.google.com/p/o3d`): Originally a browser plug-in, this is a Google library with COLLADA model support on top of the WebGL framework

- *SceneJS* (`www.scenejs.com`): Scene graphs and CAD with WebGL

- *TDL* (`https://github.com/greggman/tdl`): Low level; rendering speed is valued over ease of use; first used on Google Body and other high-performance WebGL demos

- *Three.js* (`https://github.com/mrdoob/three.js`): A lightweight 3D engine with a high level of GitHub user activity

Debugging tools

Before we begin coding, the reader should set up WebGL-Inspector from `http://benvanik.github.com/ WebGL-Inspector/`. It is currently available for Chrome and Safari and will soon be a Firefox extension as well. WebGL-Inspector lets you see the state of your buffers, texture information, individual frames, and other useful data.

The Firefox web console can also be very useful to output raw WebGL error messages. By default, the messages are not shown. You need to type about:config in the address bar and then set webgl.verbose to true.

3D refresher

This chapter expects that the reader has a basic understanding of 3D graphics. We will briefly discuss the coordinate system and transforms used in WebGL.

Coordinate system

The standard Cartesian coordinate system in three dimensions has (x, y, z) coordinate triplets. The origin (0, 0, 0) is the intersection of the x, y, and z axis. For each of the three dimensions, values increase on one side of the origin and decrease on the other. There are two separate coordinate system orientations, as shown in Figure 7-1.

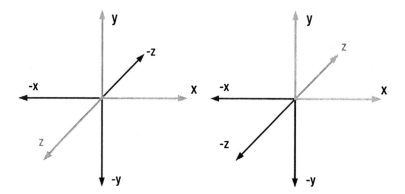

Figure 7-1. Left-hand coordinate (LHC) and right-hand coordinate (RHC) orientations. You can see that the difference between the LHC and RHC systems is which way the z axis is directed.

Transforms

Transforms alter the vertices of a figure. There are three elementary transforms: translation, rotation, and scaling, as shown in Figure 7-2.

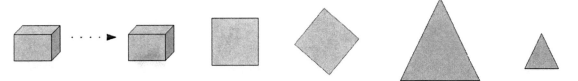

Figure 7-2. Transforms of a translation (left), a rotation (middle), and a scale (right)

Composing the scene view

To set up a scene, you have to multiply the original coordinates by three separate matrices. These are the Model, View, and Projection (MVP) matrices.

Model to world transform

The model matrix performs scaling, transformation, and rotation of the coordinates of an object from its original size, orientation, and position centered at the origin to its final place and size in the world, as shown in Figure 7-3.

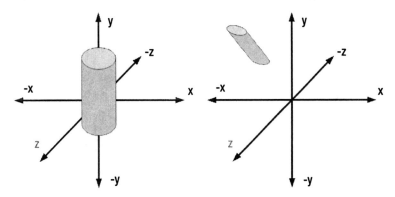

Figure 7-3. Diagram of model coordinates transformed to world coordinates

World to view transform

The view matrix transforms the world view to the "camera view" by zooming, positioning, and rotating the camera, as shown in Figure 7-4.

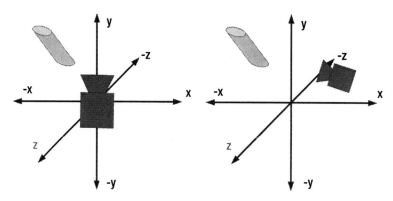

Figure 7-4. Diagram of world coordinates transformed to camera view

Often, the model and view transforms are combined into one matrix.

Projection transform

Finally, the projection matrix transforms the camera view to the screen view. There are two ways of doing this—with a perspective or with an orthogonal/parallel projection, as shown in Figure 7-5. Perspective is the realistic way in 3D and what we will use in this chapter.

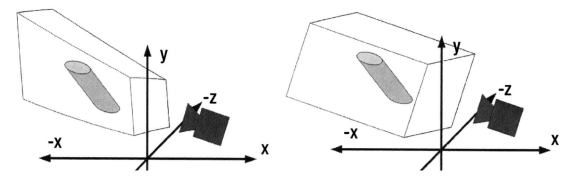

Figure 7-5. Diagram of camera coordinates transformed to screen view; left is perspective, right is orthogonal (parallel)

Viewport

The viewport sets the lower-left coordinate of the view and the width and height. Two sample viewports are shown in Figure 7-6.

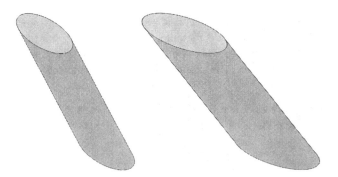

Figure 7-6. The screen on the right is a wide screen and the aspect ratio is stretched instead of maintained.

GLSL

Understanding GLSL is essential, as stated at the Khronos WebGL wiki (www.khronos.org/webgl/wiki/ Tutorial#Creating_the_Shaders): "Nothing happens in WebGL without shaders."

If shaders frighten you, feel free to skip the next couple of pages for the time being. Cut/copy the shader code examples, regard them as magic, and come back to them later.

Figure 7-7 is a simplified diagram of the steps of the graphics pipeline.

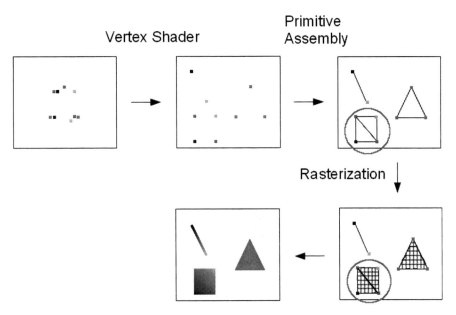

Figure 7-7. Simplified graphics pipeline

In Figure 7-7, we start with raw modelspace vertex positions. The vertex shader then transforms the vertices, usually by multiplying with the MVP matrices. Vertices are assembled into appropriate primitive types, such as points, lines, and triangles. Next the primitives are rasterized into smaller pixel fragments and passed to the fragment shader. The fragment shader interpolates color, lighting, and texture coordinates.

Vertex and fragment shaders are written in GLSL, which is a C-style language. We can include the source in a JavaScript tag or external file. The script type is "x-shader/x-vertex" or "x-shader/x-fragment" respectively.

The vertex shader is responsible for model view and projection matrices. It also does normal vector and texture coordinate generation and transformation. Per-vertex lighting can be done in the vertex shader or these values can be passed on to the fragment shader for per-pixel computation.

Minimally, a vertex shader needs to pass the original position of each vertex onto the fragment shader, as shown in Listing 7-2.

Listing 7-2. The Simplest Possible Vertex Shader, Which Passes the Input Vertex Positions to the Fragment Shader

```
<script id="shader-vs" type="x-shader/x-vertex">
        attribute vec3 aVertexPosition;
        void main(void) {
                gl_Position = aVertexPosition;
        }
</script>
```

The fragment shader operates on parts of a primitive shape. It computes per-pixel color, texture coordinates, and normals. The fragment shader also applies textures and fog. Minimally, the fragment shader needs to set the fragment color, as shown in Listing 7-3.

Listing 7-3. The Simplest Possible Fragment Shader, Which Sets Every Fragment to the Same Color (White)

```
<script id="shader-fs" type="x-shader/x-fragment">
        void main(void) {
                gl_FragColor = vec4(1.0, 1.0, 1.0, 1.0);
        }
</script>
```

Using WebGL

Drawing a simple shape

In our first example of actual WebGL usage, we will display a shaded blue square on a green background. In Listing 7-4, which is the start of our demo, we will define the basic style used, import the jQuery library from the Google CDN, and also include a local copy of the glmatrix.js file, which can be downloaded at https://github.com/toji/gl-matrix/downloads. We will also create a canvas element dimension of 500 × 500.

Listing 7-4. The Start of demo_1.html

```html
<!DOCTYPE html>
<html>
    <head>
        <style>
            body{        background: gray; }
            canvas{      background: white; }
        </style>
        <script src="http://code.jquery.com/jquery-1.6.4.min.js"></script>
        <script src="gl-matrix-min.js"></script>
    </head>
    <body>
        <canvas id="canvas" width="500" height="500"></canvas>
```

> **Note** Neither the jQuery or glMatrix libraries are necessary to program WebGL, but they do make Ajax calls and matrix manipulation easier.

In Listing 7-5, we define variables that will store the canvas WebGL context, shader program and shaders, vertex position and color attributes, vertex buffer, and modelview and projection matrices. When the DOM has finished loading, the methods initWebGL, initShaders and executeProgram are called. The initWebGL method is similar to the code in Listing 7-1. We set up the WebGL context and ensure that it is supported and set the background color. We select the canvas element with jQuery notation instead of the former document.getElementById usage. We also set the viewport dimensions to the canvas dimensions.

Listing 7-5. Initializing Variables and Defining the Component Functions of the Program

```javascript
<script>
    var gl = null,
    shaderProgram = null,
    fragmentShader = null,
    vertexShader = null,
    vertexPositionAttribute = null,
    vertexColorAttribute = null,
    squareVerticesBuffer = null,
    mvMatrix = mat4.create(),
    pMatrix = mat4.create();
    $(document).ready(function(){
        initWebGL();
        initShaders();
        executeProgram();
    });

    function initWebGL() {
        try {
            var canvas = $("#canvas").get(0);
            gl = canvas.getContext("experimental-webgl");
            gl.viewportWidth = canvas.width;
            gl.viewportHeight = canvas.height;
        } catch(e) {
            alert(e);
```

```
        }
        if (!gl) {
            alert("Error trying to initialise WebGL");
        } else {
            gl.clearColor(0.0, 0.4, 0.0, 1.0);
        }
    }
```

To understand the initShaders method, first we need to show how the flow of a shader program works.

Setting up a shader program

For both vertex and fragment shaders, we need to create a shader object, set the source for the shader, and compile it. Then we create a shader program, attach the compiled vertex and fragment shaders to it, link the program, and use it.

> **Note** *Cleaning up shaders involves the opposite process. You detach the shaders from the program, then delete the shaders, and finally delete the program.*

In the initShaders function at the bottom of Listing 7-6, we load our vertex and fragment shader source from external files, shader.vs and shader.fs, for our vertex and fragment shaders respectively. Notice that we set the parameter async: false. This ensures that the source files are fetched before we try to attach and compile the shaders. We will skip the details of the shader files until after the demo_1.html file is explained in depth.

Listing 7-6. Setting up Our Shaders

```
function makeShader(src, type){
    var shader = gl.createShader(type);
    gl.shaderSource(shader, src);
    gl.compileShader(shader);

    if (!gl.getShaderParameter(shader, gl.COMPILE_STATUS)) {
        alert("Error compiling shader: " + gl.getShaderInfoLog(shader));
    }
    return shader;
}

function attachShaders(){
    gl.attachShader(shaderProgram, vertexShader);
    gl.attachShader(shaderProgram, fragmentShader);
    gl.linkProgram(shaderProgram);

    if (!gl.getProgramParameter(shaderProgram, gl.LINK_STATUS)) {
        alert("Unable to initialize the shader program.");
    }
}

function createShaderProgram(){
    shaderProgram = gl.createProgram();
```

```
        attachShaders();

        gl.useProgram(shaderProgram);
    }

    function setupShaders(fragmentShaderSRC, vertexShaderSRC){
        fragmentShader = makeShader(fragmentShaderSRC, gl.FRAGMENT_SHADER);
        vertexShader = makeShader(vertexShaderSRC, gl.VERTEX_SHADER);

        createShaderProgram();
    }

    function initShaders() {
        var fragmentShaderSRC = null,
        vertexShaderSRC = null;
        $.ajax({
            async: false,
            url: 'shader.fs',
            success: function (data) {
                fragmentShaderSRC = data.firstChild.textContent;
            },
            dataType: 'xml'
        });
        $.ajax({
            async: false,
            url: 'shader.vs',
            success: function (data) {
                vertexShaderSRC = data.firstChild.textContent;
            },
            dataType: 'xml'
        });
        setupShaders(fragmentShaderSRC, vertexShaderSRC);
    }
```

Note To load external shader files with Ajax, you need to be running the program from a server. If you do not have a server set up, then you will have to include the shader source locally inside your program file. As a result, the code to load the source becomes simpler, but your program structure is not as modular. The alternate of using local shaders is in demo_1-2.html, with the code difference between demo_1.html shown.

```
<script id="shader-vs" type="x-shader/x-vertex">…</script>
<script id="shader-fs" type="x-shader/x-fragment"> …</script>


function initShaders() {
            var fragmentShaderSRC = $('#shader-fs').html(),
            vertexShaderSRC = $('#shader-vs').html();
            setupShaders(fragmentShaderSRC, vertexShaderSRC);

}
```

Next we pass the sources to the `setupShaders` function. That function then calls `makeShader`, which is a helper function to create a shader, set the source, and compile it. This is done by calling the WebGL functions `createShader`, `shaderSource`, and `compileShader`.

Once the individual shaders have been created, we create our shader program by calling `createShaderProgram`. This function calls the WebGL method `createProgram` and then our function `attachShaders`, which in turn calls the WebGL methods `attachShader` and `linkProgram`. Finally, we call the WebGL method `useProgram`.

Next, we call the `executeProgram` function. In Listing 7-7, we get uniform and attribute locations from our shader program and also enable attribute arrays. What are uniform and attributes in WebGL? Well they are two GLSL types. The GLSL types that we are interested in for this chapter are listed in Table 7-1.

Listing 7-7. The executeProgram Function and First Two Method Calls

```
function executeProgram(){
    getMatrixUniforms();
    getVertexAttributes();

    initBuffers();

    drawScene();
}

function getMatrixUniforms(){
    shaderProgram.pMatrixUniform = gl.getUniformLocation(shaderProgram,↪
"uPMatrix");
    shaderProgram.mvMatrixUniform = gl.getUniformLocation(shaderProgram,↪
"uMVMatrix");
}

function getVertexAttributes(){
    vertexPositionAttribute = gl.getAttribLocation(shaderProgram,↪
    "aVertexPosition");↪
    gl.enableVertexAttribArray(vertexPositionAttribute);

    vertexColorAttribute = gl.getAttribLocation(shaderProgram,
"aVertexColor");
    gl.enableVertexAttribArray(vertexColorAttribute);
}
```

Table 7-1. GLSL types and descriptions

GLSL types	Description
const	Constant throughout the program
uniform	Constant value across an entire primitive
attribute	Vertex shader per vertex information

GLSL types	Description
varying	Vertex shader write, fragment shader read
vecN	Vector of size 1 × N
matN	Matrix of size N × N
sampler	Used for textures

So the modelview and projection matrices are uniform throughout the vertex shader, while the position and colors are vertex attributes and change.

The initBuffers method in Listing 7-8 defines the vertex position and color data of our square in buffers.

In Listing 7-8, we create a buffer by calling the WebGL method createBuffer and than bind the current buffer with a bindBuffer call. Next we define the four vertex points of the cube as (x, y, z) coordinates in the vertices array and set the squareVerticesBuffer data with a bufferData call. Similarly, we set the color of each vertex in (red, green, blue, alpha) quartets (RGBA) in the colors array, and then create and bind this data to the squareVerticesColorBuffer buffer.

Listing 7-8. Vertex Buffer Assignment

```
function initBuffers() {
    squareVerticesBuffer = gl.createBuffer();
    gl.bindBuffer(gl.ARRAY_BUFFER, squareVerticesBuffer);

    var vertices = [
        1.0,  1.0, 0.0,
       -1.0,  1.0, 0.0,
        1.0, -1.0, 0.0,
       -1.0, -1.0, 0.0
    ];

    gl.bufferData(gl.ARRAY_BUFFER, new Float32Array(vertices), gl.STATIC_DRAW);

    var colors = [
        1.0,  1.0,  1.0,  1.0,  // white
        0.05, 0.05, 0.7,  1.0,  // dark blue
        0.0,  1.0,  1.0,  1.0,  // cyan
        0.0,  0.0,  1.0,  1.0   // blue
    ];

    squareVerticesColorBuffer = gl.createBuffer();
    gl.bindBuffer(gl.ARRAY_BUFFER, squareVerticesColorBuffer);
    gl.bufferData(gl.ARRAY_BUFFER, new Float32Array(colors), gl.STATIC_DRAW);
}
```

> **Note** *More information on the RGBA color format can be found on Wikipedia at http://en.wikipedia.org/wiki/RGBA_color_space.*

Our final function of the example is drawScene, shown in Listing 7-9.

Listing 7-9. The drawScene Function

```
function drawScene() {
    gl.viewport(0, 0, gl.viewportWidth, gl.viewportHeight);
    gl.clear(gl.COLOR_BUFFER_BIT);

    mat4.perspective(45, gl.viewportWidth / gl.viewportHeight, 0.1, 100.0,↪
pMatrix);

    mat4.identity(mvMatrix);
    mat4.translate(mvMatrix, [0, 0.0, -7.0]);

    setMatrixUniforms();
    gl.bindBuffer(gl.ARRAY_BUFFER, squareVerticesBuffer);
    gl.vertexAttribPointer(vertexPositionAttribute, 3, gl.FLOAT, false, 0,
0);

    gl.bindBuffer(gl.ARRAY_BUFFER, squareVerticesColorBuffer);
    gl.vertexAttribPointer(vertexColorAttribute, 4, gl.FLOAT, false, 0, 0);

    gl.drawArrays(gl.TRIANGLE_STRIP, 0, 4);
}

function setMatrixUniforms() {
    gl.uniformMatrix4fv(shaderProgram.pMatrixUniform, false, pMatrix);
    gl.uniformMatrix4fv(shaderProgram.mvMatrixUniform, false, mvMatrix);
}
```

In Listing 7-9, we set the viewport, which are the dimensions of the WebGL drawing area, and then clear the drawing area. We then set our perspective matrix attributes and store it in the pMatrix variable. We set our modelview matrix to be seven units back on the z-axis. Since our square is drawn when z=0, we need to move the camera back from the origin in order to see it. To inform our shader program the matrix values to use for modelview and projection, we call uniformMatrix4fv and pass our pMatrix and mvMatrix values to the shader program.

Now it is time to render our scene. We set our position and color buffers to the vertex position and vertex color attributes respectively. Finally, we call drawArrays with a type of TRIANGLE_STRIP. This means that our square is actually composed of four triangles, each with one vertex at the center of the square. After the triangle primitives are processed by the fragment shader, the final result is shown in Figure 7-8.

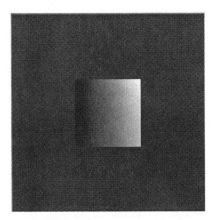

Figure 7-8. The output of Listing 7-10, a shaded square

This is a lot of work to draw a square. The good news is that advanced concepts and techniques incrementally build off of the same foundation we have just set up.

We have deferred showing our shader source until now. Listing 7-10 shows the vertex shader.

Listing 7-10. Our Vertex Shader

```
<script id="shader-vs" type="x-shader/x-vertex">
  attribute vec3 aVertexPosition;
  attribute vec4 aVertexColor;

  uniform mat4 uMVMatrix;
  uniform mat4 uPMatrix;

  varying highp vec4 vColor;

  void main(void) {
    gl_Position = uPMatrix * uMVMatrix * vec4(aVertexPosition, 1.0);
    vColor = aVertexColor;
  }
</script>
```

In Listing 7-10, our final position of each vertex is the initial position multiplied by the modelview matrix and then the projection matrix. The passed in vertex color is set in the vColor varying variable, which will be passed on to the fragment shader. The matrices are constant, while color and position change with each vertex.

> **Note** For advanced shader information covering GLSL beyond the scope of this book, please refer to www.lighthouse3d.com/tutorials/glsl-tutorial/ and the OpenGL Shading Language "Orange Book" (Addison-Wesley, 2009) by Randi J. Rost, et al. The WebGL quick reference card available at www.khronos.org/files/webgl/webgl-reference-card-1_0.pdf also has more details on GLSL.

Our fragment shader is shown in Listing 7-11.

Listing 7-11. Our Fragment Shader

```
<script id="shader-fs" type="x-shader/x-fragment">
  varying highp vec4 vColor;

  void main(void) {
    gl_FragColor = vColor;
  }
</script>
```

You can see in Listing 7-11 that we simply assigned the passed in vertex color to the final fragment color. The qualifier highp denotes the level of precision that we want.

The full listing of demo_1.html is shown in Listing 7-12.

Listing 7-12. Our Full demo_1.html Code

```
<!DOCTYPE html>
<html>
    <head>
        <style>
            body{       background: gray; }
            canvas{     background: white; }
        </style>
        <script src="http://code.jquery.com/jquery-1.6.4.min.js"></script>
        <script src="gl-matrix-min.js"></script>
    </head>
    <body>
        <canvas id="canvas" width="500" height="500"></canvas>
        <script>
            var gl = null,
            shaderProgram = null,
            fragmentShader = null,
            vertexShader = null,
            vertexPositionAttribute = null,
            vertexColorAttribute = null,
            squareVerticesBuffer = null,
            mvMatrix = mat4.create(),
            pMatrix = mat4.create();

            $(document).ready(function(){
                initWebGL();
                initShaders();
                executeProgram();
            });

            function initWebGL() {
                try {
                    var canvas = $("#canvas").get(0);
                    gl = canvas.getContext("experimental-webgl");
                    gl.viewportWidth = canvas.width;
                    gl.viewportHeight = canvas.height;
                } catch(e) {
```

```
            alert(e);
        }
        if (!gl) {
            alert("Error trying to initialise WebGL");
        } else {
            gl.clearColor(0.0, 0.4, 0.0, 1.0);
        }
    }

    function makeShader(src, type){
        var shader = gl.createShader(type);
        gl.shaderSource(shader, src);
        gl.compileShader(shader);

        if (!gl.getShaderParameter(shader, gl.COMPILE_STATUS)) {
            alert("Error compiling shader: " + gl.getShaderInfoLog(shader));
        }
        return shader;
    }

    function attachShaders(){
        gl.attachShader(shaderProgram, vertexShader);
        gl.attachShader(shaderProgram, fragmentShader);
        gl.linkProgram(shaderProgram);

        if (!gl.getProgramParameter(shaderProgram, gl.LINK_STATUS)) {
            alert("Unable to initialize the shader program.");
        }
    }

    function createShaderProgram(){
        shaderProgram = gl.createProgram();
        attachShaders();

        gl.useProgram(shaderProgram);
    }

    function setupShaders(fragmentShaderSRC, vertexShaderSRC){
        fragmentShader = makeShader(fragmentShaderSRC, gl.FRAGMENT_SHADER);
        vertexShader = makeShader(vertexShaderSRC, gl.VERTEX_SHADER);

        createShaderProgram();
    }

    function initShaders() {
        var fragmentShaderSRC = null,
        vertexShaderSRC = null;
        $.ajax({
            async: false,
            url: 'shader.fs',
            success: function (data) {
                fragmentShaderSRC = data.firstChild.textContent;
            },
            dataType: 'xml'
        });
```

```
                $.ajax({
                    async: false,
                    url: 'shader.vs',
                    success: function (data) {
                        vertexShaderSRC = data.firstChild.textContent;
                    },
                    dataType: 'xml'
                });
                setupShaders(fragmentShaderSRC, vertexShaderSRC);
            }

            function getMatrixUniforms(){
                shaderProgram.pMatrixUniform = gl.getUniformLocation(shaderProgram,↪
    "uPMatrix");
                shaderProgram.mvMatrixUniform = gl.getUniformLocation(shaderProgram,↪
    "uMVMatrix");
            }

            function setMatrixUniforms() {
                gl.uniformMatrix4fv(shaderProgram.pMatrixUniform, false, pMatrix);
                gl.uniformMatrix4fv(shaderProgram.mvMatrixUniform, false, mvMatrix);
            }

            function getVertexAttributes(){
                vertexPositionAttribute = gl.getAttribLocation(shaderProgram,↪
    "aVertexPosition");
                gl.enableVertexAttribArray(vertexPositionAttribute);

                vertexColorAttribute = gl.getAttribLocation(shaderProgram,
    "aVertexColor");
                gl.enableVertexAttribArray(vertexColorAttribute);
            }

            function executeProgram(){
                getMatrixUniforms();
                getVertexAttributes();

                initBuffers();

                drawScene();
            }

            function drawScene() {
                gl.viewport(0, 0, gl.viewportWidth, gl.viewportHeight);
                gl.clear(gl.COLOR_BUFFER_BIT);

                mat4.perspective(45, gl.viewportWidth / gl.viewportHeight, 0.1, 100.0,↪
    pMatrix);
                mat4.identity(mvMatrix);
                mat4.translate(mvMatrix, [0, 0.0, -7.0]);

                setMatrixUniforms();

                gl.bindBuffer(gl.ARRAY_BUFFER, squareVerticesBuffer);
```

```
                        gl.vertexAttribPointer(vertexPositionAttribute, 3, gl.FLOAT, false, 0,
0);

                        gl.bindBuffer(gl.ARRAY_BUFFER, squareVerticesColorBuffer);
                        gl.vertexAttribPointer(vertexColorAttribute, 4, gl.FLOAT, false, 0, 0);

                        gl.drawArrays(gl.TRIANGLE_STRIP, 0, 4);
                    }

                function initBuffers() {
                    squareVerticesBuffer = gl.createBuffer();
                    gl.bindBuffer(gl.ARRAY_BUFFER, squareVerticesBuffer);

                    var vertices = [
                        1.0,  1.0, 0.0,
                       -1.0,  1.0, 0.0,
                        1.0, -1.0, 0.0,
                       -1.0, -1.0, 0.0
                    ];

                    gl.bufferData(gl.ARRAY_BUFFER, new Float32Array(vertices),
gl.STATIC_DRAW);

                    var colors = [
                        1.0,  1.0,  1.0,  1.0,    // white
                        0.05, 0.05, 0.7,  1.0,    // dark blue
                        0.0,  1.0,  1.0,  1.0,    // cyan
                        0.0,  0.0,  1.0,  1.0     // blue
                    ];

                    squareVerticesColorBuffer = gl.createBuffer();
                    gl.bindBuffer(gl.ARRAY_BUFFER, squareVerticesColorBuffer);
                    gl.bufferData(gl.ARRAY_BUFFER, new Float32Array(colors), gl.STATIC_DRAW);
                }
        </script>
    </body>
</html>
```

Animation and depth

Our first demo renders a simple image, but has no movement or depth. In our next example, which is a modification of the previous one, we will rotate a 3D figure of an octahedron. An octahedron is simply an eight faced solid that looks like two rectangular pyramids attached at the base, as shown in Figure 7-9.

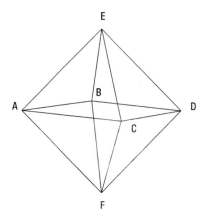

Figure 7-9. Wireframe of an octahedron with its eight faces and six vertex points

As you can see from Figure 7-9, vertices A, B, C, and D of an octahedron lie on the same plane and form a square. Vertices E and F mirror each other. The line connecting EF intersects the middle of the square—the intersection of AD and BC to be precise. EF and the plane ABCD are perpendicular.

Starting from the code in the previous demo (Listing 7-12), we remove the squareVerticesBuffer variable and define several new variables, as shown in Listing 7-13. These will be explained as they are encountered.

Listing 7-13. New Variables for Our Second Demo

```
                octahedronVertexPositionBuffer,
                octahedronVertexColorBuffer,
                octahedronVertexIndexBuffer,  //index buffer for our faces
                canvas = null,    //canvas DOM element reference
                paused = false,   //pause/resume animation flag
                height = 1.41,    //rounded square root of two
                rotationRadians = 0.0, //the amount to rotate our octahedron
                rotationVector = [1.0, 1.0, 1.0], //the axis to rotate our octahedron
                                               //experiment with other values between 0
    and 1
                rotationIncrement = 0,  //amount to increase the rotation each animation
    iteration
                x = 0, //translation amounts
                y = 0,
                z = 0,
                translationAngle = 0;   //angle used to calculate x,y,z translation
```

User input

Next, as shown In Listing 7-14, we bind the JavaScript onkeyup event to our HTML document by calling the jQuery function keyup. We also make the canvas variable global.

Listing 7-14. Keyup Handler

```
$(document).keyup(function(evt){
    if (evt.keyCode == 80) //'p'
    {
        paused =!paused;
    }
});

$(document).ready(function(){
    canvas = $("#canvas").get(0);
    …
```

Our keyup handler checks if the keyCode is 80. This corresponds to the 'p' key, which we will use to signal a pause/resume in animation.

Using requestAnimationFrame

It is a good idea to use the newer browser method, window.requestAnimationFrame, because it will not animate a scene when you are in another browser tab. This also means that extra battery life will not be needlessly wasted on mobile devices. However, the requestAnimationFrame method is fairly new and support is browser-dependant. We should test for it, reverting to the window.setTimeout fallback if it is not available. This is done by using a shim to wrap the function, such as the one shown on Paul Irish's blog at http://paulirish.com/2011/requestanimationframe-for-smart-animating/ and shown in Listing 7-15.

Listing 7-15. requestAnimationFrame Shim

```
// shim layer with setTimeout fallback
window.requestAnimFrame = (function(){
  return  window.requestAnimationFrame       ||
          window.webkitRequestAnimationFrame ||
          window.mozRequestAnimationFrame    ||
          window.oRequestAnimationFrame      ||
          window.msRequestAnimationFrame     ||
          function(/* function */ callback, /* DOMElement */ element){
            window.setTimeout(callback, 1000 / 60);
          };
})();
```

Our executeProgram function now includes an animation loop, as shown in Listing 7-16.

Listing 7-16. Animation Loop

```
function executeProgram(){
    getMatrixUniforms();
    getVertexAttributes();

    initBuffers();

    (function animLoop(){
        drawScene();
        requestAnimFrame(animLoop, canvas);
    })();
}
```

Using a function like animLoop that calls itself again is essential to animate more than one frame.

In our initWebGL function, we need to enable depth testing, as shown in Listing 7-17.

Listing 7-17. Enable gl.DEPTH_TEST

```
function initWebGL() {
    ...
    if (!gl) {
            alert("Error trying to initialise WebGL");
        } else {
            gl.clearColor(0.7, 0.7, 0.7, 1.0);
            gl.enable(gl.DEPTH_TEST);
        }
    }
}
```

If we do not check the depth of our rendered triangles, then, at times, faces of our solid that should be hidden from view are not. This gives unexpected results, as shown in Figure 7-10.

Figure 7-10. Not enabling the depth test can produce strange results

Creating movement

To move our octahedron around the screen, we need to alter its position. In this example, we use the trigonometric functions cosine and sine to alter our coordinates around circular paths. We then multiplied and/or added values to these computed magnitudes. You can play around with your coordinate generation functions to produce distinct and cool effects.

If the paused flag has been set by the user hitting the 'p' key, then we do not recalculate the

(x, y, z) coordinates or rotationRadians and do not increment our rotationIncrement or translationAngle variables.

Listing 7-18. Calculating Our Translation and Rotation After Each Frame

```
mat4.translate(mvMatrix, [3*x, y, -12.0 + 5*z]);

if(!paused){
    x = Math.cos(translationAngle);
    y = x;
    z = Math.sin(translationAngle);
    rotationRadians = rotationIncrement/(180/Math.PI);

    rotationIncrement++;
    translationAngle += .01;
}
mat4.rotate(mvMatrix, rotationRadians, rotationVector);
```

Using an index buffer

In this demo, we will use gl.TRIANGLES instead of a gl.TRIANGLE_STRIP. While it is still possible to use a TRIANGLE_STRIP here, doing so is much more complicated.

```
gl.bindBuffer(gl.ELEMENT_ARRAY_BUFFER, octahedronVertexIndexBuffer);
gl.drawElements(gl.TRIANGLES, octahedronVertexIndexBuffer.numItems, gl.UNSIGNED_SHORT,
0);
```

The initBuffers function (from Listing 7-12) has been completely replaced, as shown in Listing 7-19. Our vertex and fragment shaders remain exactly the same.

Listing 7-19. Our Octahedron Buffer Initialization Function

```
function initBuffers() {

    octahedronVertexPositionBuffer = gl.createBuffer();
    gl.bindBuffer(gl.ARRAY_BUFFER, octahedronVertexPositionBuffer);
    vertices = [
        // top faces
        0.0, height, 0.0,
        1.0, 0.0, 1.0,
            -1.0, 0.0, 1.0,

        0.0, height, 0.0,
        1.0, 0.0, -1.0,
            -1.0, 0.0, -1.0,

        0.0, height, 0.0,
        1.0, 0.0, 1.0,
        1.0,  0.0, -1.0,

        0.0, height,  0.0,
            -1.0, 0.0,  1.0,
            -1.0,  0.0,  -1.0,

        //bottom faces
        0.0, -height, 0.0,
        1.0, 0.0, 1.0,
```

```
            -1.0, 0.0, 1.0,

        0.0, -height, 0.0,
        1.0, 0.0, -1.0,
            -1.0, 0.0, -1.0,

        0.0, -height, 0.0,
        1.0, 0.0, 1.0,
        1.0,  0.0, -1.0,

        0.0, -height,  0.0,
            -1.0, 0.0,  1.0,
            -1.0, 0.0,  -1.0
];
gl.bufferData(gl.ARRAY_BUFFER, new Float32Array(vertices), gl.STATIC_DRAW);

octahedronVertexPositionBuffer.itemSize = 3;
octahedronVertexPositionBuffer.numItems = 24;

colors = [
    [1.0, 0.0, 0.0, 1.0], // red
    [0.0, 1.0, 0.0, 1.0], // green
    [0.0, 0.0, 1.0, 1.0], // blue
    [1.0, 1.0, 0.0, 1.0], // yellow

    [1.0, 1.0, 1.0, 1.0], // white
    [0.0, 0.0, 0.0, 1.0], // black
    [1.0, 0.0, 1.0, 1.0], // magenta
    [0.0, 1.0, 1.0, 1.0]  // cyan
];


var unpackedColors = [];
//8 colors by 4 channels - rgba
for(var i=0; i < 8; ++i){
    for(var k=0; k < 3; ++k){
        var color = colors[i];
        unpackedColors = unpackedColors.concat(color);
    }
}

octahedronVertexColorBuffer = gl.createBuffer();
gl.bindBuffer(gl.ARRAY_BUFFER, octahedronVertexColorBuffer);
gl.bufferData(gl.ARRAY_BUFFER, new Float32Array(unpackedColors),↪
gl.STATIC_DRAW);

octahedronVertexColorBuffer.itemSize = 4;
octahedronVertexColorBuffer.numItems = 24;

var octahedronVertexIndices = [
    //top
    0, 1, 2,       3, 4, 5,
    6, 7, 8,       9, 10, 11,
    //bottom
    12, 13, 14,    15, 16, 17,
```

```
        18, 19, 20,   21, 22, 23
    ];

    octahedronVertexIndexBuffer = gl.createBuffer();
    gl.bindBuffer(gl.ELEMENT_ARRAY_BUFFER, octahedronVertexIndexBuffer);
    gl.bufferData(gl.ELEMENT_ARRAY_BUFFER, new↪
Uint16Array(octahedronVertexIndices), gl.STATIC_DRAW);
    octahedronVertexIndexBuffer.itemSize = 1;
    octahedronVertexIndexBuffer.numItems = 24;
}
```

> **Note** *Even though we want to render the vertices in groups of three (triangles), the itemSize of the indices buffer is one. Each element represents one vertex. WebGL will assemble triplets of vertex indices when we render and specify gl.TRIANGLES.*

Figure 7-11 is a composite of three screenshots of our second demo, which demonstrates the animation in the program.

Figure 7-11. Octahedron rotating around the screen

To create the figure of the octahedron, there are actually only six distinct vertices. However, we want each face to be a different color. If we used only six vertices in our vertex buffer, than we could only have six colors—one for each vertex, not the eight needed for each of the eight faces to be different. Furthermore, even if the number of vertices was equal or greater than the number of faces (as in the case of a cube) then vertices are shared across different faces. You cannot define a buffered vertex to be a different color based on its usage and because of this, blending will occur (see Figure 7-12). To bypass this issue, we will need to define each vertex-color pair separately.

Referring again to Figure 7-9, when the octahedron is centered at the origin (0,0,0) and vertices A, B, C, D lie on the plane formed by y=0, than the vertex points are:

A: (-width, 0, -width)

B: (width, 0, -width)

C: (width, 0, width)

D: (-width, 0, width)

E: (0, height, 0)

F: (0, -height, 0)

We have chosen 1 for the width and the square root of 2 (1.41) for the height.

Each buffer specifies the itemSize, which is the number of sub-elements per item. For vertex position, this is 3, corresponding to the three position values (x, y, z). For vertex color, it is 4, corresponding to the four color channels (r, g, b, a). The numItems is how many items, each with the itemSize sub-elements that you have. So for an itemSize of 3 with 24 numItems, your buffer would hold 3 × 24 = 72 values, while an itemSize of 4 with 24 numItems requires 4 × 24 = 96 values.

If we did not care about faces having blended colors, we could have defined six vertices and used the index buffers shown in Listing 7-20.

Listing 7-20. Using Six Vertices Instead of Twenty-four

```
vertices = [
    0.0, height, 0.0,
    width, 0.0, width,
    -width, 0.0, width,
    -width, 0.0, -width,
    width, 0.0, -width,
    0.0, -height, 0.0,
];

octahedronVertexPositionBuffer.itemSize = 3;
octahedronVertexPositionBuffer.numItems = 6;

//A,B,C,D = 1,2,3,4  E = 0, F = 5
var octahedronVertexIndices = [
    //top
    0, 1, 2,        0, 1, 4,
    0, 2, 3,        0, 3, 4,
    //bottom
    5, 1, 2,        5, 1, 4,
    5, 2, 3,        5, 3, 4,
];

octahedronVertexIndicesBuffer.itemSize = 1;
octahedronVertexIndicesBuffer.numItems = 24;
```

If you do not modify the color code, then only the first six colors are used—three red and three green, as shown on the left of Figure 7-12. If you do modify the code to remove the k loop, and use six of your eight colors, then you get the result on the right of Figure 7-12.

Listing 7-21. Defining Six Colors Instead of Twenty-four

```
for(var i=0; i < 6; ++i){
        var color = colors[i];
        unpackedColors = unpackedColors.concat(color);
}

octahedronVertexColorBuffer.itemSize = 4;
octahedronVertexColorBuffer.numItems = 6;
```

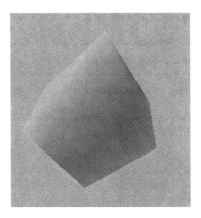 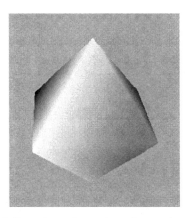

Figure 7-12. Two colors on the left, six colors on the right. Both illustrate varying vertex colors per face, resulting in blended faces. You may want this effect, just be aware that one color per vertex will not result in solid faces if at least two vertices differ in color.

The full source code is available on the book web site at octahedron.html. As you can see, even a simple shape involves a high number of vertices. Creating images quickly becomes tedious and error-prone from inputting raw data by hand. A better solution is to load existing models.

Loading a complex model

Higher-level libraries will load wavefront obj files, collada, and other model file formats. The most common way to load data is using Ajax and JSON or XML.

The program Blender, available at www.blender.org, is an open-source 3D suite. A script to export Blender models in JSON format is available at http://code.google.com/p/blender-webgl-exporter/.

A basic game

When creating a game, you should plan what you wish to accomplish and how to implement it (at a high level) before you write any code. This can always be modified during development. but is a good start.

Planning

Game:	A simple dart game.
Models:	A 2D dartboard/target will be rendered in a circular shape using triangle primitives and a textured image. A 3D "dart," an elongated tetrahedron, will be rendered.
Input:	We will use mouse events to throw the dart and an HTML form button to reset the dart.
Collision Detection:	The dart will stop when it reaches the dartboard z position.
Scoring:	We will use dart position to find the score associated with a dartboard circular segment.

Adding a texture

We will generate a triangle fan and then texture it to produce our dartboard. This is shown in Listing 7-22.

Listing 7-22. Our Dartboard Variables and Buffer Initialization

```
...
dartboardVertexPositionBuffer = null,
dartboardVertexTexCoordBuffer = null,
dartboardTexture = null,
dartboardDiameter = 2.5,
dartboard_sections = 20, //number of circular sections
dartboard_z = -7.0,
...

function initDartboardBuffer(){
        var vertices = [0,0,0], //center vertex
        texCoords = [0,0],
        x,
        y,
        radians = 0;

        //programatically create vertices.
        //will divide circle into 20 sections = 18 degrees each
        for(var i=0; i < dartboard_sections; i++){
            radians = i * 2.0 * Math.PI/dartboard_sections;

            x = Math.cos(radians);
            y = Math.sin(radians);

            vertices = vertices.concat([x*dartboardDiameter, y*dartboardDiameter,↵
    dartboard_z]);
            texCoords = texCoords.concat([x/2.0 + .5, y/2.0 + .5]);
        }
```

```
            dartboardVertexPositionBuffer = gl.createBuffer();
            gl.bindBuffer(gl.ARRAY_BUFFER, dartboardVertexPositionBuffer);
            gl.bufferData(gl.ARRAY_BUFFER, new Float32Array(vertices), gl.STATIC_DRAW);
            dartboardVertexPositionBuffer.itemSize = 3;
            dartboardVertexPositionBuffer.numItems = (dartboard_sections + 1);

            dartboardVertexTexCoordBuffer = gl.createBuffer();
            gl.bindBuffer(gl.ARRAY_BUFFER, dartboardVertexTexCoordBuffer);
            gl.bufferData(gl.ARRAY_BUFFER, new Float32Array(texCoords), gl.STATIC_DRAW);
            dartboardVertexTexCoordBuffer.itemSize = 2;
            dartboardVertexTexCoordBuffer.numItems = (dartboard_sections + 1);
        }
```

In Listing 7-22, we create a circular shape comprised of triangular sections by programmatically computing coordinates. We could have textured the square enclosure of the dartboard with only two triangles using a texture that had a transparent background. However, if we wanted to texture every *n*th section or blend color or discard certain regions, then the triangles are essential. If we are combining lighting operations with a texture, then accurate vertex points are also important.

Each (x, y) coordinate will be in the range -1 to 1. To generate the corresponding texture coordinate, we then divide each (x, y) coordinate by 2 and add .5. This clamps the texture coordinate (s, t) to the range of 0 and 1. Next, to load our texture image and set the type of filtering, we need the code in Listing 7-23.

Listing 7-23. Loading and Initializing Our Texture

```
        function initTexture(){
            dartboardTexture = gl.createTexture();
            dartboardTexture.image = new Image();
            dartboardTexture.image.onload = function() {
                handleLoadedTexture(dartboardTexture)
            }

            dartboardTexture.image.src = "dartboard.gif";
        }

        function handleLoadedTexture(texture) {
            gl.bindTexture(gl.TEXTURE_2D, texture);
            gl.pixelStorei(gl.UNPACK_FLIP_Y_WEBGL, true);
            gl.texImage2D(gl.TEXTURE_2D, 0, gl.RGBA, gl.RGBA, gl.UNSIGNED_BYTE, ⮬
texture.image);
            gl.texParameteri(gl.TEXTURE_2D, gl.TEXTURE_MAG_FILTER, gl.NEAREST);
            gl.texParameteri(gl.TEXTURE_2D, gl.TEXTURE_MIN_FILTER, gl.NEAREST);
            gl.bindTexture(gl.TEXTURE_2D, null);
        }
```

Now, we have generated texture coordinates and want to texture the dartboard. We just want to color our dart in this example and so we have two options. We can use a single shader program and set a uniform flag that determines whether we want the shader to use a texture for each object in our scene, or we can create and bind multiple shader programs, switching them as needed. We will go with the second option. The following code modification redefines our variables as arrays:

```
        COLOR_SHADER = 0,
        TEXTURE_SHADER = 1,
```

```
            NUM_SHADERS = 2,
            shaderPrograms = [],
            fragmentShaders = [],
            vertexShaders = [],
            vertexPositionAttributes = [],
            vertexColorAttributes = [],
            textureCoordAttributes = [],
```

Our shaders are physically stored in the files shader.vs, shader.fs, tex_shader.vs, and tex_shader.fs. The first two shader files remain the same as in the previous example. The last two now include texture processing and do not pass in color data.

Listing 7-24. Vertex and Fragment Shader for a Textured Object

```
<script id="shader-vs" type="x-shader/x-vertex">
  attribute vec3 aVertexPosition;
  attribute vec2 aTextureCoord;

  uniform mat4 uMVMatrix;
  uniform mat4 uPMatrix;

  varying highp vec2 vTextureCoord;

  void main(void) {
    gl_Position = uPMatrix * uMVMatrix * vec4(aVertexPosition, 1.0);
    vTextureCoord = aTextureCoord;
  }
</script>

<script id="shader-fs" type="x-shader/x-fragment">
  varying highp vec2 vTextureCoord;
  uniform sampler2D uSampler;

  void main(void) {
        gl_FragColor = texture2D(uSampler, vec2(vTextureCoord.s, vTextureCoord.t));
  }
</script>
```

We also parameterize our shader functions so that they can be reused, as shown in Listing 7-25.

Listing 7-25. Parameterized Shader Functions

```
        function initShaders() {
                var fragmentShaderSRC = null,
                vertexShaderSRC = null;

                var shaderFilenames = ['shader', 'tex_shader'];
                for(var i=0; i< NUM_SHADERS; ++i){
                    $.ajax({
                        async: false,
                        url: shaderFilenames[i] + '.fs',
                        success: function (data) {
                            fragmentShaderSRC = data.firstChild.textContent;
                        },
```

```
                    dataType: 'xml'
                });
                $.ajax({
                    async: false,
                    url: shaderFilenames[i] + '.vs',
                    success: function (data) {
                        vertexShaderSRC = data.firstChild.textContent;
                    },
                    dataType: 'xml'
                });
                setupShaders(fragmentShaderSRC, vertexShaderSRC, i);
            }
        }

        function attachShaders(i){
            gl.attachShader(shaderPrograms[i], vertexShaders[i]);
            gl.attachShader(shaderPrograms[i], fragmentShaders[i]);
            gl.linkProgram(shaderPrograms[i]);

            if (!gl.getProgramParameter(shaderPrograms[i], gl.LINK_STATUS)) {
                alert("Unable to initialize the shader program.");
            }
        }

        function createShaderProgram(i){
            shaderPrograms[i] = gl.createProgram();
            attachShaders(i);
        }

        function setupShaders(fragmentShaderSRC, vertexShaderSRC, i){
            fragmentShaders[i] = makeShader(fragmentShaderSRC, gl.FRAGMENT_SHADER);
            vertexShaders[i] = makeShader(vertexShaderSRC, gl.VERTEX_SHADER);

            createShaderProgram(i);
        }
```

As shown in Listing 7-26, next we set up our vertex uniforms and attributes for each program. The texture shader sets a sampler uniform. We use the vertex attribute in our color shader and texture coordinate attribute in our texture shader.

Listing 7-26. Setting Our Shader Uniform and Attributes

```
        function getMatrixUniforms(i){
                shaderPrograms[i].pMatrixUniform = gl.getUniformLocation(shaderPrograms[i],↪
    "uPMatrix");
                shaderPrograms[i].mvMatrixUniform = gl.getUniformLocation(shaderPrograms[i],↪
    "uMVMatrix");

                if( i==TEXTURE_SHADER ){
                    shaderPrograms[i].samplerUniform = gl.getUniformLocation↪
    (shaderPrograms[i], "uSampler");
                }
            }
```

```
function setMatrixUniforms(i) {
    gl.uniformMatrix4fv(shaderPrograms[i].pMatrixUniform, false, pMatrix);
    gl.uniformMatrix4fv(shaderPrograms[i].mvMatrixUniform, false, mvMatrix);
}

function getVertexAttributes(i){
    vertexPositionAttributes[i] = gl.getAttribLocation(shaderPrograms[i],↪
"aVertexPosition");
    gl.enableVertexAttribArray(vertexPositionAttributes[i]);

    if(i == TEXTURE_SHADER){
        textureCoordAttributes[i] = gl.getAttribLocation(shaderPrograms[i],↪
"aTextureCoord");
        gl.enableVertexAttribArray(textureCoordAttributes[i]);
    }else if(i == COLOR_SHADER){
        vertexColorAttributes[i] = gl.getAttribLocation(shaderPrograms[i],↪
"aVertexColor");
        gl.enableVertexAttribArray(vertexColorAttributes[i]);
    }
}

function executeProgram(){
    for(var i=0;i<NUM_SHADERS; ++i){
        getMatrixUniforms(i);
        getVertexAttributes(i);
    }

    initBuffers();

    (function animLoop(){
        drawScene();
        requestAnimFrame(animLoop, canvas);
    })();
}
```

In Listing 7-27, we refactor our initBuffers and drawScene methods to call the octahedron (dart) and dartboard method calls.

Listing 7-27. Drawing Our Scene and the Dartboard

```
function initBuffers() {
    initOctahedronBuffer();
    initDartboardBuffer();
}

function drawScene() {
    gl.viewport(0, 0, gl.viewportWidth, gl.viewportHeight);
    gl.clear(gl.COLOR_BUFFER_BIT | gl.DEPTH_BUFFER_BIT);

    mat4.perspective(45, gl.viewportWidth / gl.viewportHeight, 0.1, 100.0,↪
pMatrix);

    drawDartboard();
    drawDart();
```

```
        }

    function drawDartboard(){
        //draw dartboard
        gl.useProgram(shaderPrograms[TEXTURE_SHADER]);

        mat4.identity(mvMatrix);
        mat4.translate(mvMatrix, [0, 0, dartboard_z]);
        setMatrixUniforms(TEXTURE_SHADER);

        gl.activeTexture(gl.TEXTURE0);
        gl.bindTexture(gl.TEXTURE_2D, dartboardTexture);
        gl.uniform1i(shaderPrograms[TEXTURE_SHADER].samplerUniform, 0);

        gl.bindBuffer(gl.ARRAY_BUFFER, dartboardVertexPositionBuffer);
        gl.vertexAttribPointer(vertexPositionAttributes[TEXTURE_SHADER], 3,↪
gl.FLOAT, false, 0, 0);

        gl.bindBuffer(gl.ARRAY_BUFFER, dartboardVertexTexCoordBuffer);
        gl.vertexAttribPointer(textureCoordAttributes[TEXTURE_SHADER], 2,↪
gl.FLOAT, false, 0, 0);

        gl.drawArrays(gl.TRIANGLE_FAN, 1, dartboard_sections);
    }

    function drawDart (){
        //draw dart
    }
```

In the drawDartboard function, we use the texture shader, reset the view to the identity, and then translate the dartboard back along the z-axis. We set the active texture and a sampler uniform, which the fragment shader uses. We bind our buffer data and draw the dartboard by calling drawArrays.

Figure 7-13. Dartboard image textured onto a triangle fan

Drawing our dart

Our dart will be a stretched version of the octahedron we rendered in our previous demo, using only two colors, gold and blue.

```
...
octahedronVertexPositionBuffer = null,
octahedronVertexColorBuffer = null,
octahedronVertexIndexBuffer = null,
dartScale = .5,
dartWidth = .2 * dartScale
dartHeight = 2.0 * dartScale,
dartSkew = .5,
dart_x = 0.0,
dart_y = 0.0,
dart_z = 0.0,
dart_z_velocity = 0.0,
DART_START = [0.5, -0.5, -2.0],
...
```

We now have formally set variables for the dart properties. Next we initialize the dart buffer, as shown in Listing 7-28.

Listing 7-28. Initializing the Dart Buffer

```
function initOctahedronBuffer(){
            octahedronVertexPositionBuffer = gl.createBuffer();
            gl.bindBuffer(gl.ARRAY_BUFFER, octahedronVertexPositionBuffer);
            var vertices = [
                // top faces
                0.0, dartHeight, 0.0,
                dartWidth, 0.0, dartWidth,
                    -dartWidth, 0.0, dartWidth,

                0.0, dartHeight, 0.0,
                dartWidth, 0.0, -dartWidth,
                    -dartWidth, 0.0, -dartWidth,

                0.0, dartHeight, 0.0,
                dartWidth, 0.0, dartWidth,
                dartWidth,  0.0, -dartWidth,

                0.0, dartHeight,  0.0,
                    -dartWidth, 0.0,  dartWidth,
                    -dartWidth,  0.0,  -dartWidth,

                //bottom faces
                0.0, -dartHeight * dartSkew, 0.0,
                dartWidth, 0.0, dartWidth,
                    -dartWidth, 0.0, dartWidth,

                0.0, -dartHeight * dartSkew, 0.0,
                dartWidth, 0.0, -dartWidth,
```

```
                    -dartWidth, 0.0, -dartWidth,

            0.0, -dartHeight * dartSkew, 0.0,
            dartWidth, 0.0, dartWidth,
            dartWidth,  0.0, -dartWidth,

            0.0, -dartHeight * dartSkew,  0.0,
                -dartWidth, 0.0,  dartWidth,
                -dartWidth,  0.0,  -dartWidth
        ];
        gl.bufferData(gl.ARRAY_BUFFER, new Float32Array(vertices), gl.STATIC_DRAW);
        octahedronVertexPositionBuffer.itemSize = 3;
        octahedronVertexPositionBuffer.numItems = 24;

        colors = [
            [1.0, 0.7, 0.0, 1.0], // gold
            [1.0, 0.7, 0.0, 1.0], // gold
            [1.0, 0.7, 0.0, 1.0], // gold
            [1.0, 0.7, 0.0, 1.0], // gold

            [0.0, 0.0, 1.0, 1.0], // blue
            [0.0, 0.0, 1.0, 1.0], // blue
            [0.0, 0.0, 1.0, 1.0], // blue
            [0.0, 0.0, 1.0, 1.0], // blue
        ];
        var unpackedColors = [];
        //8 colors by 4 channels - rgba
        for(var i=0; i < 8; ++i){
            for(var k=0; k < 3; ++k){
                var color = colors[i];
                unpackedColors = unpackedColors.concat(color);
            }
        }

        octahedronVertexColorBuffer = gl.createBuffer();
        gl.bindBuffer(gl.ARRAY_BUFFER, octahedronVertexColorBuffer);
        gl.bufferData(gl.ARRAY_BUFFER, new Float32Array(unpackedColors),↪
gl.STATIC_DRAW);

        octahedronVertexColorBuffer.itemSize = 4;
        octahedronVertexColorBuffer.numItems = 24;

        var octahedronVertexIndices = [
            //top
            0, 1, 2,      3, 4, 5,
            6, 7, 8,      9, 10, 11,
            //bottom
            12, 13, 14,   15, 16, 17,
            18, 19, 20,   21, 22, 23
        ];

        octahedronVertexIndexBuffer = gl.createBuffer();
        gl.bindBuffer(gl.ELEMENT_ARRAY_BUFFER, octahedronVertexIndexBuffer);
        gl.bufferData(gl.ELEMENT_ARRAY_BUFFER, new Uint16Array↪
```

```
(octahedronVertexIndices), gl.STATIC_DRAW);
                octahedronVertexIndexBuffer.itemSize = 1;
                octahedronVertexIndexBuffer.numItems = 24;
        }
```

Now it is time for us to draw the dart, as shown in Listing 7-29.

Listing 7-29. Drawing the Dart

```
function drawDart(){
                gl.useProgram(shaderPrograms[COLOR_SHADER]);

                if(!paused){
checkIfReachedBoard();
                }
mat4.identity(mvMatrix);
                dart_z += dart_z_velocity;
                dart_z  = Math.max(dart_z, dartboard_z);
                mat4.translate(mvMatrix, [dart_x, dart_y, dart_z]);
                mat4.rotate(mvMatrix, 225, [1, 0, 0]);

                setMatrixUniforms(COLOR_SHADER);

                gl.bindBuffer(gl.ARRAY_BUFFER, octahedronVertexPositionBuffer);
                gl.vertexAttribPointer(vertexPositionAttributes[COLOR_SHADER], 3,↪
    gl.FLOAT, false, 0, 0);

                gl.bindBuffer(gl.ARRAY_BUFFER, octahedronVertexColorBuffer);
                gl.vertexAttribPointer(vertexColorAttributes[COLOR_SHADER], 4,↪
    gl.FLOAT, false, 0, 0);

                gl.bindBuffer(gl.ELEMENT_ARRAY_BUFFER, octahedronVertexIndexBuffer);
                gl.drawElements(gl.TRIANGLES, octahedronVertexIndexBuffer.numItems,↪
    gl.UNSIGNED_SHORT, 0);
                }
```

In Listing 7-29, we use the color shader and check if our dart has reached the dartboard. We reset the matrix to the identity and then translate and rotate our dart. We bind our buffers and draw the triangle elements as usual.

Mouse events

To determine where our dart should end up, we keep track of the vector between the initial and final mouse position when the user clicks the mouse, moves it with the mouse down, and then releases the mouse. We also calculate the "velocity" of this event, which is the distance divided by event duration. We attach mousedown and mouseup event handlers to the canvas DOM element. We have also added a HTML <button> to reset the dart position.

Listing 7-30. User Interaction and Mouse Events

```
<button id="reset" >Reset</button>
...
positionStart = [],
```

```
        positionChange = [],
        timeChange = 0.0;

$(document).ready(function(){
    var canvasObj = $("#canvas")
    canvas = canvasObj.get(0);

    canvasObj.mousedown(function(e){
        positionStart = [e.pageX, e.pageY];
        timeChange = new Date().getTime();
    });

    canvasObj.mouseup(function(e){
        positionChange = [e.pageX - positionStart[0], e.pageY - positionStart[1]]
        timeChange = new Date().getTime() - timeChange;
        if(paused && (positionChange[1] < 0)){
            throwDart();
        }
    });

    $("#reset").click(function(){
        resetDart();
    });

    initWebGL();
    initShaders();
    initTexture();
    resetDart();

    executeProgram();
});
function resetDart(){
    paused = true;
    dart_x = DART_START[0];
    dart_y = DART_START[1];
    dart_z = DART_START[2];
    translation_angle = 0.0;
    dart_z_velocity = 0.0;
    $("#reset").attr("disabled", true);
}
```

To throw the dart, we take the positionChange array and find the inverse angle, by calling Math.atan2. Then we set the x position to the cosine of this angle. To find the y position, we take the difference of the mouse throw velocity and a precomputed expected velocity. Admittingly, the calculations of these values could use an improved model. For example, a moving lever that the user clicks on to determine their aim, like the type found in many golf simulators, could be a better user interface.

Listing 7-31. Throwing the Dart

```
function throwDart(){
    resetDart();
    paused = false;
    var angle = Math.atan2(positionChange[1], positionChange[0]);
```

```
    dart_x = Math.cos(angle) * dartboardDiameter;
    if(Math.random() < 0.5){
            dart_x *= -1;
    }
    var velocity = (
    Math.sqrt(positionChange[0]*positionChange[0] +
positionChange[1]*positionChange[1])/
            timeChange
    );
    var yAngle = (velocity - .6);
    dart_y = Math.sin(yAngle) * dartboardDiameter;
    dart_z_velocity = -0.1;
}
```

Basic collision detection

For our darts game, the only collision detection we will do is to determine if the dart has reached the dartboard z-axis. In fact, it does not even need to fall within the bounds of the board. We will stop the dart whenever it reaches the z depth of the dartboard.

```
function checkIfReachedBoard(){
    if(dart_z == DART_START[2] || Math.abs(dart_z - dartboard_z) < 0.001){
        paused = true;
        $("#reset").attr("disabled", false);
        calculateAndDisplayScore();
    }
}
```

Scoring

To calculate the score of the dart throw, we define an array of segment values. Then we calculate the angle of the throw and which segment it is in. Finally, we look up the value of the segment and display it in an HTML paragraph. This is shown in Listing 7-32.

Listing 7-32. Scoring

```
function calculateAndDisplayScore(){
    var scores = [13,4,18,1,20,
        5,12,9,14,11,
        6,10,15,2,17,
        3,19,7,16,8];
    var final_angle = Math.atan2(dart_y, dart_x);
    var final_angle_degrees = final_angle * 180/Math.PI;
    var landed_section = Math.floor(final_angle_degrees/↩
(360.0/dartboard_sections));

    if(landed_section < 0){ landed_section = Math.abs(landed_section)+10; }
    if(Math.sqrt(dart_x*dart_x + dart_y*dart_y) < (dartboardDiameter/2.0)){
        $("#score").html("<strong>Nice Throw: (" + scores[landed_section] +↩
")</strong>");
    }else{
        $("#score").html("Practice is needed");
    }
}
```

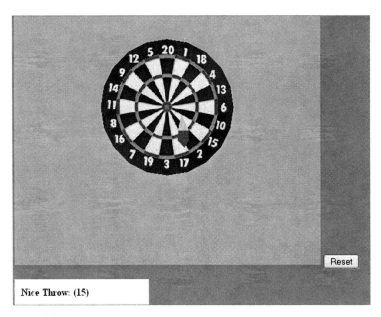

Figure 7-14. Our completed dart game

The full source of the program is available online in the file `darts.html`. The following are some improvements you could make to the game:

- More precise scoring. Calculating double and triple score areas and separating the two bull's-eye areas.

- Making the throwing smoother and more realistic. Adding gravity and a throwing arc.

- Throwing multiple darts.

- Keeping track of high scores.

- Improving the graphical realism of the dart model.

Summary

In this chapter, WebGL was introduced and we went through the steps involved in setting up a basic scene. Learning how to set up a scene yourself is good not only for a theoretical understanding of what is going on, but it can also give you an appreciation of how using one of the existing WebGL frameworks can improve productivity.

I hope you are excited with what you have learned so far with WebGL and are ready to explore the *Cycleblob* chapter, which features an interactive 3D game—*Cycleblob*! In that chapter, you will learn more advanced WebGL techniques such as lighting, creating an active camera, blending, and loading in complex models.

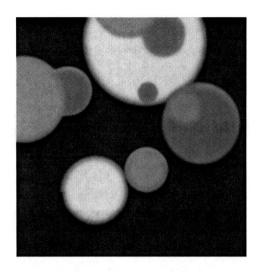

Chapter 8

CycleBlob: A WebGL Lightcycle Game

I started learning JavaScript and WebGL for fun in my free time on evenings and weekends. For most of my career, I've programmed large enterprise applications in C++ and, on occasion, I've written some data visualizations using desktop OpenGL. 3D content on the web is something that I've been waiting for a while to happen, so when the news of the upcoming WebGL specification arrived, I could not wait to try it out. The technological opportunity coincided with an idea I've been nurturing for a while: taking the concept of an old '80s game that is usually played in a 2D setting and somehow translating it into the 3D world. Some ideas that I considered include:

- A *PAC-MAN* game in a maze situated on a deformed, closed surface.

- A *Qix*-like game (aka *Xonix*, *Volfied*) where the player needs to conquer as much area as possible of the surface of a 3D shape, trying to avoid enemies and obstacles.

- *Scorched Earth*, a turn-based warfare game between players on a small, 3D planet floating in space.

- *Q*bert*, which features a little creature that paints stairs as he steps on them, trying to cover an entire staircase. Instead of filling just one flight of stairs, play on a complete, 3D world made of cubes.

Eventually, the idea that appealed to me the most was that of the lightcycle game. Inspired by the 1982 movie *TRON*, lightcycles are sort of like motorcycles that move on a flat grid and leave a wall trail behind them. The goal is to avoid crashing into walls and remain the last player alive. Players can block other cycles on the grid, causing them to crash because they have nowhere to turn. Players can also work in teams to better their chances of winning. My version of the game takes place on a closed, 3D surface instead of a flat, walled arena. After two months of full-time work (between jobs), I came up with CycleBlob (http://cycleblob.com), a full, 3D lightcycle game that runs in the browser using WebGL.

What is WebGL?

WebGL (Web-based Graphics Library) is a port of the OpenGL ES API to the web browser. It allows JavaScript code to directly display and manipulate 3D scenes on an HTML5 canvas embedded in a web page.

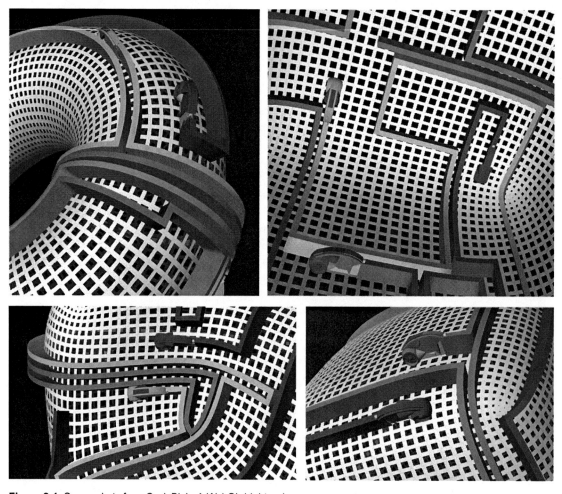

Figure 8-1. Screenshots from CycleBlob: A WebGL Lightcycle game

With some minor exceptions, (until WebGL arrived) interactive 3D content has been largely confined to monolithic applications that the user downloads and runs on a desktop computer. Back in the '90s, we had VRML, an XML-like language that described 3D models and worlds. VRML had very few mechanisms for interacting with the user and it was primarily used for displaying static, 3D content. Its current incarnation—in the form of X3D—addresses this issue to a large extent, adding mechanisms for creating fully interactive worlds. X3D, however, is not intended to allow full programmability the way JavaScript does. X3D is a declarative language that allows the programmer to describe what objects to display and what the relations between those objects are. WebGL, on the other hand, comes from the *imperative* paradigm: the programmer writes the exact instructions on *how* to draw every element of the scene. This opens up a whole new world of options and flexibility—compared to what is possible with X3D. Another drawback of X3D is that like VRML, it requires the user to install a plug-in to the browser. WebGL, on the other hand, is an integral part of the HTML5 standard and does not require an external plug-in in the browsers that support it.

WebGL is fully supported by the latest versions of Mozilla Firefox and Google Chrome, and is in development for Safari and Opera. This support, however, still depends on the OS being fairly recent and updated, and on the hardware and drivers to be fairly up-to-date. Microsoft Internet Explorer still does not support WebGL; furthermore, Microsoft has explicitly stated its distrust of WebGL technology due to possible security concerns. I expect, however, that with the current trend towards HTML5 and away from Flash and Silverlight, and with the sincere intent of the WebGL community to address security issues, Microsoft will turn around and eventually align with the rest.

Starting with WebGL

The basic tutorials from `http://learningwebgl.com` are a good starting point for a newcomer to 3D graphics. These tutorials are a port to WebGL by the renowned NeHe OpenGL tutorials. I started by copying one of the tutorial's code for a basic rendering engine, then adding features on top of it; copying from other tutorials to load meshes and add lighting; and adding my own code for animation. After a while, I found myself gradually refactoring out the tutorial code, replacing it with more generic code in some places and code specialized for my own needs in others. Working with the tutorials allowed me to quickly get off the ground and have something working and rendering in a short time. Once you have a 3D image visible, you know you're on the right track. With every step and feature added, you can easily check that nothing broke down and that you still get a proper 3D rendering.

Work environment setup

Like any programming activity, writing and debugging a web application requires a small amount of setup to enable you to write code and see it working. An absolute minimal setup consists of the following:

- A text editor for writing code. On Windows, even Notepad.exe can be used for this purpose.
- A folder with all the files that make up the application—HTML and JavaScript files.
- A browser to view the results.

Working with this setup is similarly simple. You write the HTML and JavaScript using the editor, save them to your project folder, and double-click the HTML file to open it in the browser to see if it works.

This setup is sufficient for the first few attempts at tinkering with web applications, but pretty soon, it becomes evident that it is not an ideal environment.

The problem with local disk files

When you double-click an HTML file on a local disk, the browser treats it differently than a page downloaded from a real web server. The page may not be able to refer to other files unless they are in a specific folder structure; JavaScript code may not be able to perform AJAX requests; and features may be disabled or enabled according to various security considerations. The exact differences depend on the browser, but common to all browsers is that to a certain extent, working with local disk files is inherently different from working with a real web server. The indication that you are working with a local file is that the address bar says something like `file:///C:/webgl/myapp.html`, instead of a regular web address. In order to simulate real working conditions for our web application, we will need an actual web server.

WampServer (`www.wampserver.com/en`) is a very convenient package for Windows. It can be downloaded for free. The simple installer creates a fully-configured web development environment, ready for use. To see it work, do the following:

- After installation, make sure the Wamp service is running. You can see its status icon in the notification area of the taskbar. The icon should be green.

- Go to the folder where Wamp is installed (say `C:\wamp`) and go to the sub-folder called `www`. Create a new folder for your work called `myapp` (for example). Copy your HTML and JS files to this folder and make sure that the main HTML file is called `index.html`.

- Now open the browser and direct it to `http://localhost/myapp`. If everything is working as it should, you will see your application page.

What happens behind the scenes is that WampServer opens a port 80 (TCP port for HTTP protocol) locally on your computer. When you direct the browser to go to the address `localhost`, it tries to access your computer as if it were a web server. WampServer then sends him the files found under the folder `www`.

By default, WampServer only enables a local browser to access the content under `www`. The port is not opened on any outbound interface, so no one other than you can access this page.

"Wamp" is an acronym for Windows, Apache, MySQL, PHP. It is a play on the common "LAMP" acronym (Linux, Apache, MySQL, PHP) that describes the common internet web server setup.

Debugging JavaScript

Modern browsers almost invariably contain some facilities for debugging JavaScript code.

- The basic JavaScript console gives basic indications of errors that may have occurred or warnings about unexpected behavior. The console also allows immediate access to the JavaScript interpreter command line for evaluating short snippets.

- The latest versions of Chrome and IE contain a full debugger out of the box. It allows setting breakpoints in the JavaScript code, debugging it step-by-step, and examines variables in a watch window.

- For Firefox, there is an add-on called Firebug (http://getfirebug.com) that is also a full debugger. It contains similar features to the Chrome and IE built-in debuggers.

It is important to become familiar with these tools before setting off on any non-trivial debugging session.

A better editor

The Windows Notepad can save text files, but it is hardly ideal for programming. For my JavaScript coding, I use ActiveState Komodo Edit (www.activestate.com/komodo-edit), a convenient and free editor that can do syntax highlighting for JavaScript (and other languages). A nice feature of this editor is that it can open and save files directly to FTP servers. This is useful when working in a development environment on a remote server.

3D models and geometry

A minimal WebGL rendering engine allows for displaying a simple, 3D object centered on the 3D canvas. An initial code base that does this is the foundation for any WebGL application. The specific details for implementing it are described in Chapter 7 of this book and in the learningwebgl.com tutorials. In this section, I will discuss what is usually the next step in writing a 3D application: getting or creating the actual 3D models to be displayed. The most common representation of a 3D model is a triangle mesh, otherwise known as a "triangle soup." A triangle mesh is a collection of triangles in 3D space that are connected along their edges.

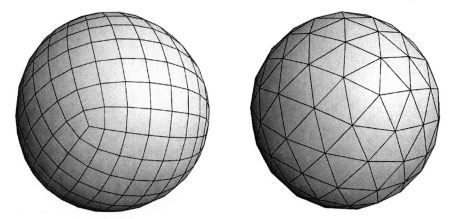

Figure 8-2. Two 3D models of a sphere. The right is a triangle mesh, the left is quad mesh.

A convenient and efficient way to represent a triangle mesh in a program is using three lists, as follows:

- **Vertices list**: Contains the 3D coordinates of all points where triangles meet. A point in a triangle mesh is usually a meeting point of three to six triangles. An edge between two triangles spans between two vertices.

- **Triangles list**: Contains an entry for every triangle that needs to be drawn for the model. Each triangle is made of three indices of vertices from the vertices list. The vertices are referenced by index so that their coordinates are not repeated.

- **Normal vectors list** (optional): A normal is a 3D vector that indicates a direction in 3D that is perpendicular to the surface and pointing outward from the object. The normals are used in lighting calculations, among other things. We usually specify a normal for every vertex of the mesh, so the normal vectors list is identical in length to the vertices list. A later section will describe a method to calculate normals in case they are not given.

In the game's JavaScript code, these lists are further simplified by flattening them into arrays of numbers. A triangle mesh can be defined by an object that contains the following arrays of numbers:

- **The vertices array**: A list of floating-point numbers. Every triplet of consecutive numbers defines the x, y, and z coordinates of a point in space.

- **The triangles indices array**: A list of integer numbers. Every triplet of consecutive integers defines the three corner points of a triangle. The numbers are zero-based indices to the vertices array. The order of the three indices in each triplet is significant. This will be discussed later.

- **The normals array** (optional): A list of floating-point numbers, similar to the vertices array. Every consecutive triplet of floats defines the x, y, and z components of the normal vector of a vertex.

The following is an example of a simple, 3D model of a tetrahedron (without normal definitions) in JSON format (JavaScript Object Notation).

```
var mesh {
"vertexPositions" :
  [ 1.0, -1.0, -1.0,    // vertex 0
   -1.0,  1.0, -1.0,    // vertex 1
   -1.0, -1.0,  1.0,    // vertex 2
    1.0,  1.0,  1.0 ],  // vertex 3
"trianglesIndices" :
  [1, 2, 3,
   0, 2, 1,
   3, 2, 0,
   0, 1, 3]
}
```

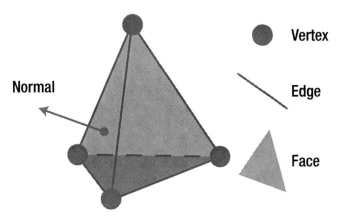

Figure 8-3. The tetrahedron model in 3D has four vertices, four faces, and six edges. Any point on the surface may have a normal, but only one is shown.

From these JavaScript arrays, the code can directly construct the typed arrays that are sent to the WebGL API. From the typed arrays, WebGL constructs vertex buffer objects to be rendered on the canvas.

Another popular mesh representation that I'm going to use is a quad mesh. A quad mesh is very similar to a triangle mesh, but it is made of rectangles instead of triangles. In the mesh representation, a rectangle is defined by four indices instead of three. WebGL is not capable of directly rendering rectangles, so before rendering, the model needs to pass through some processing that will break each rectangle into two triangles. This is trivially achieved if the rectangles are convex.

A straightforward generalization of the idea of the triangle and quad meshes is a general *polygon mesh*. In a polygon mesh, every face of the model is a flat shape with an arbitrary number of vertices. As before, any polygon can be divided into triangles using a process called "triangulation," and thus any polygon mesh can be converted into a triangle mesh. We will not use any polygon meshes in this chapter.

For reference, the following is a short list of some mesh geometry definitions that will be used throughout this chapter:

- **Vertex**: A point in 3D space defined by three coordinate numbers for x, y and z.

- **Edge**: A segment line that spans between two vertices.

- **Face**: A flat surface, usually a triangle or a rectangle that spans between three or four vertices.

- **Mesh**: A collection of connected faces that together make up a shape. If the surface forms a closed shape, that shape has an "inside" space and an "outside" space.

- **Normal**: A vector perpendicular to a surface at a certain point. That surface may be a single face or a complete mesh. As a matter of convention, normals of a closed shape are set to point toward the outside of the shape.

Models classification

The geometric models in CycleBlob can be divided into three categories.

- Static "artistic" models that are simply moved around in the scene and are not manipulated in any way. The player bike and the bonus ball are such models. In a well-funded game produced by a game studio, such models are usually created by 3D-modelling artists. In the case of CycleBlob, I used the Google SketchUp 3D repository to find these models.

- Dynamic models that are generated purely in JavaScript code at runtime. The wall trail behind the bikes and the explosion effect are such models. The JavaScript code of the game explicitly generates the arrays of data for these meshes in real time. These models are changed and updated in almost every single frame to account for the movement of the bikes and the progress of time.

- Static models that go through some geometric processing before being displayed in 3D. The model of the 3D world on which the game is played ("the grid") is such a model.

The following sections describe each of these in detail.

Static models

Before being displayed to the user, the models first need to find their way to the user's browser. Since models can be rather big at times, this is most conveniently achieved using XMLHttpRequest transfers after the page has loaded—to avoid having the user wait for a long time before anything is displayed.

3D models come in various shapes and formats: from complex scenes that include lighting, camera positions, and animation produced with an editor-like Autodesk 3ds Max, to simple objects that don't include much more than a triangle mesh definition. One popular format for such simple meshes is the wavefront .obj format.[1] This simple textual format is widely supported by 3D editors and viewers, which can export or convert files to it.

The tetrahedron example in the .obj format looks like this:

```
v 1.0 -1.0 -1.0
v -1.0 1.0 -1.0
v -1.0 -1.0 1.0
v 1.0 1.0 1.0

f 2 3 4
f 1 3 2
f 4 3 1
f 1 2 4
```

[1] For more information, visit http://en.wikipedia.org/wiki/Wavefront_.obj_file.

Vertices are specified by lines starting with the letter "v" and mesh faces are specified with "f" lines that, as before, specify the vertices' indices. In this format, the vertices are specified as one-based indices, not zero-based. The full .obj format specifies other types of lines for normal and texture coordinates.

A WebGL application can be set up to download .obj files directly from the server and parse them in JavaScript to create the arrays for display. In CycleBlob, I opted for a slightly different approach. I wrote a small C++ program that reads .obj files and converts them into the JSON representation. The WebGL game then downloads the JSON files and converts them to JavaScript objects using the built-in JSON library. This approach saves the time and code it takes to parse .obj files and is less prone to errors.

After reading the JSON files into JavaScript objects, the code converts the JavaScript arrays into Float32Array and Int16Array typed arrays that are going to be sent to WebGL. The process culminates to an eventual call to gl.bufferData() for every typed array. This call sends the data to the GPU and after it, the JSON objects and the typed array can be safely discarded.

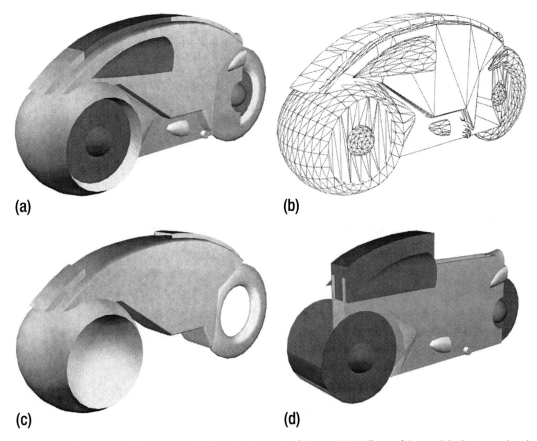

(a)

(b)

(c)

(d)

Figure 8-4. (a) The rendered bike model. (b) The triangle mesh of the model. (c) Parts of the models that are colored according to the player color. (d) The rest of the model with constant color.

The bike model in CycleBlob is made of not one, but several distinct meshes—each with a different color. The JSON file of this model contains the lists of vertices and triangles for each of the meshes, along with the definition of its color. One of the meshes has a special "placeholder" color that indicates that it needs to be displayed in a color specific for the player being drawn (red, blue, yellow, etc.).

Dynamic models

Building typed array objects (Float32Arrays, Int16Array) from JavaScript arrays and sending them to the GPU with gl.bufferData() can be a time-consuming operation. It requires copying a lot of data and relying on the garbage collector to claim the unneeded arrays. Dynamic models change in every frame, it is therefore crucial that their handling be as fast as possible. Instead of building the complete set of typed arrays from scratch in every frame, it is possible to make incremental updates to existing buffers using gl.bufferSubData(). This call allows for appending data and changing the content of existing buffers.

As a case study, we'll look at the generation of the wall that trails behind the bike as it progresses in the game. The wall is made of three, long strips of triangles—two for the left and right sides, and one for the top. Each strip is generated and rendered separately. The triangle construction looks like Figure 8-5.

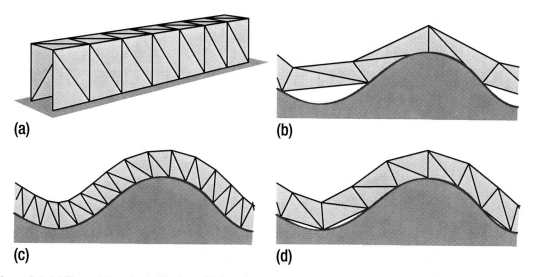

(a)

(b)

(c)

(d)

Figure 8-5. (a) The wall triangles in 3D. (b, c, d) Views from the side of a wall on a curved surface. The wall segments need to be short enough to adjust properly to the surface curvature.

To adjust to the curvature of the grid surface, each wall segment has to be quite short.

The last segment, the one closest to the bike, is the only part that is updated in every frame. The animation engine advances the bike slightly forward each frame and the wall construction advances by the same amount. Just before a frame is rendered, the very last two triangles of each of the three strips are erased and overwritten by two similar triangles that are slightly longer. After incrementing past a certain length, the construction skips one erasure, leaving behind a completed segment and starting a new one. In total, only six triangles are updated—every frame for each wall—and processing time is kept to a minimum.

Geometric processing

Downloading a complete model from the server can become an issue if the model is considerably large and download speed is slow. Common solutions to this problem, such using gzip compression in the http level or using a binary data format instead of textual JSON, don't address the underlying fact that a model may inherently contain a lot of information.

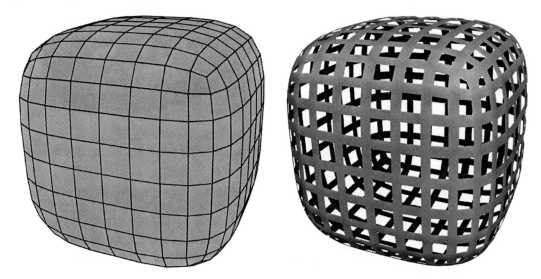

Figure 8-6. (a) The simple quad mesh the grid is based on. (b) The desired grid effect.

Often in algorithms design, a significant performance gain is achieved by changing the actual algorithm rather than by making tweaks and micro-optimizations in the code level. In the context of 3D models, this is analogous to using a different, simpler model instead of optimizing the details of format and transport efficiency. In CycleBlob, the world grid is based on a quad mesh, which is essentially a simple structure. However, for display, I wanted the grid to have holes through which the rest of the world can be visible. This effect can generally be created through various means, which I've considered when writing the game.

- Rendering the grid using thick line primitives. In addition to polygons, the graphics hardware is also able to draw lines from vertex to vertex. To draw the grid, thick lines are stretched between two neighboring vertices (see Figure 8-7). This option requires the model data to specify line segments, rather than triangles or rectangles, so some data conversion needs to take place. The main drawback of this method is that thick lines don't appear as realistic as polygons when it comes to creating the illusion of a surface. Line primitives are drawn as thick, 2D strips, so under close examination they appear to add a certain, unaesthetic thickness to the surface. Moreover, with thicker lines, small gaps between segments become visible.

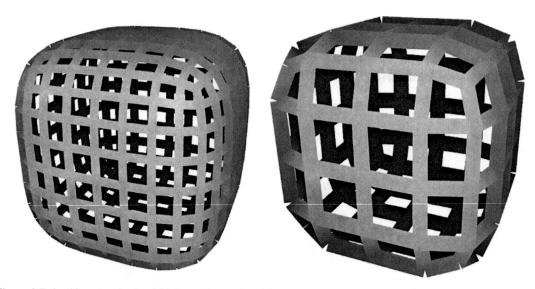

Figure 8-7. A grid rendered using thick lines. The rendered lines have a constant width regardless of the view point. This creates an unaesthetic "thickness" at the edges of the shape, as well as small gaps between adjacent lines.

- Writing a fragment shader that discards the inside of the rectangles, leaving only a frame for display (see Figure 8-8b). The upside of this approach is that it is straightforward to implement and that the rectangle model can be rendered with minimal modification (dividing each rectangle into two triangles). The downside is that the fragment shader is only capable of discarding whole pixels. If the underlying WebGL environment supports antialiasing through multisampling, as is currently the case with Google Chrome, the discarded pixels would create unaesthetic, jagged edges inside the holes.

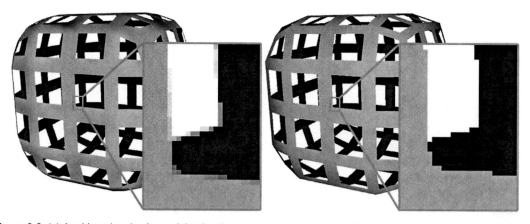

Figure 8-8. (a) A grid rendered using a plain triangle mesh on a display with multi sampling. (b) A grid rendered using a shader that calls discard.

- The direct approach. Rendering a model that explicitly looks like a grid with holes (see Figure 8-9). This option means that the displayed mesh is a plain, triangle mesh—no tricks or shortcuts. With this option, the edges of the grid are made of normal polygons so a multisampling implementation can work correctly to avoid jagged edges. This approach, despite being more resource intensive, allows fine control over the look of the mesh surface. This is the approach I've chosen to implement for the grid model display in CycleBlob.

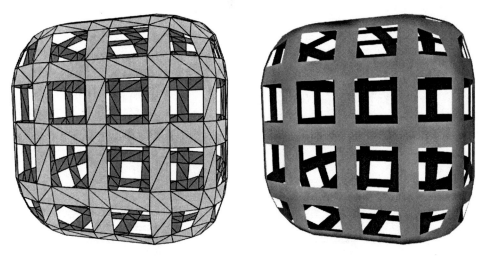

Figure 8-9. (a) The triangle mesh of the grid mode. (b) The grid model rendered with lighting.

With modern desktop OpenGL, the programmer can write a geometry shader that generates the complex grid model on the fly from the data of the simple, underlying mesh. WebGL, however, does not yet expose a geometry shader functionality since only relatively recent desktop graphics cards support it. Therefore, we have to explicitly load the mesh grid in JavaScript and render it in the same way as regular static models.

Figure 8-6 shows the original quad mesh and the resulting grid mesh. The numbers in Table 8-1 show the order-of-magnitude difference in the sizes of these models. The model of the grid with holes is substantially bigger than the quad mesh it is based on. Downloading the grid mesh from the server would take too much time, so only the simple quad mesh is downloaded and a processing stage generates the grid model in JavaScript when the game is initialized. The processing stage takes a quad mesh as input and generates a triangle mesh of the model with holes, as shown in Figure 8-10.

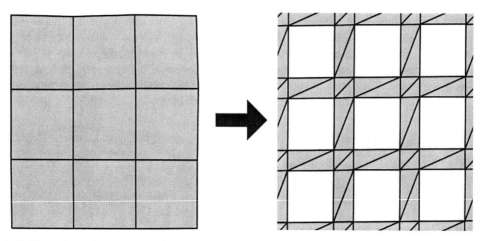

Figure 8-10. The plain quad mesh passes through a pre-processing stage that generates the triangle mesh that's going to be used for display.

Table 8-1. Difference in Data Volume of the Two Grid Models

	No. of faces	No. of vertices	Size of model file
Input quad mesh	384	386	16.7 KB
Output triangle mesh with holes	2300	1536	127 KB

For the remainder of the chapter, I will refer to the original quad mesh of the grid as the "grid mesh" and the triangle mesh that has holes as the "grid model." The grid mesh is used intensively for the various calculations that make the game mechanics work. The grid model is used only for display on the 3D view.

You may wonder at this point about the origin of the grid meshes used in the game levels. How were they produced? Before starting work on the game, I wrote a little C++ program that takes as input a definition of a simple quad mesh—say a cube with six faces—and performs a Catmul–Clark subdivision on it. This algorithm takes every face of the mesh and subdivides it into smaller and "smoother" faces. With repeated iterations of the process, the mesh becomes denser and smoother. The tool I wrote is called "KawaiiGL" and it is available as open source at `http://sourceforge.net/projects/kawaiigl/`*.*

Another, more conventional, way to create geometric models is by simply using one of the many available 3D-modelling applications out there, such as Maya, 3ds Max, or LightWave 3D. I did not make use of these tools for creating geometry for CycleBlob, however, since I have little experience working with them.

Movement and positioning

One of the key characteristics of a computer game is the mechanics of the movement and animation. Coming up with a natural and streamlined look and feel for a game is often as crucial as the basic concept and art design. Indeed, some common categories of games such as "first-person shooter" or "platformer," for example, refer to these look-and-feel properties rather than other aspects of the game. This section discusses in detail a few such topics implemented in CycleBlob.

Situating on a grid

In the 2D lightcycle game, situating the bike on the grid is simply a matter of moving the player model or sprite to a point and rotating it around its axis in multiples of 90 degrees. Situating the bike on the 3D grid is the base concept of CycleBlob and is a slightly more challenging task. The bike model now needs to be moved in 3D space, to be rendered above an arbitrary point on the surface, and to be rotated in 3D to create the illusion that it is actually driving on the surface. Luckily, there is a simple mathematical trick called "coordinate base transformation" that allows doing this potentially complex rotation and translation in only one step.

When drawing a model, we're sending sets of x, y, z coordinates to the graphics hardware and then telling it to connect them with triangles. These x, y, z coordinates are relative to some axis origin, orientation, and scale that define their coordinate system. The bike model from Figure 8-4, for example, has the following coordinate system (see Figure 8-11a):

- Its axis origin is centered at the exact middle of the model.

- The positive Y-axis points towards the back of the bike.

- The positive Z-axis points from bottom to top.

- The positive X-axis points from the right of the bike to its left.

- The height of the bike is about one unit and its length is about two units.

The square grid model has a similar coordinate system (see Figure 8-11b):

- The axis origin is in the middle of the object.

- The grid faces and the edges are aligned with the major axis.

- The height, width, and length of each face are all approximately one unit.

If we were to draw the bike and the grid model using the same coordinate system without a coordinate transformation between them, they would appear one inside the other, as in Figure 8-11c. That is clearly not what we want to do. Instead, we scale the bike and apply the coordinate base transformation on its coordinates before drawing it. The coordinate base transformation moves the scaled bike to the intended point on the grid and rotates it in all three axes so that it appears upright on the grid and faces toward its current forward direction (see Figure 8-11d).

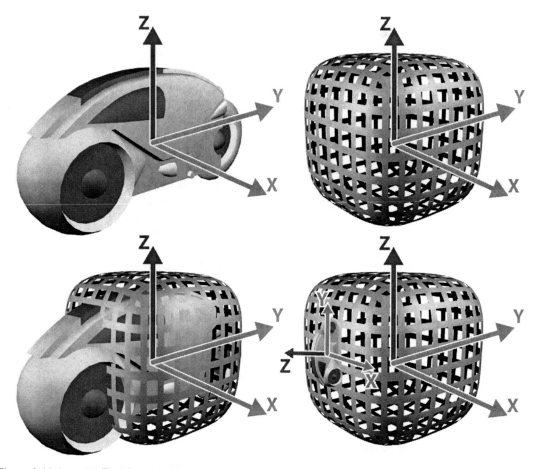

Figure 8-11. (a and b) The bike and grid models with their coordinates axis. (c) Drawing both models in the same coordinate system. (d) Drawing with the coordinate base transformation.

The coordinate base transformation is a 4 × 4 matrix that we build using the data from the scene by following a simple procedure.

Given the following input:

Point P: The point on the grid surface over which the bike should appear. This point may not coincide with an actual vertex of the grid mesh, but it is usually a point on an edge between two vertices.

Point Q = (Qx, Qy, Qz): The position coordinates where the bike should be moved. This point is closely related to P. Also called the "translation vector" since we "translate" (move) the model from the axis origin (0,0,0) by this vector.

Vector N = (Nx, Ny, Nz): The normal of the surface at point P. This is the vector perpendicular to the surface at point P, pointing to the outside of the shape.

Vector F = (Fx, Fy, Fz): The forward direction of the bike. This is the direction the bike moves in when no turns are taken. It's a vector tangent to the surface at point P and is also perpendicular to N. (More on how to find this vector to come.)

Both N and F need to be normalized to the length of 1.

To create the transformation, we first calculate the vector R:

R = N × F

Vector R, which stands for "right," is composed of the elements (Rx, Ry, Rz). It is a vector tangent to the surface, like F, and it points to the right-hand side of the bike.

With these vectors, we construct the 4 × 4 transformation matrix:

M=

(Fx Rx Nx Qx)

(Fy Ry Ny Qy)

(Fz Rz Nz Qx)

(0   0   0   1)

The vectors N, F, and R make the orthogonal coordinate base to which we want to transform the bike model. They are copied to the first three columns of the matrix. The fourth and final "homogeneous" column makes the translation to point Q.

To apply this transformation to the bike model, we use it like any other rotation or translation transformation in the rendering engine. The transformation matrix is pushed to the model-view matrix stack. This causes the transformation it represents to be applied to the vertices of the bike model in the code of the vertex shader.

Transformation components

So far, we've defined the meaning of each of the components of the transformation, but the practice of calculating them may still not be clear.

Normal vectors are usually provided with the model we're rendering for lighting purposes. If the model is generated in code or does not contain normals, a good approximation of the normal data can be easily computed from just the mesh triangles data. The general process for this is as follows:

1. Calculate the normal of every triangle individually.

2. Approximate the normals of the surface on each of the vertices of the mesh.

3. From the vertices normals, smoothly approximate a normal vector for every point of the surface.

To understand this procedure, remember that the triangle mesh is considered as only a discrete sampling of an ideal, smooth 3D surface. This is why normals on different parts of the same flat triangle may differ slightly in direction and not be exactly equal to the triangle normal—the vector perpendicular to the triangle plane. This effect is the most frequently used method to achieve real-time, smooth lighting in 3D rendering.

Taking a cross product of the vectors induced by two edges of a triangle gives the direction of its normal (shown in Figure 8-12). For a triangle stretched between vertices a, b, and c, the normal would be:

$$N = normalize(\ (b - a) \times (c - a)\ ) = (b - a) \times (c - a)\ /\ |(b - a) \times (c - a)|$$

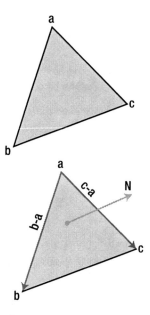

Figure 8-12. Extracting a normal from a triangle.

The length of the cross-product vector is equal to twice the area of the triangle, so we normalize it to a size of 1 by dividing it by its own length.

A consistent orientation of normals means that all normals of the mesh consistently point either to the inside or to the outside of the mesh. The orientation of the normal vector is determined by the order of the elements in the cross product, so to get a consistent orientation, the order of the vertices of the triangle is important. An often-used convention is that when you look at the mesh from outside, all the polygons should be specified in clockwise order. For the triangle shown in Figure 8-12, the order should be (a,b,c) and not, for instance, (c,a,b).

With a normal for each triangle, the normal of a vertex is calculated as the average of the normals of the triangles that touch it. Figure 8-13 exemplifies this.

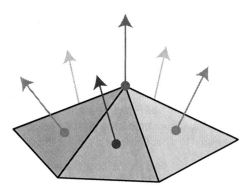

Figure 8-13. Calculating a normal for a vertex (purple) as the average of faces normals (green).

If the mesh contains a large variation of triangle sizes, a better approximation is achieved by weighing the average by the area of the triangles.

The resulting average normal would not generally be a length of 1.0, so another division by length is needed.

Up to this point, all this normal calculation work is done in a pre-processing stage. With a normal for every vertex calculated in advance, it is now possible to quickly calculate a smooth normal for every point on the surface as a linear combination of the normals of the surrounding vertices. We are, however, only interested in normals on the edges of the grid. For example, if the bike is situated a third of the way on the edge between vertices A and B, the normal we'll use for the coordinate base transformation is:

$N_p = 0.33 * N_A + 0.66 * N_B$

Where N_A and N_B are the normals of vertex A and vertex B, respectively.

Finding the forward direction of the bike is easier than finding the normal. The bike movement is always constrained to be between two vertices that are adjacent in the original quad mesh of the grid model. When the bike travels from vertex A to vertex B, a good approximation of the forward direction is the direction vector between A and B. This vector is calculated as the subtraction of the coordinates of the two vertices:

$F' = B - A$

Similar to normals, we refer to this as an approximation—since the desired movement on the surface should be as smooth as possible, while the edges and triangles are straight and flat. This curvature is expressed by the smooth normals we calculated, so this approximation of the forward vector is not guaranteed to be exactly perpendicular to the calculated normal. Slight distortions in the movement may be noticeable if we'll use F' from the formula. To calculate the exact forward direction, and simultaneously the R vector, we perform two cross product calculations:

$R = normalize(N \times F')$

$F = R \times N$

The vector F is now exactly perpendicular to N and is situated on the plane created by N and F'. It is better than F' in that it is tangential to the smooth surface represented by the mesh. Vector R is perpendicular to F and N and, after normalization to the length of 1, is identical to the R vector mentioned earlier.

Last, but not least, for the transformation, calculating the coordinates Q, to which the bike model is going to be moved. Q should be a constant distance above the surface, so we take a short offset in the direction of N above point P. Since the axis origin of the bike model is in its center, without this offset in the direction of N, the bike would appear half above and half below the grid. To create the illusion that the bike rides on the surface, the offset needs to be equal to about half the height of the bike model.

The vectors N, F, and R and point Q are not only for the coordinate transformation; they are also the basis for all the display items that pertain to the bikes. The following are a few other uses:

- **Animation**: The bike is animated to move along the direction of the F vector as time progresses.

- **Player control**: When the bike is instructed to turn, its direction is changed to either R for right or to (-R) for left. That direction then becomes the forward direction.

- **Wall generation**: The height of the wall is constructed perpendicular to the surface using N. R is used to create the thickness of the wall.

- **Explosion model**: When the bike hits a wall, the explosion animation is positioned perpendicular to F and centered at point P.

- **Camera positioning**: More on this in the following section.

Camera positioning

A common difficulty in 3D game design is where and how to position the camera so that everything the player needs to see is clearly visible. The approach I implemented in CycleBlob is extremely simple and seems to work well most of the time.

I wanted the game world to feel like it's a small planet floating in space, so the basic idea of a top view camera was there from the beginning. To achieve the final look, several other details needed to be worked out.

- **Camera relation to the bike**: As the bike turns, should the camera be rotated with it? Or should it remain more or less in constant orientation relative to the grid? With a camera that "sticks" relative to the bike, the bike is always seen driving toward the top of the screen and the world looks like it's spinning in front of it. One can imagine a long, invisible rod sticking out of the back of the bike and holding the camera that films it from above. With such a camera, the most natural control system is one that turns the bike either left or right from its current heading using the left and right arrow keys. The main downside I found to such a camera is that it is easy to lose orientation and miss an upcoming turn in order to avoid hitting a wall. This is the main reason that in the final implementation I chose to keep the camera constant to the grid and to control the bike using the Up, Down, Left, and Right keys for constant directions. When the user hits the Up key, the bike turns to the direction that corresponds to the top of the screen. When the user hits Left, the bike turns to the left of the screen, and so on.

- **Center of view**: What part of the scene should be displayed at the exact center of the screen? The obvious answer that comes to mind is that the player's bike should be there. Although this sounds logical, it may often not be the best choice. The player's bike is often found on corners and edges of the grid. Centering the view on the player in these cases obscures most of the grid surface from view and prevents the player from seeing the big picture of the game. Furthermore, it often leaves large portions of the screen empty, wasting valuable screen space. The next simplest option is to center the view at the center of the mesh. With this option, the player is likely to have good visibility of most of what's going on and the screen is guaranteed to be full at all times.

The center of the mesh is easily calculated as the average of all coordinates' positions, or more simply as the center of the axis-aligned bounding box of the grid.

With these details decided upon, creating the transformation matrix for the camera positioning is a simple matter of taking the right vectors and coordinates and plugging them into the matrix formula of the gluLookAt() function. gluLookAt() is a function from the GLU API found in desktop OpenGL implementations. It provides a useful abstraction to setting up a camera viewpoint and can be reimplemented in JavaScript quite easily. gluLootAt() takes nine float arguments that make two sets of 3D coordinates and one 3D vector (see Figure 8-14 for an overview).

gluLookAt(eyeX, eyeY, eyeZ, centerX, centerY, centerZ, upX, upY, upZ);

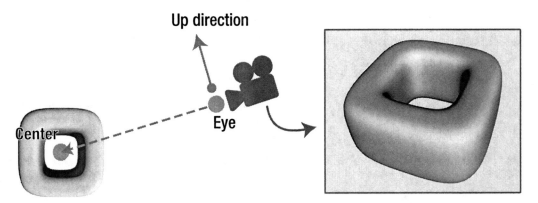

Figure 8-14. The glLookAt() parameters in a 3D scene and the 3D rendered result.

- **Center coordinates**: The point in the scene at which the camera is looking. As described earlier, this point is set to be the center of the grid model.

- **Eye coordinates**: The point in the scene where the camera is positioned. This point is set to be directly above the bike. The normal of the surface at the point where the bike is displayed is used for computing this point.

- **Up vector**: This vector defines the orientation of the camera around the axis established by the center and eye coordinates. The game maintains a vector that always points to the top of the screen and uses it as the camera up vector. When the bike moves to the right of the screen, the up vector is its right-hand side. When the bike moves towards the top of the screen, the up vector is its forward direction. With each turn the player makes in the game, this vector is updated. Taking the camera up vector to always be only the forward direction of the bike would have resulted in a camera that sticks to the bike rather than to the grid.

The glLookAt() matrix is the first matrix that is pushed to the model-view stack when drawing the scene. This is closely followed by the rendering of the grid model (more on this later in this chapter).

Due to its simplicity, the camera positioning in CycleBlob is not perfect and has been the source of much of the user feedback I've received. A few notable disadvantages include:

- The inability to see around sharp corners. Since the camera is positioned directly above the bike, it is difficult to predict what lies beyond a sharp edge of the grid. This is especially notable in the tetrahedron grid in the third level.

- The obstruction of the view by the grid itself. If the grid contains tunnels or concave regions, the view of the player can get obstructed by the grid itself. This is the case, for instance, in the torus grid in the eighth level (also in the custom-level screen).

These two problems are the result of the same principle that allows for the simplicity of the camera system: that the eye and center coordinates are derived from the geometry of the grid without taking other factors, like visibility, into consideration.

The ultimate solution to both problems would be to define an optimal viewpoint above the surface for every vertex of the grid mesh, instead of relying on the normal, and to linearly interpolate the camera position between these optimal points. To see around sharp edges for instance, the camera point could be set to advance a little further ahead of the edge to provide a better view of what's beyond it. To have the bike visible even as it enters the torus hole, the camera can delay at a safe distance, where the bike and its surroundings are still visible, and then to pass quickly through the hole.

Defining the optimal viewpoints for every vertex would require a considerable amount of manual labor. Another option is to code a rule set that can define these points automatically, but that would also require a comparable amount of work and involve considerable complexity.

An option for camera positioning that I have yet to discuss is that of a "first person" perspective. With a first-person camera, the player sees the game through the eyes of the rider of the bike. He sees the grid directly underneath him and the obstacles directly in front of him. The original *TRON* film contains a few cuts rendered from exactly this perspective.

In an early version of the game, I performed a few experiments with this viewpoint and it turned out to be extremely confusing and disorienting. The game was practically unplayable since it was difficult to know where on the grid the bike stood; where the enemies were in relation; and how far the bike was from an upcoming wall. This has an interesting implication on the realism of the scenes that the movie portrays.

A similar option, which may be more playable, is a middle ground between the first-person view and the top view. The camera is situated slightly above and behind the bike so that its surroundings are still visible and distance estimation is easier than in pure, first-person view. This option may be implemented for user selection in a future version of the game.

Animation engine

Smooth animation is a key factor in making a game look good and fun to play. If the animation is choppy or delayed or contains unaesthetic artifacts, the player is going to run out of patience fast, leave, and never return—even if the game concept is amazing in every other respect.

Animation in CycleBlob occurs in several objects:

- The bikes move across the grid

- A wall is constructed in real-time behind the bikes

- The camera follows the player's bike

- When a bike crashes, there's a short "crash" animation that features circles and sparks

- Rotating bonus objects appear and disappear on the grid

- A rotating "lives" count appears in the upper-left corner of the screen

To make the animation as smooth as possible, every one of these objects gets updated in every displayed frame. In this section, I'll delve into the details of the bike movement to demonstrate how this is done. The animation of the other objects is performed using very similar methods.

As mentioned earlier, the bikes move on the edges of the quad mesh on which the grid model is based. At any point in time, the game maintains the exact position on the grid of every bike in the game using the following three parameters:

- A: The index of the grid vertex just behind the bike

- B: The index of the grid vertex just in front of the bike

- T: A float value between 0 and 1 that indicates how far between these vertices the bike is. If the bike is a third of the way between A and B, then this value would be 0.33. If the bike is just about to reach vertex B, this value is something like 0.95.

These three parameters are enough to display the bike anywhere it is capable of reaching on the grid. Updating the bike animation comes down to maintaining these values up-to-date and displaying the result.

At the beginning of the game, every bike is assigned a random initial starting point vertex and a random initial heading. This defines the first A and B the bikes starts with. T is initialized to 0 to mean that the bike stands on A, its starting-point vertex.

With each animation step, the game does the following to maintain the animation parameters A, B, and T:

- Advance T according to the bike speed.

- If T reaches a value greater than 1, it means that it passed over vertex B to the edge after it. The game uses the grid mesh data to find the index of the next vertex and makes the transition to a new edge. A is updated to the value of B and B is updated to the value of the new vertex index. T is subtracted by 1 since the bike is now between the two new vertices.

To clarify this procedure, let's look at an example. We have indices A and B, which are the vertex indices of the edge the bike is currently on. T is being advanced from 0.95 to 1.1, which means that it passes over vertex B by 0.1 of the distance between A and B and that the bike should be displayed on the next edge. The next vertex, C, is located, and we perform the following assignments:

```
A = B;
B = C;
T = T - 1; // value= 0.1
```

Notice that this 0.1 actually refers to the tenth of the distance between the A and B we started with. We now use it, however, as the tenth of the distance between B and C. This approximation works since in the grid models that I use in the game, the variation between adjacent edges lengths is small. The distance between A and B is usually very close to the distance between B and C, so the effects of this inaccuracy are not noticeable to the user.

Finding vertex C depends on the direction that the bike is heading. It's worth delving on how the game finds this vertex. In the mesh pre-processing stage, for each of the mesh vertices we find and save a list of its neighboring vertices. Two vertices of the grid are called "neighbors" if an edge passes between them.

When passing over vertex B in game-play time, we know that the next vertex we want to find has to be a neighbor of B. So we only need to go over B's neighbors and choose the one that is aligned with the bike's forward direction. The following simple procedure (in pseudo-code) does this.

```
Given starting vertex B, set of neighboring vertices NB and forward direction F do:
var minDot = -INFINITY;
var chosenC = none;
for each vertex V in NB:
    var toV = normalize(V - B);
    var neiDot = dot(F, toV);
    if (neiDot > minDot)
        minDot = neiDot;
        chosenC = v;
return chosenC;
```

The vector "toV" is the direction from vector from B to its neighbor V.

The procedure uses the dot product between F and toV to find which neighbor is best considered in-line with the forward direction F. It takes advantage of the useful fact that if two vectors of size 1 are pointing in approximately the same direction, their dot product is close to 1, and if they are pointing in approximately opposite directions, it is close to -1.

The procedure returns the optimal selection for the next vertex in the most general case where a vertex has any number of neighbors. In CycleBlob, however, all of the grid meshes are quad meshes and the great majority of vertices in these meshes have exactly four neighbors. The cube grid of the first level, for instance, has 1,538 vertices, all of which (except six) have four neighbors; the remaining six vertices are the ones at the corners of the cube—they have three neighbors.

For vertices that have exactly four neighbors, the game doesn't use this general procedure and instead does something a lot simpler. When reaching vertex B, the player has only three choices. He can either do nothing and let the bike continue forward, or he can turn left or turn right. For each of these choices, only one of the four neighbors is acceptable. One of the neighbors of B is the vertex we just came from, A, and it can't be reached again because the bike can't turn 180 degrees on its axis.

Knowing where neighbor A is, we can start going clockwise around B and find the vertex that we will turn to if the user turns to the left. Going clockwise again, we find the vertex to go to if the bike just continues forward. Going a third time clockwise around B brings us to the vertex we'll choose if we want to make a right turn (see Figure 8-15). With the proper pre-processing performed on the mesh data, selecting the next vertex with this procedure consists of just a few array lookups and doesn't require multiple vector math operations like subtraction and dot products. This optimization may seem redundant when we need to find the next vertex for only two to six bikes, but it becomes significant for the artificial intelligence module that often looks 20 or 30 steps ahead before making the decision to turn the bike.

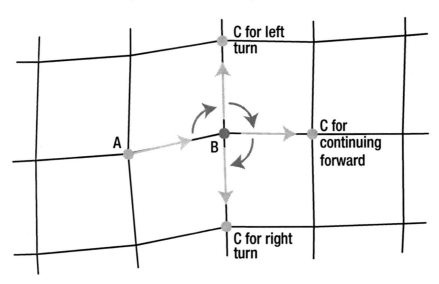

Figure 8-15. Selecting the next vertex to move to from B when there are only four neighboring vertices is done by going clock-wise around B from neighbor to neighbor, starting with neighbor A.

Speed and measurements

An issue that I've yet to address is units of measurement. What are the units for distance and velocity in a 3D scene? Are we dealing with meters? Inches? Pixels? It doesn't really matter because everything is relative. We can think of the numbers we pass around the application in whatever measurement system we want. The only thing that does matter is the relationships between sizes in the scene. The ratio between the grid size, bike size, and bike speed, for instance, should remain constant. Otherwise, the bike may appear disproportionate to the grid and it may travel slower or faster than what the level designer intended. Say the grid is a cube with a total length, depth, and height equal to 50 units (meters, inches—doesn't matter) and the vertices of the grid are 2.5 units apart. If that is the case, I'd like the bike to measure 10 units of length and the speed to be 3.75 units per second.

Defining these sorts of relationships between measurements can become tricky, so it's useful to establish a common basis for measurement that expresses every measurement. In CycleBlob, the common basis for all length- and size-related measurements is the average distance between two adjacent vertices of the grid. This distance, call it Dv, gives a good estimate of the scale of the grid model and is useful for measuring other objects.

- The bike should be approximately 4*Dv

- The height of the wall left behind the bike should be 2*Dv units and its width 0.2*Dv

- The speed of the bike should be 1.5*Dv per second

Part of the pre-processing stage for a grid model is measuring Dv and setting an absolute value to all these constants.

Animation timing

We now know that the bike speed is given as units of length per second. However, the T parameter discussed earlier is a unitless number between 0 and 1. To determine the amount needed to advance T, we need to know:

- The distance between vertices A and B on the grid. This is easy to compute using the grid mesh. We'll call this d(A,B)

- The amount of time that has passed since the last update. We'll call this Δt (delta-t).

The amount we need to increase T is determined by:

ΔT = (speed * Δt) / d(A,B)

(speed * Δt) gives the distance the bike travels in Δt divided by d(A,B) we get the distance normalized to the range of [0,1]. If we sort out the units of the elements in this assignment, we see that indeed, ΔT is a unitless measure, like T itself. Notice that there are two "delta tees" here. Δt is the amount of time that passed while ΔT is the difference in the animation T parameter.

The ΔT formula takes into consideration the exact amount of time that passed and the exact distance traveled since the last update. Taking these variables into consideration is essential for achieving smooth animation in which the bike looks like it is traveling at a constant speed. A simpler approach that was used in an early version of the game was to just set ΔT to a constant value, say 0.5. This basically means that in every update, the bike traverses half of the edge it is currently on. The simplicity of this approach, however, creates two problems:

- A variation exists in the edges lengths across the grid. For instance, in the cube model, the edges at the center of the cube faces are longer than those at the corners of the cube. Setting ΔT to a constant 0.5 means that it takes two updates to traverse any edge, no matter where it is. This makes the bike move faster on a long edge and slower on a short edge. This becomes most noticeable when two bikes ride parallel to one another, one in the center of the cube and one on the side of the cube. The bike in the center looks like it travels faster. Another effect of this issue is that the player's bike looks like it changes its velocity as the length of the edges changes. When it reaches longer edges, the speed seems to increase, and on shorter edges, decrease.

- The length of time between updates depends on the hardware being used, the workload of the system and browser at a given time, and many other variables. Setting a constant ΔT assumes all these variables are constant. A value of, say 0.25, makes an implicit assumption on the frame rate in which the game is going to run. Let's say we expect the game to always run at 30 frames per second (fps), this would make the bike traverse 7.5 edges per second, which is an OK rate. Running the game now on a slower machine that is only capable of 20 fps will make the bike travel only five edges per second. The game runs slower that expected and the player gets bored. On the flip side, running the game on a new machine and possibly a newer browser capable of 60 fps makes the bike travel 15 edges per second, which is unplayably fast.

Frame rate control

There are several popular ways in JavaScript to establish a more or less constant frame rate. Two of them use timers and one uses a new capability added to JavaScript with HTML5.

The first option and the one most traditionally used for JavaScript animation is using setTimeout(func, timeout). This function causes func() to be called approximately timeout milliseconds after the call. Setting up frame rendering with this function often looks like this:

```
function main() {
    // do some initializations
    tick();
}

function tick() {
    setTimeout(tick, 16);
    // do rendering, animation
}
```

The main() function starts the animation by making the first call to tick(), which is responsible for displaying and processing the animation of a single frame of the game. The very first thing that tick() does is to set up the next call to tick(), 16 milliseconds into the future. A delay of 16 ms between frames produces a frame rate of approximately 60 fps. When using this method, it is important that the call to setTimeout() will be performed before any rendering or processing to ensure that the interval between frames will be as close as possible to 16 ms. The rendering and processing stages of tick() may take a few milliseconds, and making the setTimeout() call at the end of the function would make the total time of a single frame longer than 16 ms (see Figure 8-16).

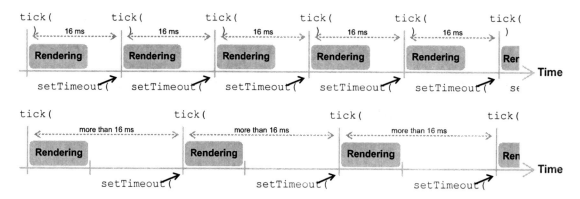

Figure 8-16. Possible timelines using setTimout() for frame-rate control. Calling setTimeout() at the end of tick() may cause the complete frame cycle to be longer than the required timeout and cause a frame-rate lower than expected.

Another traditionally common option is using setInterval(func, timeout). This function is similar to setTimeout()—but with one difference. Whereas setTimeout() triggers func() only once and requires an additional call setTimeout() for the next frame, setInterval() triggers func()—again and again, every timeout interval, without intervention—until it is stopped with clearInterval(). A basic setup with this function looks like this:

```
function main() {
    // do some initializations
    setInterval(tick, 16);
}

function tick() {
    // do rendering, animation
}
```

setInterval() brings a higher level of automation to the process of repeated execution while setTimeout() provides a higher grain of control and flexibility. With setTimeout() the programmer can decide, for instance, to stop the ticks for a while, say when the player paused the game, or to generate faster ticks during important bits of the animation that should appear smoother than the rest. setInterval() and setTimeout() are concerned only with elapsed time and can be used for any task that requires execution at a specific timing.

The third and final option is using requestAnimationFrame(). This function is different from the previous two in that it is specifically designed to be used for animation frame rate control. Instead of specifying a time interval, it tells the browser to decide the best rate of animation frames and call tick() at that rate. Using this function in code is similar to using setTimeout() in that each call needs to make a request for the next call after it, as follows:

```
function main() {
    // do some initializations
    tick();
```

```
}

function tick() {
    requestAnimationFrame(tick, 16);
    // do rendering, animation
}
```

This approach shifts the responsibility of determining the right frame rate for the game from the programmer to the browser. The browser is almost always more capable of estimating the different variables that this decision entails. If, for instance, the user opened multiple tabs with resource-demanding WebGL content, the browser may decide to only allow each of them to display their content at 30 fps instead of 60 fps. This prevents one window from starving others for resources. Another example, which occurs with tabbed browsing, happens when the game is running in a tab that is not visible by the user. In this situation, the game may find that it is only allowed to display one or two frames per second since the browser doesn't want to waste resources on displaying animation that the user never sees. Such performance optimizations are naturally browser dependent and the programmer can't rely on them in any way.

Using requestAnimationFrame() is currently the recommended method of making animation in HTML5. Since it doesn't make any guarantees on the time interval between calls to tick(), using the ΔT formula is essential for smooth and platform-independent animation. A call to tick() may be deliberately delayed by the browser due to a global policy, like in the case of an inactive tab, or it can be delayed by other influences, like garbage collection triggering, or even external influences in the host machine that causes a slow down. It is up to the code in tick() to maintain accurate time measurement for the formula to work.

The first call to tick() does nothing but take a sample of the current time by doing:

```
lastTickTime = new Date().getTime();
```

Every subsequent call to tick() calculates the time that passed from the previous call:

```
var timeNow = new Date().getTime();
var delta_t = lastTickTime - timeNow;
lastTickTime = timeNow;
```

lastTickTime is updated to be used in the next call to tick() and from this point on delta_t (lowercase t) is going to be used for updating the animation. This calculated value of delta_t is useful for the animation as long as there are no unexpectedly long delays. A sudden long delay sets a high value to delta_t and causes the animation to jump ahead abruptly, allowing the animation to essentially "run away." The player sees the bike at one place on the grid, then suddenly the animation freezes and the next thing he sees after half a second is the bike a few edges ahead, without a smooth transition. This may even cause the player to crash and loose the game if he didn't have the chance to make a turn at the right moment. When we get the call to tick() after an unexpectedly long delay, the damage of a frozen animation was already done and the best we can do now is to avoid further inconvenience to the player. A runaway animation is avoided by limiting delta_t to an upper bound:

```
if (delta_t > 50) { // milli-seconds
    delta_t = 50;
}
```

Of course, a better solution would be to prevent these delays in the first place, but most of the causes for such delays are outside the control of the programmer. One can only hope that as browser technology progresses and WebGL becomes more robustly supported, the guarantees on frame rate will become more robust as well. Using `requestAnimationFrame()` to drive your animation holds a certain promise that as these advances are made, your application stays on the front lines of achievable performance.

Code structure

A hobby project like CycleBlob, developed by a sole programmer, can quickly become a tangled mess of functions that an outsider would find hard to penetrate. Two months of full-time work took the code base from the bare minimum of the `learningwebgl.com` tutorials to a full and complete game with a well-established concept, players, levels, menus, sounds, help page, error pages for non-supporting browsers, and a small artificial intelligence module. Although maintaining order in the code was often a technical chore to be delayed until late at night, the upside of refactoring code into proper OOP objects bore almost immediate fruits in the form of greater convenience in navigating the code and understanding what fits where.

The final sections of this chapter contain brief descriptions of the different modules of the code and explain how they interact with each other.

The code for the game is available for download at `https://github.com/shooshx/CycleBlob`.

Starting up

Like anything else on the web, it all starts from an HTML page. The HTML page of CycleBlob is quite short and straightforward:

- The file starts with an `<!doctype html>` declaration, the standard for HTML5.

- Two `<canvas>` elements, one on top of each other. The bottom canvas is for 3D content and is the one initialized with a WebGL context. The top canvas is for 2D graphics, like menus and text, and is initialized with a regular 2D context. The 2D canvas is mostly transparent so that the 3D content under it is visible.

- `<audio>` tags to load the sound files along with the page.

- `<img>` tags made invisible using `style="display:none"` that pre-load the images used in the menu system.

- Some `<meta>` tags for search engine goodness.

- A link to the minified JavaScript file that contains all of the code of the game and a link to the jQuery minified source. jQuery is used sparingly for easy access to the HTML DOM.

- Some boilerplate JavaScript code from Google Analytics that allows me to keep track of the number of visitors to the site.

- An `<iframe>` that contains the shaders code used by WebGL. The game uses only a single pair of vertex-shader/fragment-shader for all rendering. These shaders are fairly standard and implement the basic Phong lighting model with a single light source.

- A link to the feedback page and a small Facebook "Like" button that is not used often enough by visitors of the site.

- Finally, a call to `webGLStart()` that occurs in response to the `onload` event of the page. This function is called automatically when all of the resources listed on the page are fully loaded and the code of the game is ready to be started.

Using two canvases one above the other is the simplest method of superimposing 2D graphics over a 3D scene. It requires some basic knowledge of the 2D canvas graphics API, which is vastly different from WebGL but rather simple to pick up. Tasks like selecting fonts for text, drawing curved lines, and stroking them are quite a bit simpler with the 2D canvas API than using WebGL.

The converse option is, of course, to use just a single canvas with a WebGL context and to do both 2D and 3D drawing exclusively with WebGL. Going this path would require using a viewport that is appropriate for 2D drawing and an orthogonal projection transformation matrix that is naturally different from the one used for 3D rendering. With this method, drawing text and menu buttons is done using WebGL vertices buffers, triangles, and textures, which can take considerably more code and debugging effort than using the 2D API. On the other hand, creating the menu and text elements in WebGL allows a more unified and streamlined user experience, as well as better graphic quality for the 2D elements in case the browser supports antialiasing for WebGL. You'll notice that suspiciously missing from the list of downloaded resources are the 3D models used in the game. Adding the models as objects to be downloaded from the HTML would mean that the browser would download them before `webGLStart()` is called. Since the models are fairly big in comparison to the rest of the downloaded resources, downloading them before the application starts would cause a significant delay before the user sees any UI element displayed.

Instead of adding them in the HTML, the 3D models are downloaded using `XmlHttpRequests` in an asynchronous manner by the JavaScript code in the initialization procedure. During their download, the user can interact with the main menu of the game and even view the instructions screen.

The function `webGLStart()` resides in the file `main.js` in the non-minified source repository. It performs the initialization of the game, as follows:

- Accesses the two `<canvas>` elements in the HTML and creates the corresponding WebGL and 2D contexts.

- Sets a handler for the resize event of the page. The handler recalculates the projection transformation and changes the size of 2D elements to fit the size of the canvas.

- Compiles the single shader program used for all rendering.

- Starts the download of static models—the bike model and the life bonus model. The download proceeds asynchronously and the code receives a notification when the download is complete.

- Generates the model of the explosion animation. The basic geometry elements of the explosion are a concentric circle model and an exploding spark model. During the explosion animation, these static models are scaled and colored but their vertices are not modified (see Figure 8-17).

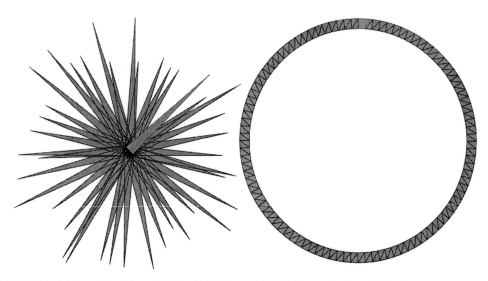

Figure 8-17. The static models of the explosion effect. The spark model is a collection of thin triangles in random lengths and orientation that are all on the same plane. The ring model is a just a round triangle strip. These models are generated in the initialization of the game.

- Initialization of the sound module with the files loaded by the ‹audio› tags. The sound module is quite simple, but is outside the scope of this chapter.

- First call to tick() to start the animation engine.

- Setting up a timed event with setInterval() for the appearance and disappearance of bonus objects on the grid. The interval is set to 1 second and in each call, the game randomly decides if it's time for a bonus to appear or not.

- Finally, a call is made to the 2D graphics module to display the main starting menu of the game on the 2D canvas. Aside from displaying the start menu and setting up keyboard and mouse controls for it, this function also starts an asynchronous download of the grid model of the first level. This action happens here rather than in the main initialization function since the game possibly needs to load these models each time the main menu is reached.

webGLStart() returns rather quickly, but the events and timers it established will drive the game from here on. The majority of the functionality originates in the tick() function.

The tick() function

The tick() function is called repeatedly by the JavaScript runtime in response to repeat calls to requestAnimationFrame(). The calls to tick() continue the entire time the game is running, without exception, even when it is paused or a 2D menu is shown. When no 3D content needs to be visible, the function just skips over the scene-rendering phase. In practice, the situation where absolutely no 3D content is shown happens only when the main menu of the game is active. At any other time, there is some 3D content to be displayed. Stopping and restarting the calls to tick() would complicate the logic of the menu system with no consequential performance gains.

The tick() function is where most of the real-time game play occurs. The following is an outline of the major blocks of this function.

Frame rate mechanics: Calls requestAnimationFrame() to schedule the next frame and calculates the time elapsed from the previous tick() call.

Keyboard input sampling: function sampleKeys(): Keyboard events onkeydown() and onkeyup() are received from the document object in an asynchronous manner. The key codes from these asynchronous events are pushed into a FIFO (First in First out) queue. This queue is then emptied in the next tick() function after the presses are made. This method of user-input capture ensures that even if the user made a quick succession of presses to two or more keys in between frames, no key press will get lost. This is especially important in a game like CycleBlob, where quick and precise keyboard action can save the player from crashing into a wall.

Artificial Intelligence decisions: The AI module of each computerized player is given a chance to evaluate the state of the game and possibly make a decision to turn the bike either left or right, or continue forward in the current direction.

Animation step: function animate(): Lets every animated object advance its animation state according to the amount of elapsed time. First and foremost, the players' positions are updated. After that, all animated special effects are updated. This includes the following:

- Explosions quickly grow and fade away

- The wall of a recently-crashed player changes color and drops down into nothing

- Bonus objects that reside on the grid; there is animation for their appearance, disappearance, and rotation

- Number of live objects displayed on the top-left corner of the screen; these also have animations for appearance, disappearance, and rotation

Notice that at this stage, nothing was yet displayed in this call to tick(). Only the *state* of the animations was updated. For example, in the explosion animation, the state consists of the radius of the rings and the scale factor of the spark model. For player bikes, the state consists of the A and B vertices and the T parameter that tells how far between them the bike is.

Render 3D menu items: Some 3D items are not part of real-time game play and don't depend on the state of the player. The rotating models of the lives-count in the top-left corner are such objects, as well as the 3D objects on the instructions page (enemy and player bikes, an example rotation bonus object).

Render the main 3D scene of the game: function drawScene(): This function draws all of the elements that take part in the game-play. It sets up the needed transformations and renders the following:

- The pre-processed grid model

- For every player, the bike and the wall behind it

- Any explosions that may be occurring

- Any bonus objects that reside on the grid

All the efforts invested thus far in loading and generating models, animating them, and lighting them culminate into a single, rendered frame. This function tells WebGL to communicate with the graphics hardware and kick it into action. In most modern machines, this is where the majority of the time the tick() call is spent. Anything else the game does takes a fraction of the time the rendering takes.

In Firefox and Chrome, the currently stable WebGL implementation, calling requestAnimationFrame() repeatedly when the tab is active maintains a frame rate of approximately 60 fps. This is generally considered the upper frame rate bound since most modern LCD displays cannot refresh at a higher rate. (This is in contrast to older CRT displays, which could reach refresh rates as high as 120 fps.) For 60 fps, a call to tick() should occur approximately every 16 ms. This optimal frame rate can be maintained only as long as the tick() call returns in less that 16 ms. If it doesn't, the next call can't be triggered. Since all of JavaScript events are triggered from the same OS thread, if that thread is busy executing the previous call to tick(), it will lag in handing the next call and the effective frame rate would decrease from 60 fps. Anything done in tick() should be extremely efficient and anything that can be performed in a pre-processing stage should be done at that time.

Data structures

The flow of data in CycleBlob is fairly straightforward. Several global objects hold all of the persistent information the game uses and maintains. A brief discussion of the major ones follows.

var resources (loadManager.js): A repository that maintains a list of resources that were downloaded from the server using XmlHttpRequest and possibly processed in code. Currently, the resources managed here are only mesh models, but the name of the variable implies possible future extension for other resources, like audio files and images. Every resource has a name and before using a resource, the code needs to check that it actually exists. If it doesn't, then the resource needs to be downloaded and possibly processed before it can be used. Grid models are downloaded in batches of three at a time, for the next three levels the user is going to play. After the player advances to the next level, the processed grid model is removed and reclaimed by the garbage collector to avoid a heavy memory footprint.

var levels (gameControl.js): Defines the core parameters for every level of the game. This includes the URL to the grid model that needs to be downloaded, the number of players participating, and the level of artificial intelligence they have. This data is never changed and is considered to be constant.

var players (main.js): This holds a list of the players (human and artificial intelligence) that are currently participating in the game. The Player object (player.js) contains everything there is to know about a player, as follows:

- Whether it is alive or dead

- Its color

- A reference for the bike model from the resources repository (a future version may have different bike models for each player)

- Parameters required for movement and animation: forward direction, normal, and the A, B, and T parameters

- A Wall object that holds the model of the wall trailing behind the player

- References to possible special-effect animation objects that may be occurring for the player. When an object exists here, it receives a call from the global `tick()` function with the amount of time that elapsed to update its animation state.

- An optional reference to an `AI` object that's responsible for the decision making of a computerised player

`var world (main.js)`: This object is responsible for the grid mesh and its state. A reference from this object to the processed model in the resources repository defines the mesh that the current game play occurs on. The grid mesh object remains constant throughout the game and an additional "live map" is maintained beside it. Most aspects of the mechanics of the game rely heavily on this map. It keeps track of where a wall erects and where a bonus objects rotates, and it ultimately decides the fate of who loses and who wins the game by detecting crashes between players and walls.

The map contains a state variable for every vertex of the grid. A vertex can be in one of the following states:

- **Free**: The vertex is free to be moved onto by a player.

- **Occupied by a player's bike**: The movement procedure of the player maintains which are the next and previous vertices the player occupies (A and B). This information is used to detect bike-to-bike collisions where two bikes crash into one another and die.

- **Occupied by a player's wall**: Left behind the bike, a player that bumps into one crashes and dies. A few seconds after the player's death, its own wall vanishes and the vertices occupied by it become free.

- **Occupied by a bonus object**: A bonus object occupies a small circle of five adjacent vertices on the map. A player that bumps into either of them "eats" the bonus and the bonus vanishes.

A human player avoids collisions with walls and other bikes by looking at the rendered frames and making split-second decisions to turn the bike. A computerized player, however, does not have the luxury of a visual cortex; so instead, it uses the map information to "see" what's going on on the grid. The map information is used by the AI module to avoid collisions with walls, plan its steps going forward, and perform rudimentary attempts at winning the game.

Automatic players of the 2D lightcycle game have been a hot topic for research and online programming competitions. The so-called "intelligence" implemented in the computerized player of CycleBlob is extremely simple and not all that intelligent in comparison to how sophisticated these players can get. Still, among the most common feedback comments that I get for the game is that the AI is too hard to beat. Perhaps it is the added complexity of the game mechanics that make the AI players appear smarter than they are.

Conclusion

Like many personal projects online, CycleBlob is a work in progress. Occasionally, I take a weekend to add a few more features and tune the code for greater performance or to review recent requests from users. Some of the things that I hope to be able to work on in the near future include:

- More bonus options. Currently the only bonus in the game is to give the player one more life. Some of the more interesting options I'm considering are bonuses that allow one player to be faster than the others for a period of time, to allow him to break or jump over walls, or even shoot projectiles at other players. Maintaining the balance of the game with these new bonuses is going to be challenging. With new features for the human users, the AI players will need to get smarter as well, since I don't want the game to be too easy to win.

- More grid models from a wider variety of shapes. The current camera control system limits the types of grid models to shapes that have a well-defined center and with a surface that is mostly visible from the outside. Working up a finer level of camera control will allow a wide variety of interesting grid meshes; for instance, the ones in Figure 8-18.

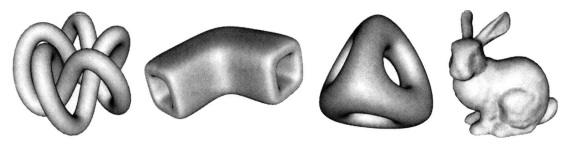

Figure 8-18. Grid models that would be possible for play with a better camera control scheme.

One possible future extension that seems natural for a game like CycleBlob is online multiplayer play. One promising direction for that is the use of HTML5 WebSockets for two-way communications between clients and a server that is responsible for maintaining the shared state of the game. Implementing a real-time state for multiple players over the internet is a challenge, even for commercial games fully backed by a team of experts and implemented in C++. I expect that making multiplayer work well for CycleBlob would require at least as much time as it took to implement the game itself, so that may be difficult to achieve in the near future.

Reference

Table 8-2 lists mathematical symbols used in this chapter for reference. Coordinates and vectors are an ordered set of three floating-point numbers (x,y,z).

Table 8-2. Mathematical Symbols Used in This Chapter

Symbols	Definition
a,b,c	(coordinates) Vertices of a single triangle when calculating its normal
P	(coordinates) A point on the surface of the grid mesh over which the player's bike is situated

Symbols	Definition
Q	(coordinates) The point to which the bike model is translated to; this point is slightly above P
N	(vector) The normal vector of the surface where the bike is situated; a vector perpendicular to the surface
F	(vector) The current forward direction of the bike, tangential to the surface where the bike is situated
R	(vector) The current right-hand side of the bike, tangential to the surface where the bike is situated
M	(4 × 4 matrix) The transformation matrix that situates the bike on the grid
A,B	(integer numbers) The indices of the vertices between which the bike is situated
T	(floating point in the range [1,0]) the distance between A and B that the bike is situated; using A,B, and T, we can calculate P
Dv	(floating-point number) The average distance between two neighboring vertices of the grid mesh; the value is calculated in the grid pre-processing and used as the basis of all other measurements.
d(A,B)	(floating-point number) The distance between vertex A and vertex B of the grid mesh
Δt, delta-t	(floating-point number) The amount of time between two consecutive updates of the animation
ΔT, delta-T	(floating-point number) The addition to T in an animation update

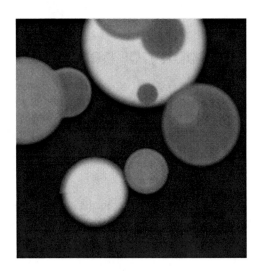

Chapter 9

A Real-Time Multiplayer Game Using WebSockets

In this chapter, we will walk through the creation of a simple multiplayer game. We will use the HTML5 canvas to display graphics to the user, WebSockets to facilitate communication with our server, and node.js to create the server.

WebSockets are truly a boon to game development on the web. Before the advent of WebSockets, game clients had to speak to the game's server by polling with XMLHttpRequest or by using Flash. The former has many drawbacks—particularly that it is very wasteful of bandwidth, and the latter is something that we, as HTML5 developers, should like to avoid. WebSockets, on the other hand, are native to the browser, with a simple JavaScript interface. Data sent over WebSockets doesn't carry HTTP headers, so it is much more efficient than XMLHttpRequest.

The WebSocket protocol has gone through several iterations since 2010, but now appears to be converging to a final version. Browser support for WebSockets has been notoriously spotty, but the September 2011 releases of Chrome 14 and Firefox 7, both supporting the same version ("hybi-10") of the WebSocket protocol, are a good sign that things are settling down. Internet Explorer 10, not yet released at the time of this writing, will also implement that version. Browser support will only improve from here.

WebSockets are easy to implement and extremely useful. Let us begin, then, to develop an online bumper car game!

Philosophy of netcode

In a multiplayer game, nothing ruins the experience quite like somebody cheating. Unfortunately, there will always be somebody who tries to cheat at your game. Even more unfortunately, "cheating" in a JavaScript game, such as the one we will soon construct, is extremely simple. JavaScript is not even compiled! The raw source code is available to anybody playing your game. Using Chrome's developer tools, the Firebug browser add-on, and so forth, they can even change the code of the game and the contents of variables as the game runs. All of a sudden, that puny starter weapon jumps from doing 5 damage per hit to 50,000 damage per hit. Uh oh.

For a single player game, this is arguably not an issue. If the player wants to hack around with the game and change it, then it's his fault if it breaks and it affects no one else. Obviously, though, a multiplayer game needs some sort of protection against this abuse. One way to have that protection is to make the server authoritative. In other words:

> **Tip** *Never trust the user! Always expect users to be malicious, and therefore do all important processing on the server side.*

The game's logic should be executed on the server which is, presumably, impervious to corruption by a would-be cheater. In a sense, the server will be the only computer running the "real" copy of the game. Periodically, it tells the players what's going on, and that is what shows up on their screens. Of course, the players can also supply input (to control their characters, etc.) that the server processes. In this scheme, the cheater fires his ultra-powerful gun, but the server doesn't know or care that the cheater intends for it to do 50,000 damage. All the server receives is a command to fire, and then it fires the regular old 5 damage bullet.

This sounds like an airtight solution, but can it be put to practical use in a game? Yes it can, with some caveats. To illustrate one shortcoming, imagine we make a game where we execute the game logic and then draw the game's graphics to a JPEG file, all on the server side. Then, the server simply sends out this JPEG to all the players and the game's "client" just draws that JPEG and processes user input. This is the epitome of simplicity, but unfortunately it would be borderline unplayable—it would be very choppy. Even supposing the server sends the game state (i.e., the JPEG) to the players ten times per second, the animation on the player's computer will run at just ten frames per second (even less if we consider network latency). We can make it smoother by sending out game state more often, but bandwidth costs will shoot up (even if we're not being silly and sending an image file).

It's really not necessary, though, to have the server telling the client 1000 times per second what's going on. The conditions in your game are probably not changing on such a fine timescale. Ten updates per second, or something on that order of magnitude, is usually enough to accurately portray to the players the correct state of the game. In between these updates, we can have the game client execute its own copy of the game logic, so that things continue to move in predictable, non-choppy ways, and the game doesn't feel unresponsive. The next time an update arrives from the server, it will replace whatever the local game client has done, because the server is authoritative. If the time between server updates is short, then the client's depiction and the server's depiction of the game won't differ much, and the gameplay will be smooth. This simple idea, simulating the game locally while the real game is being played on the server, is sometimes called "dead reckoning."

Ideally, we can share the code for the game logic between the client side (for responsiveness) and the server side (for actually running the game). That way, we don't need to have two separate copies of complicated code that perform very similar tasks. It's not always true that this can be done. In fact, JavaScript has been, until recently, totally confined to users' web browsers. Only now, with JavaScript interpreters like Google's V8 (http://code.google.com/p/v8/) and Mozilla's Rhino (www.mozilla.org/rhino/), can JavaScript code be run outside the context of any browser. In this chapter, we will write our game logic *once*, in JavaScript, and then use it for both the game client and for the game server, which will run on node.js, built atop V8.

Designing the bumper cars game

Now let's make a game! The game will be simple in concept: each player controls a bumper car. He can move his car around and bounce off of other players' cars and off of the rigid walls. For simplicity of physics, we'll take the cars to be circular. We'll split up the program into a few parts with well-defined purposes.

- **game.js**: This file will contain the game logic, i.e. the collision detection. This file will be used by both the client (the player in his web browser) and the server (in node.js) to run their game loops. game.js will have a routine RunGameFrame(Cars) that will be called over and over again to progress the game's status. The argument, Cars, will be a collection of data about all of the cars' positions, velocities, and so forth, so that they may be processed. game.js will also have a set of game options controlling things like the size of the game environment, strength of friction, etc.

- **client.js**: This file will run a game loop and draw the game on an HTML canvas. We will first create a "local" game client (client-local.js) that will operate entirely within the browser, and then upgrade it to the real game client (client-multiplayer.js) that will connect to the WebSocket server and communicate with it (sending user input and receiving game state).

- **server.js**: This file, to be executed under node.js, will run the "real" game loop, keeping a list of the players and their car data. server.js will establish a WebSocket server and communicate with the clients (receiving user input and sending game state).

- **bumper.htm**: This file will be a bare-bones HTML page serving as the game client. It will refer to game.js, client.js, and have an HTML canvas.

The game logic

The logic in our game is all related to detecting and handling collisions. Because the focus of this chapter is netcode, the explanation of the physics involved will be cursory. Conceptually, it is simple: the bumper cars will collide elastically (conserving both momentum and energy) with each other and with the walls. We will take the cars to be circular (of fixed radius) to maximize symmetry. The collision detection presented here is very good, but not perfect. For our purposes, it more than suffices.

With a little bit of clairvoyance, we begin the game engine, game.js, with the list of game properties that we'll need (see Listing 9-1). These will, in the final product, apply simultaneously to the client and the server. There is certainly virtue in not having two such lists maintained separately.

Listing 9-1. Global Properties of the Game

```
var GP =
        {
                    GameWidth: 700,              // In pixels.
                    GameHeight: 400,             // In pixels.
                    GameFrameTime: 20,           // In milliseconds.
                    CarRadius: 25,               // In pixels.
                    FrictionMultiplier: 0.97,    // Unitless
                    MaxSpeed: 6,                 // In pixels per game frame.
                    TurnSpeed: 0.1,              // In radians per game frame.
                    Acceleration: 0.3            // In (pixels per game frame) per game frame.
        };
```

Now, in Listing 9-2, let's outline the code for the game loop method, RunGameFrame(Cars). The argument, Cars, will be a collection of the car data, namely their positions and velocities. Those two pieces of information, in some sense, *are* the car: they are all we need, internally, to keep track of. We'll store cars as simple JavaScript objects: { X, Y, VX, VY }. We will add some properties later on, but these are the only essentials. The position will be in pixels and the velocity will be in pixels per "game frame." A game frame is the basic unit of timing that we use. It means, simply, one iteration of the game loop.

> ***Tip*** *In general, timing for logic in your game should be done by counting game frames and not by using built-in timing functions such as JavaScript's setInterval. Those functions will be irregular depending on CPU load, browser throttling, and so forth. While that is not a bad thing in and of itself, you will have a hard time giving a consistent game experience for different users unless you do your timing by counting game frames.*

In each game frame, we have to

- update the cars' positions

- check for collisions after they're in their new positions

- react to those collisions

Listing 9-2. Outline of RunGameFrame

```
function RunGameFrame(Cars)
{
        // Move the cars and collect impulses due to collisions.

        // Apply impulses.

        // Enforce speed limit and apply friction.
}
```

This type of collision detection, where we move the cars regardless of environment and *then* check for collisions, has some drawbacks. The only serious one that we will consider here is that two cars might pass each other in one time step with no collision registered. Say one car at x=0 is moving to the right at 100 pixels per game frame and the other car, at x=50, is sitting still. One game frame later, the first car has passed the second car but we didn't account for it! A simple way to correct many instances of this is to enforce a maximum speed, small in comparison to the diameter of the bumper cars, so the collision will be registered during some time step.

The result of every collision is to change the momentum of the involved cars (momentum is equivalent to velocity in this formulation—all cars will have unit mass). If a car incurs multiple collisions in one game frame, the collisions can be treated independently and the changes in momentum from each (called "impulses" in physics parlance) simply add up. Therefore, we will look at each car, enumerate its collisions in that game frame (i.e., is its center sufficiently close to any other car or to the walls?), and then compute and store the impulses from those collisions. Afterwards, we will add those impulses onto the car's velocity.

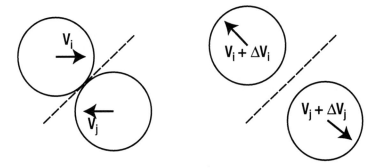

Figure 9-1. A glancing collision and the trajectories resulting from it

When car i and car j, with positions r_i and r_j and velocities v_i and v_j, collide elastically, they receive the impulses shown in Figure 9-2.

$$\Delta v_i = \frac{(r_j - r_i) \cdot (v_j - v_i)}{|r_j - r_i|^2}(r_j - r_i)$$

$$\Delta v_j = -\Delta v_i$$

Figure 9-2. The impulses received by the colliding cars. All quantities are vectors and the dot is the vector dot product.

The first block of code in RunGameFrame is shown in Listing 9-3.

Listing 9-3. Collision Detection Implementation

```
// Move the cars and collect impulses due to collisions.

// Each impulse will be an array in the format
```

```
// [ Index of first car, Index of second car, X impulse, Y impulse ].
var Impulses = [];
for (var i = 0; i < Cars.length; i++)
{
    // Move the cars. X and Y are the coordinates of the center of the car.
    Cars[i].X += Cars[i].VX;
    Cars[i].Y += Cars[i].VY;

    // Check for proximity to the left and right walls.
    if (Cars[i].X <= GP.CarRadius || Cars[i].X >= GP.GameWidth - GP.CarRadius)
    {
        // If we are going towards the wall, then give an impulse. Note that, in the
        // game frame following a collision with the wall, the car may still be in close
        // proximity to the wall but will have velocity pointing away from it. We should
        // not treat that as a new collision. That is the reason for this code.
        if ((Cars[i].X <= GP.CarRadius && Cars[i].VX <= 0)
            || (Cars[i].X >= GP.GameWidth - GP.CarRadius && Cars[i].VX >= 0))
        {
            Impulses.push([i, null, 2 * Cars[i].VX, 0]); // Turn the car around.
        }

        // Make the walls truly rigid. If the car pushed into the wall, push it back out.
        if (Cars[i].X <= GP.CarRadius) Cars[i].X = GP.CarRadius;
        if (Cars[i].X >= GP.GameWidth - GP.CarRadius)
            Cars[i].X = GP.GameWidth ñ GP.CarRadius;
    }

    // Same as above, but now for the top and bottom walls.
    if (Cars[i].Y <= GP.CarRadius || Cars[i].Y >= GP.GameHeight - GP.CarRadius)
    {
        if ((Cars[i].Y <= GP.CarRadius && Cars[i].VY <= 0)
            || (Cars[i].Y >= GP.GameHeight - GP.CarRadius && Cars[i].VY >= 0))
        {
            Impulses.push([i, null, 0, 2 * Cars[i].VY]);
        }

        if (Cars[i].Y <= GP.CarRadius) Cars[i].Y = GP.CarRadius;
        if (Cars[i].Y >= GP.GameHeight - GP.CarRadius)
            Cars[i].Y = GP.GameHeight ñ GP.CarRadius;
    }

    // Now that collisions with walls have been counted, check for collisions between
    // cars. Two cars have collided if their centers are within 2 * GP.CarRadius, i.e.
    // if they overlap at all.
    // Note the bounds of this for loop. We don't need to check all the cars.
    for (var j = i + 1; j < Cars.length; j++)
    {
        // Euclidean distance between the centers of the two cars.
        var DistSqr = (Cars[i].X - Cars[j].X) * (Cars[i].X - Cars[j].X)
                    + (Cars[i].Y - Cars[j].Y) * (Cars[i].Y ñ Cars[j].Y);

        if (Math.sqrt(DistSqr) <= 2 * GP.CarRadius)
        {
            // The impulses from a two dimensional elastic collision.
            // Delta = (r_j - r_i) . (v_i - v_j) / |r_j - r_i|^2.
```

```
                    // Impulse 1 = -Delta * [ DX, DY ].
                    // Impulse 2 = Delta * [ DX, DY ].
                    var DX = Cars[j].X - Cars[i].X;
                    var DY = Cars[j].Y - Cars[i].Y;

                    var Delta = (DX * (Cars[i].VX - Cars[j].VX)
                                   + DY * (Cars[i].VY - Cars[j].VY)) / (DX * DX + DY * DY);

                    // If they're proceeding away from the collision,
                    // (r_j - r_i) . (v_i - v_j) <= 0,
                    // then we already dealt with the collision. This is similar to the
                    // consideration we made for collisions at the wall.
                    if (Delta <= 0) continue;

                    Impulses.push([i, j, Delta * DX, Delta * DY]);
                }
            }
        }
```

This is the meat of the game's physics. Every collision, even with walls, gives rise to an impulse that will change the cars' velocities. Now, applying the impulses is very straightforward, as shown in Listing 9-4.

Listing 9-4. Continuation of RunGameFrame

```
// Apply impulses.
for (var i = 0; i < Impulses.length; i++)
{
    // Wall collisions specify null for one of the car indices, because there is no
    // second car involved. Therefore we are careful not to refer to an index which
    // doesn't belong to the Cars array.
    if (Impulses[i][0] in Cars)
    {
        Cars[Impulses[i][0]].VX -= Impulses[i][2];
        Cars[Impulses[i][0]].VY -= Impulses[i][3];
    }

    if (Impulses[i][1] in Cars)
    {
        Cars[Impulses[i][1]].VX += Impulses[i][2];
        Cars[Impulses[i][1]].VY += Impulses[i][3];
    }
}
```

Finally, we can't let things get too crazy, so we enforce the speed limit mentioned earlier. We also throw in friction for good measure, as shown in Listing 9-5.

Listing 9-5. Continuation of RunGameFrame

```
// Enforce speed limit and apply friction.
for (var i = 0; i < Cars.length; i++)
{
// Scale down the car's speed if it's breaking the speed limit.
var Speed = Math.sqrt(Cars[i].VX * Cars[i].VX + Cars[i].VY * Cars[i].VY);
if (Speed >= GP.MaxSpeed)
{
```

```
        Cars[i].VX *= GP.MaxSpeed / Speed;
        Cars[i].VY *= GP.MaxSpeed / Speed;
    }

    // Friction will act on the cars at all times, eventually bringing them to rest.
    Cars[i].VX *= GP.FrictionMultiplier;
    Cars[i].VY *= GP.FrictionMultiplier;
    }
```

That's all for the `RunGameFrame` method. In fact, that is *all* of the game logic, and there wasn't very much! We complete game.js by adding the lines in Listing 9-6.

Listing 9-6. Code Required for node.js Compatibility

```
if (typeof exports !== "undefined")
{
    exports.GP = GP;
    exports.RunGameFrame = RunGameFrame;
}
```

These lines will allow us to use game.js within node.js when we write our server in a later section.

The game client, Part 1

The game client—what shows up in the user's browser—is slightly more complicated than game.js. We need to

- open a WebSocket connection

- transmit user input to the server

- receive game state from the server

- draw the game

Before diving into the multiplayer stuff, let's just get the game client working on its own. First, make a simple HTML file, bumper.htm, to house the game, as shown in Listing 9-7.

Listing 9-7. bumper.htm

```
<!DOCTYPE html>
<html>

<head>
<title>Bumper Cars</title>
<script language="JavaScript" src="game.js"></script>
<script language="JavaScript" src="client-local.js"></script>
</head>

<body style="text-align: center">
<canvas id="BumperCanvas" style="border: 1px solid black">
Your browser does not support HTML canvas!
</canvas>
```

```
</body>

</html>
```

Now, in client.js, we'll define a few variables specific to the game client, as shown in Listing 9-8.

Listing 9-8. Global Variables in client.js

```
var GraphicsContext;
var Cars = [];
var MyCar = null;
var KeysPressed = 0; // Bit 0: up. Bit 1: left. Bit 2: right.
```

GraphicsContext will refer to the HTML canvas's drawing context, Cars will contain all of the data for the cars that we'll display to the user, and MyCar will be a reference to that element of Cars that the player is in control of. The most interesting of these is KeyPressed, and we will discuss it in a moment.

We'll be displaying a little graphic, car.png, and we load it here (see Listing 9-9) so that the browser caches it.

Listing 9-9. Image Preloading Code

```
var CarImage = new Image();
CarImage.src = "car.png";
```

The player will control the car with his arrow keys. We'll make it so that left and right turn the car, while up makes the car accelerate. In that case, it's necessary to store an orientation for the car, augmenting the short list of car properties from the previous section. This will be an angle that the car makes with some arbitrary axis. Pressing left or right increases or decreases the orientation.

In order to process multiple keys at once, we have to think a bit outside the box—simply responding to keydown events is not sufficient here. What we need to know during a given game frame is whether those three keys are pressed down or not. The KeysPressed variable will serve that purpose. We'll use its bits as flags, setting bit #0 if the up key is pressed down, bit #1 if the left key is pressed down, and bit #2 if the right key is pressed down. If this is unfamiliar to you, imagine we have three light switches, each going on when a certain key is pressed down and going off when that key is released. The KeysPressed variable keeps track of which lights are on. The event handlers to achieve this functionality are as shown in Listing 9-10.

Listing 9-10. Handling Keyboard Input

```
document.addEventListener("keydown",
    function(E)
    {
        if (E.which == 38 && (KeysPressed & 1) == 0) KeysPressed |= 1; // Up.
        else if (E.which == 37 && (KeysPressed & 2) == 0) KeysPressed |= 2; // Left.
        else if (E.which == 39 && (KeysPressed & 4) == 0) KeysPressed |= 4; // Right.
    }
```

```
            );

    document.addEventListener("keyup",
        function(E)
        {
            if (E.which == 38) KeysPressed &= ~1; // Up.
            else if (E.which == 37) KeysPressed &= ~2; // Left.
            else if (E.which == 39) KeysPressed &= ~4; // Right.
        }
    );
```

The & and | are the "bitwise and" and "bitwise or" operators, respectively. Once the page loads, we get our drawing context from the canvas and then proceed into the game loop, as shown in Listing 9-11.

Listing 9-11. Starting the Game Loop on Window Load

```
    window.addEventListener("load",
        function()
        {
            var BumperCanvas = document.getElementById("BumperCanvas");
            BumperCanvas.width = GP.GameWidth;
            BumperCanvas.height = GP.GameHeight;
            GraphicsContext = BumperCanvas.getContext("2d");

            // Set up game loop.
            setInterval(
                function()
                {
                    if (MyCar)
                    {
                        if (KeysPressed & 2) MyCar.OR -= GP.TurnSpeed; // Turn left.
                        if (KeysPressed & 4) MyCar.OR += GP.TurnSpeed; // Turn right.
                        if (KeysPressed & 1) // Accelerate.
                        {
                            MyCar.VX += GP.Acceleration * Math.sin(MyCar.OR);
                            MyCar.VY -= GP.Acceleration * Math.cos(MyCar.OR);
                        }
                    }

                    RunGameFrame(Cars);
                    DrawGame();
                },
                GP.GameFrameTime);
        }
    );.
```

What you see in Listing 9-11 is the entire game loop. Every 20 milliseconds (this value is stored in GP.GameFrameTime), we process the input captured in Listing 9-11 (the OR property of a car is its orientation), run a game frame (that method belongs to game.js), and then draw the game. When the up key is pressed, the car accelerates along the car's current orientation. The factors of sine and cosine can be understood with a little bit of geometry, taking into account the wonky HTML canvas coordinates where the positive y direction is down and angles are measured clockwise.

Now, the only thing missing from this non-multiplayer client is to draw the game. Listing 9-12 is a straightforward exercise in using the `canvas`.

Listing 9-12. DrawGame method

```
function DrawGame()
{
    // Clear the screen
    GraphicsContext.clearRect(0, 0, GP.GameWidth, GP.GameHeight);

    for (var i = 0; i < Cars.length; i++)
    {
        GraphicsContext.save();
        GraphicsContext.translate(Cars[i].X | 0, Cars[i].Y | 0);
        GraphicsContext.rotate(Cars[i].OR);
        GraphicsContext.drawImage(CarImage, -CarImage.width / 2 | 0, ⮎
  -CarImage.height / 2 | 0);
        GraphicsContext.restore();
    }
}
```

There are a few interesting points to be raised here:

- The `x | 0` trick takes the integer part of the number x (and it's much faster than `Math.round`, etc.).

- In current implementations of `canvas`, content may be drawn either aliased or anti-aliased depending on whether the command specifies integer or fractional pixel values. It is a good idea to only draw at integer values so that the moving car's appearance doesn't change as it moves through non-integer coordinates.

- Saving and restoring canvas state is very useful, and a good habit to have.

The client is done! Load it up, and it does... nothing. Well, there are no cars. So, let's add some cars to test it out.

Listing 9-13. Initializing the Local Client with Some Cars

```
Cars.push({ X: 200, Y: 200, VX: 0, VY: 0, OR: 0 });
Cars.push({ X: 100, Y: 100, VX: 5, VY: 0, OR: 0 });
Cars.push({ X: 300, Y: 300, VX: -1, VY: -1, OR: Math.PI });
MyCar = Cars[0];
```

This code can go anywhere that's not in a function, so put it at the end of the file. Next we'll implement the server using node.js and then revisit the game client in order to bring it online.

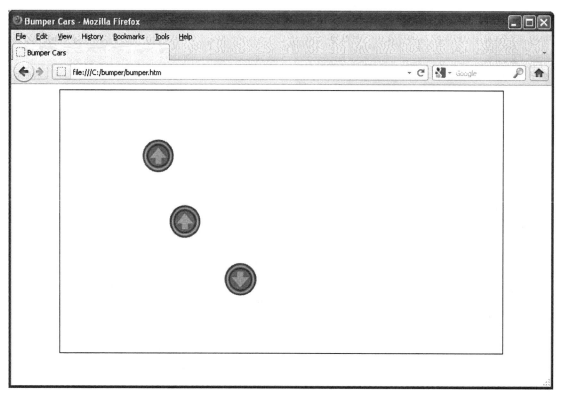

Figure 9-3. The offline game client created in this section

The game server

To set up the game server, you will need access to some computer running node.js (www.nodejs.org). This can be your own computer (there is a Windows port of node.js) or some remote server. We are going to run a WebSocket server on node.js. A WebSocket server can be written in a number of different languages, but using node.js is the most convenient for us because we can share our JavaScript game logic, with no modifications whatsoever, between the client and the server.

At the time of this writing, there are a few node.js add-on modules for creating WebSocket servers, but the one we will use is called WebSocket-Node (https://github.com/Worlize/WebSocket-Node). First install npm, the node.js package manager, and then issue the command npm install websocket to get the module just mentioned. More explicit instructions for getting node.js up and running are found in this chapter's appendix.

Our server.js will need to

- establish a WebSocket server

- run a game loop, maintaining the authoritative state of all the players' cars

- receive and act on player input

- periodically send out game state to all the players

We'll begin by importing the modules that we need (similar to using `#include` in C), as shown in Listing 9-14.

Listing 9-14. Importing node.js Modules

```
var System = require("util");
var HTTP = require("http");
var WebSocketServer = require("/path/to/websocket").server;
var Game = require("/path/to/game");
```

The `sys` and `http` modules come with node.js, but the `websocket` module is what we downloaded a moment ago, and the `game` module is actually just our game.js. You can either put these files (the `websocket` module and game.js) where node.js knows to look for them or you can specify the full paths explicitly (if game.js is located at `/home/user123/bumper/game.js`, you will do `require("/home/user123/bumper/game")`). The `exports` code we added at the end of game.js is important here: only those variables exported by game.js will be accessible to server.js. Now, as shown in Listing 9-15, some global variables that we'll use throughout server.js.

Listing 9-15. Global Variables for the Server

```
var Frame = 0;
var FramesPerGameStateTransmission = 3;
var MaxConnections = 10;
var Connections = {};
```

`Frame` will count game frames, though we won't do any intricate timing in this example game. `FramesPerGameStateTransmission` will control how often game state is broadcasted to players; in this case it's after every three game frames. In game.js, we specified `GameFrameTime` to be 20 milliseconds, so updates will be sent out about every 60 ms, or approximately 17 times per second. `MaxConnections` will limit the number of connections we allow on our server. `Connections` will contain data about the players, including their car state but also stuff about the WebSocket connection: IP address, and so forth.

At this point we can immediately accomplish our first goal. It is very simple to set up a WebSocket server in the environment we've chosen (see Listing 9-16). A WebSocket server piggybacks on a regular old HTTP server, and node.js can create an HTTP server for us in one line.

Listing 9-16. Setting Up the WebSocket Server

```
// Creates an HTTP server that will respond with a simple blank page when accessed.
var HTTPServer = HTTP.createServer(
            function(Request, Response)
            {
                Response.writeHead(200, { "Content-Type": "text/plain" });
                Response.end();
            }
        );

// Starts the HTTP server on port 9001.
HTTPServer.listen(9001, function() { System.log("Listening for connections on port
9001"); });

// Creates a WebSocketServer using the HTTP server just created.
var Server = new WebSocketServer(
            {
                httpServer: HTTPServer,
                closeTimeout: 2000
            }
        );
```

> **Tip** Generally, ports 0–1023 are reserved for system processes, but you are free to choose any higher numbered port for your WebSocket server. In this case, we arbitrarily choose 9001. Make sure that the port you choose is not being blocked by a firewall.

It's really that simple (on our end—of course there is some heavy stuff going on behind the scenes). If we were to run this code, we would have a working WebSocket server at this point. It wouldn't do anything, but it would be there. The next thing we do is subscribe to the WebSocket server's `request` event, which is raised when somebody connects to the server. When that happens, we want to add that client to the `Connections` object and then throw them into the fray with a bumper car. Actually, we'll put off giving the new player a car until he sends a handshake message with an in-game handle, but more on that in a minute.

Listing 9-17. Reacting to Clients Connecting to WebSocket Server

```
// When a client connects...
Server.on("request",
    function(Request)
    {
            if (ObjectSize(Connections) >= MaxConnections)
            {
                Request.reject();
                return;
            }

            var Connection = Request.accept(null, Request.origin);
            Connection.IP = Request.remoteAddress;

            // Assign a random ID that hasn't already been taken.
```

```
        do
            {
                Connection.ID = Math.floor(Math.random() * 100000)
            } while (Connection.ID in Connections);

        Connections[Connection.ID] = Connection;

        Connection.on("message",
            function(Message)
            {
                // All of our messages will be transmitted as unicode text.
                if (Message.type == "utf8")
                    HandleClientMessage(Connection.ID, Message.utf8Data);
            }
        );

        Connection.on("close",
            function()
            {
                HandleClientClosure(Connection.ID);
            }
        );

        System.log("Logged in " + Connection.IP + "; currently " +
                ObjectSize(Connections) + " users.");
    }
);
```

Note that the Server object (our WebSocket server) registers event listeners using on(), in the same way that addEventListener is used for DOM objects in the browser. The method is relatively straightforward. In summary, we do the following:

- Check that we're not running afoul of the connection limit (this connection limit is not needed, but it is here to illustrate rejecting a connection).

- Call accept (as opposed to reject) on the Request object.

- Store the client's IP address and assign a unique ID number to the client for internal use.

- Attach event listeners to this player's Connection object (close is raised when the connection is closed and message is raised whenever that player sends us data).

You may have noticed ObjectSize being applied to Connections. We can't get the size of Connections using Connections.length because it's an object rather than an array. So, we implement this simple counting routine ourselves, as shown in Listing 9-18.

Listing 9-18. Generic Method to Count Size of JavaScript Objects

```
function ObjectSize(Obj)
{
    var Size = 0;
    for (var Key in Obj)
        if (Obj.hasOwnProperty(Key))
```

```
                Size++;

        return Size;
    }
```

The event handler for the player disconnecting is very simple. Notice that in Listing 9-18 we directed that event to a function called HandleClientClosure (see Listing 9-19).

Listing 9-19. HandleClientClosure method

```
    function HandleClientClosure(ID)
    {
        if (ID in Connections)
        {
            System.log("Disconnect from " + Connections[ID].IP);
            delete Connections[ID];
        }
    }
```

Likewise, when we receive data from a player, we process it in HandleClientMessage. Let's outline the behavior of that function in Listing 9-20.

Listing 9-20. HandleClientMessage outline

```
    function HandleClientMessage(ID, Message)
    {
        // Check that we know this client ID and that the message is in a format we expect.

        // Handle the different types of messages we expect:
        // - Handshake message where the player tells us his name
        //      --> Create his car object and send everybody the good news.
        // - Key was pressed.
        //      --> Update the player's personal KeyPressed bitfield.
        // - Key was released.
        //      --> Ditto.
    }
```

It is completely up to us to choose a message format. Using JavaScript, a natural choice is JSON that is nothing more than a standardized way of encoding JavaScript variable data. We could easily make our messages shorter or more obscure, but there is no benefit to that in the present case. JSON support is ubiquitous, with all modern browsers (and node.js) supporting the routines JSON.stringify() for encoding and JSON.parse() for decoding. Therefore, we will choose our server-bound messages to be JSON-encoded JavaScript objects in the format { Type: ..., Data: ... }. The three types of messages will be "HI" for handshake, "U" for key up, and "D" for key down. Now, in Listing 9-21, let's fill out HandleClientMessage.

Listing 9-21. HandleClientMessage Method

```
    function HandleClientMessage(ID, Message)
    {
        // Check that we know this client ID and that the message is in a format we expect.
        if (!(ID in Connections)) return;
```

```
        try { Message = JSON.parse(Message); }
        catch (Err) { return; }
        if (!("Type" in Message && "Data" in Message)) return;

        // Handle the different types of messages we expect.
        var C = Connections[ID];
        switch (Message.Type)
        {
            // Handshake.
            case "HI":
                // If this player already has a car, abort.
                if (C.Car) break;

                // Create the player's car with random initial position.
                C.Car =
                    {
                        X: Game.GP.CarRadius + Math.random() * (Game.GP.GameWidth↪
- 2 * Game.GP.CarRadius),
                        Y: Game.GP.CarRadius + Math.random() * (Game.GP.GameHeight↪
- 2 * Game.GP.CarRadius),
                        VX: 0,
                        VY: 0,
                        OR: 0,
                        // Put a reasonable length restriction on usernames.
                        // Usernames will be displayed to all players.
                        Name: Message.Data.toString().substring(0, 10)
                    };

                // Initialize the input bitfield.
                C.KeysPressed = 0;
                System.log(C.Car.Name + " spawned a car!");

                SendGameState();
                break;

            // Key up.
            case "U":
                if (typeof C.KeysPressed === "undefined") break;

                if (Message.Data == 37) C.KeysPressed &= ~2; // Left
                else if (Message.Data == 39) C.KeysPressed &= ~4; // Right
                else if (Message.Data == 38) C.KeysPressed &= ~1; // Up
                break;

            // Key down.
            case "D":
                if (typeof C.KeysPressed === "undefined") break;

                if (Message.Data == 37) C.KeysPressed |= 2; // Left
                else if (Message.Data == 39) C.KeysPressed |= 4; // Right
                else if (Message.Data == 38) C.KeysPressed |= 1; // Up
                break;
        }
}
```

Notice that we again augmented, for the final time, the list of data stored per car. We're now keeping track of the user's handle (username) and it will be displayed on the cars once we revisit the game client.

> ***Caution*** *Always perform strict data validation on any input received from users! It is very simple for a user to change the game client and send messages out of order or send messages that the server does not understand. If you are not careful, these can crash your server or worse.*

Of course, the method SendGameState, called after the handshake, is all-important. It will broadcast all of the game data to all of the players several times per second. In a more complicated game, especially one with many users, this will be something that you want to optimize for speed and bandwidth efficiency. In our case, these aren't important concerns. We proceed pretty naively, then in Listing 9-22.

Listing 9-22. SendGameState Method

```
function SendGameState()
{
    var CarData = [];
    var Indices = {};

    // Collect all the car objects to be sent out to the clients
    for (var ID in Connections)
    {
        // Some users may not have Car objects yet (if they haven't done the handshake)
        var C = Connections[ID];
        if (!C.Car) continue;

        CarData.push(C.Car);

        // Each user will be sent the same list of car objects, but needs to be able to pick
        // out his car from the pack. Here we take note of the index that belongs to him.
        Indices[ID] = CarData.length - 1;
    }

    // Go through all of the connections and send them personalized messages. Each user gets
    // the list of all the cars, but also the index of his car in that list.
    for (var ID in Connections)
        Connections[ID].sendUTF(JSON.stringify({ MyIndex: Indices[ID], Cars: CarData
}));
}
```

The message we send out is a JSON-encoded string made from the object { MyIndex: ..., Cars: ... }. Each user will get a personalized message like this, with all the car information (including his own car), as well as the index of his car in the group. The way we send data is very simple: each element of Connections has the method sendUTF() (part of WebSocket-Node's type, WebSocketConnection) that accepts a string as input.

The only remaining piece of server.js is the game loop (see Listing 9-23). We already constructed a game loop in client.js, and this one will be very similar.

Listing 9-23. Setting up the Game Loop on the Server

```
// Set up game loop.
setInterval(function()
    {
        // Make a copy of the car data suitable for RunGameFrame.
        var Cars = [];
        for (var ID in Connections)
        {
            var C = Connections[ID];
            if (!C.Car) continue;

            Cars.push(C.Car);

            if (C.KeysPressed & 2) C.Car.OR -= Game.GP.TurnSpeed;
            if (C.KeysPressed & 4) C.Car.OR += Game.GP.TurnSpeed;
            if (C.KeysPressed & 1)
            {
                C.Car.VX += Game.GP.Acceleration * Math.sin(C.Car.OR);
                C.Car.VY -= Game.GP.Acceleration * Math.cos(C.Car.OR);
            }
        }

        Game.RunGameFrame(Cars);

        // Increment the game frame, which is only used to time the SendGameState calls.
        Frame = (Frame + 1) % FramesPerGameStateTransmission;
        if (Frame == 0) SendGameState();
    },
    Game.GP.GameFrameTime
);
```

The variables exported from game.js are referenced as Game.RunGameFrame and Game.GP, where Game was defined all the way at the top of server.js when we called require().

Now all of server.js is put together, but our game client is stuck in the Stone Age. Time to bring it online!

The game client, Part 2

The game client is going to assume a subordinate role now that we have an authoritative server. Every time the server calls SendGameState(), the game client will receive the list of car data and overwrite whatever it had previously. We still have a game loop and still respond to keyboard input, but only to make the game experience smoother as we discussed in an earlier section. The main client changes, therefore, are to establish a WebSocket connection and then handle messages from the server, and to pass along keyboard data to the server.

As shown in Listing 9-24, we'll keep two global variables more than we had in the old game client.

Listing 9-24. New Global Variables for the Client

```
var Socket = null;
var GameTimer = null;
```

The first is our WebSocket and the second will be used to stop the game loop if the WebSocket connection is aborted. When the page loads, we'll ask the player for a handle and then connect to the WebSocket server. So, in our window-load event handler, we add the code as shown in Listing 9-25.

Listing 9-25. Modification of Window Load Event Handler in the Client

```
...
GraphicsContext = BumperCanvas.getContext("2d");

var Name = prompt("What is your username?", "Anonymous");
GraphicsContext.textAlign = "center";
GraphicsContext.fillText("Connecting...", GP.GameWidth / 2, GP.GameHeight / 2);

try
{
    if (typeof MozWebSocket !== "undefined")
        Socket = new MozWebSocket("ws://SERVERIP:9001");
    else if (typeof WebSocket !== "undefined")
        Socket = new WebSocket("ws://SERVERIP:9001");
    else
    {
        Socket = null;
        alert("Your browser does not support websockets. We recommend that you use➥
 an up-to-date version of Google Chrome or Mozilla Firefox.");
        return false;
    }
}
catch (E) { Socket = null; return false; }
```

At the time of this writing, Firefox calls its WebSocket type MozWebSocket. That may change in the future. For the time being, the code in Listing 9-25 is compatible with both Firefox and Chrome. Of course, SERVERIP should be replaced by the IP address of the server running server.js, be it 127.0.0.1 or the IP address of a remote server.

Next, in Listing 9-26, we listen for events raised by the WebSocket, and then we will be done with the window-load event handler.

Listing 9-26. WebSocket Event Handlers

```
Socket.onerror = function(E) { alert("WebSocket error: " + JSON.stringify(E)); };

Socket.onclose = function (E)
    {
        // Shut down the game loop.
        if (GameTimer) clearInterval(GameTimer);
        GameTimer = null;
    };

Socket.onopen = function()
```

```
    {
        // Send a handshake message.

        // Set up game loop.
    };

Socket.onmessage = function(E)
    {
        // Parse the car data from the server.
    };
```

The latter two event handlers require some more detail. When the WebSocket connection succeeds in opening, the open event is raised, meaning that it is ready to send and receive data. At that point, we want to send a handshake message to the server telling it the player's name. Then, we'll begin a game loop.

Listing 9-27. WebSocket "open" Event Handler

```
Socket.onopen = function()
    {
        // Send a handshake message.
        Socket.send(JSON.stringify({ Type: "HI", Data: Name.substring(0, 10) }));

        // Set up game loop.
        GameTimer = setInterval(
            function()
            {
                // Supposing MyCar is not null, which it shouldn't be if we're
                // participating in the game and communicating with the server.
                if (MyCar)
                {
                    // Turn and accelerate the car locally, while we wait for the
                    // server to respond to the key presses we transmit to it.
                    if (KeysPressed & 2) MyCar.OR -= GP.TurnSpeed;
                    if (KeysPressed & 4) MyCar.OR += GP.TurnSpeed;
                    if (KeysPressed & 1)
                    {
                        MyCar.VX += GP.Acceleration * Math.sin(MyCar.OR);
                        MyCar.VY -= GP.Acceleration * Math.cos(MyCar.OR);
                    }
                }

                RunGameFrame(Cars);
                DrawGame();
            },
            GP.GameFrameTime);
    };
```

There is not much new in this game loop besides the fact, which must be stressed again, that the game loop is only being run for a smooth user experience. The actual game logic is being computed on the server and sent to us. Now we receive and handle the server's game state messages, as shown in Listing 9-28.

Listing 9-28. WebSocket "message" Event Handler

```
Socket.onmessage = function(E)
    {
        var Message;

        // Check that the message is in the format we expect.
        try { Message = JSON.parse(E.data); }
        catch (Err) { return; }
        if (!("MyIndex" in Message && "Cars" in Message)) return;

        // Overwrite our old Cars array with the new data sent from the server.
        Cars = Message.Cars;
        if (Message.MyIndex in Cars) MyCar = Cars[Message.MyIndex];
    };
```

Keyboard input from the user should now send a message to the server. It's not necessary to send a message every time a keydown event is fired—if the key is held down there will be a ton of those events. So, we implement this as shown in Listing 9-29.

Listing 9-29. New Multiplayer-Enabled Keyboard Handlers

```
document.addEventListener("keydown",
    function(E)
        {
            var Transmit = true;
            if (E.which == 38 && (KeysPressed & 1) == 0) KeysPressed |= 1; // Up.
            else if (E.which == 37 && (KeysPressed & 2) == 0) KeysPressed |= 2; // Left.
            else if (E.which == 39 && (KeysPressed & 4) == 0) KeysPressed |= 4; // Right.
            else Transmit = false;

            // Only send to the server if the key is one of the three we care about, and only
            // if this key press wasn't already reflected in the KeyPressed bitfield.
            if (Transmit && Socket && Socket.readyState == 1)
                Socket.send(JSON.stringify({ Type: "D", Data: E.which }));
        }
    );

document.addEventListener("keyup",
    function(E)
        {
            var Transmit = true;
            if (E.which == 38) KeysPressed &= ~1; // Up.
            else if (E.which == 37) KeysPressed &= ~2; // Left.
            else if (E.which == 39) KeysPressed &= ~4; // Right.
            else Transmit = false;

            // For "keyup", we just have to check that it's one of the keys we care about.
            if (Transmit && Socket && Socket.readyState == 1)
                Socket.send(JSON.stringify({ Type: "U", Data: E.which }));
        }
    );
```

Sending the data is as simple as calling the send() method on the WebSocket object. The WebSocket's readyState property has the value 1 when it is open and functioning correctly. With those changes, we're totally online-enabled! One last tweak to make is to draw player names above their cars. The DrawGame method is shown in Listing 9-30.

Listing 9-30. Modification of DrawGame Method in the Client

```
function DrawGame()
{
    // Clear the screen
    GraphicsContext.clearRect(0, 0, GP.GameWidth, GP.GameHeight);

    GraphicsContext.save();
    GraphicsContext.font = "12pt Arial";
    GraphicsContext.fillStyle = "black";
    GraphicsContext.textAlign = "center";
    for (var i = 0; i < Cars.length; i++)
    {
        GraphicsContext.save();
        GraphicsContext.translate(Cars[i].X | 0, Cars[i].Y | 0);
        GraphicsContext.rotate(Cars[i].OR);
        GraphicsContext.drawImage(CarImage, -CarImage.width / 2 | 0, ↪
-CarImage.height / 2 | 0);
        GraphicsContext.restore();


        if (Cars[i].Name)
        {
            GraphicsContext.fillText(
                (Cars[i] == MyCar ? "Me" : Cars[i].Name.substring(0, 10)),
                Cars[i].X | 0,
                (Cars[i].Y - GP.CarRadius - 12) | 0
                );
        }
    }
    GraphicsContext.restore();
}
```

And we are ready to play. Invite all your friends!

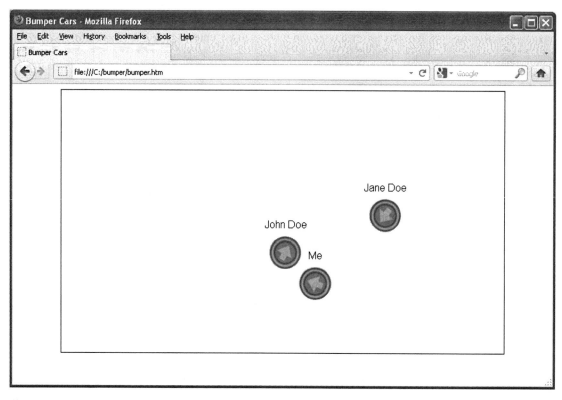

Figure 9-4. The final game client, with three players online

Conclusion

WebSockets and the HTML5 canvas open up all sorts of possibilities to developers. These technologies are still brand new, but we should expect to see them really take off in the years ahead. In this chapter, we've created a prototype game and hopefully you will agree that it wasn't exceedingly difficult. Nobody can argue the fact that this was a walk in the park compared to making the same bumper car demo as a standalone application in a traditional language like C++.

You may point out that the ease of development owes to offloading all of the heavy lifting to the web browser. This is certainly true, but in the context of many games and applications, the benefits outweigh the downsides. The performance hit you take, relying on a browser rather than optimizing your own standalone application, is getting smaller every day (not to say that it will ever be non-existent). Web browsers are continually improving thanks to intense competition for market share.

On the other hand, you get portability and high-level access to sockets, graphics, sound, user input, and so forth, all with comparatively minimal effort on your part. Clearly, this is an option worth considering for development of any small or mid-sized games. I hope to see yours online soon!

Appendix: Setting up node.js

Let's walk through getting node.js up and running. We'll do it first on Windows and then make some comments about doing it on a UNIX-based system.

Windows

Download the latest Windows version of node.js from www.nodejs.org. As of this writing, the version is 0.6.2. The installer unpacks node.exe (the thing that will run our JavaScript code) and appends the appropriate directory (for me, C:\Program Files\nodejs) to the environment path variable. You should find that directory (if you are having trouble, search your hard drive for node.exe) and make a note of it.

On Windows, there is no Node Package Manager (npm) utility to automate installation of node.js libraries, so we'll have to install the websocket library manually. To do that, visit the project's web page, https://github.com/Worlize/WebSocket-Node, and find the option to download the repository as a zip file. Extract that zip file to the same directory as node.exe. Alongside node.exe, there should now be a directory with a name like Worlize-WebSocket-Node-0d04b73 (the string you find at the end may be different). Rename that directory to "websocket". That's it! The library is installed.

Now, you should place all the source files associated with the bumper car game in a directory of your choosing. I put mine in c:\bumper, so we'll use that for what follows. We need to update server.js so that it knows where to find our libraries. Open up server.js and find the lines beginning "var WebSocketServer = ..." and "var Game = ...". Replace those with:

```
var WebSocketServer = require("c:/program files/nodejs/websocket").server;
var Game = require("c:/bumper/game");
```

where the directories correspond to those on your system. Notice that the slashes are backwards from normal Windows paths.

Next, in client-multiplayer.js, find the two instances of "ws://SERVERIP:9001". If your port 9001 is open to external traffic, then you can replace SERVERIP by your IP address. If not, and you just want to try it out locally, then replace SERVERIP by localhost (or, equivalently, 127.0.0.1). Go to the command line and execute

```
node c:\bumper\server.js
```

If you get a complaint that it can't find node, then navigate to the directory containing node.exe and try executing it again. Finally, update bumper.htm to make sure that it refers to client-multiplayer.js rather than client-local.js, and then load up bumper.htm in a web browser (or two)!

UNIX

To install node.js on a UNIX-based operating system, you should first check if there is a pre-compiled package available for you, following the instructions located at https://github.com/joyent/node/wiki/Installing-Node.js-via-package-manager. If not, you will have to build node.js from its source code. There are comprehensive instructions for doing that available at https://github.com/joyent/node/wiki/Installation.

After installing node.js, you will want to install the Node Package Manager (npm), by executing the following command: `curl http://npmjs.org/install.sh | sh`

and then install the `websocket` module by running npm:

```
npm install websocket
```

If you have issues installing or using npm, you can perform a manual installation instead, as described in the Windows walkthrough. At this point, node.js should be all set up and it remains just to direct server.js, client-multiplayer.js, and bumper.htm to the correct places.

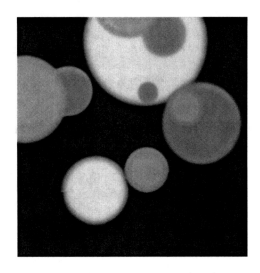

Chapter 10

Hard-Pressed for a Choice of Technology

Browser-based games have been around for as long as there have been browsers, and one can easily retrace the evolution of browsers by following the evolution of browser-based games. At first games were text-based—this was the evolution of multi-user dungeons. MUDs were mainly turn-based due to the limitations of HTTP, but then developers started adding images, chats, and player interaction. However, the stagnation in HTML development, which followed the first browser war, resulted in most games of the 2000s being developed with third-party plug-ins, as the multimedia capabilities of HTML4 were humble, to say the least.

The new round of browser wars, which began in 2009, saw HTML5 become both a major force in browser multimedia technology and a popular choice among developers. Its incredible pace of progress was instrumental in this. What we saw in 2008 were simple HTML-based casual games at best, whereas today, it is hardly amazing to see real-time battles and full, 3D gaming in a browser—with no additional plug-ins.

A key advantage of HTML5 over various aging technologies like Flash and Silverlight is its support and advancement by mobile platforms. The staggering growth in the number of devices running Android and iOS makes it a highly promising technology.

What is particularly inspiring is that browser developers are not just adding new technologies, but promoting HTML5 as a platform for game development. The release of IE9 in the spring of 2011 saw Microsoft hold the {Dev:unplu99ed} contest for games and multimedia developers offering a total of $40,000 in prizes. Google Inc. operates Game Developer Central (http://code.google.com/games), which provides developer tools, and Chrome Web Store to promote browser-based games. Mozilla proved the quickest of all, holding the Game On 2010 contest for developers of browser-based games, with industry professionals from Zynga, Facebook, SixToStart, and many other companies serving as judges. My team's project, FAR7, won the Best Technology category. As the CTO, I would like to discuss the crucial and most complicated stage of development, which is choosing the technology.

Why the choice is so hard to make

Being game developers, we must squeeze everything we can out of the possibilities offered by web browsers and find workarounds for the limitations that still exist. The limitations of browser capabilities warrant comparisons of browser game developers' current situation with that of game developers from the '80s, who were fighting for every bit of data and FPS while making simple (yet not a tiny bit less exciting) games for a budding market. Just as it was back then, we now have to worry about buffering and extra screen refresh; optimized sprites and stored data for the best performance; packing files for fast download; and much more.

The rapid progress of technology and a new round of the browser wars further complicate choosing the right technology (with HTML being one notable example).A great number of new technologies have been introduced in the span of a mere two years. Many of these have similar functionality, and it is sometimes extremely difficult to make the right choice. For instance, it is simply impossible to choose between canvas and SVG, or WebSockets and Server-Sent Events, without researching and studying their respective backgrounds.

Before we start developing, we must identify our target market, clearly define the game genre, and assess available resources. By the way, the latter is critical for indie games and start-ups, which often do not even live to see the first prototype solely because the developers fail to choose technologies with optimum labor intensity. As for the genre, it can pose stringent requirements to an engine part. FPS games call for short ping times, whereas an RPG may require a large cache.

Until a standard game development stack takes shape, each developer must make his own choice, combining what he sees as essential technologies to build his own game engine. It is this choice that will determine how successful the engine is; which, in turn, will affect the success and popularity of the game.

No market player knows for sure the right way to make games, but it is apparent to everyone these technologies have a great future. This is the motivation behind frequent developer conferences, the most notable of these being hackathons held by the Facebook crew, featuring speeches by organizers and guests from well-known companies, such as Zynga, Three Rings, and other HTML5 game development pioneers. One of these hackathons saw the making of an application named JSGameBench (`https://github.com/facebook/jsgamebench`), designed to analyze the performance of various technologies in different browsers. JSGameBench is continuously updated, and I strongly recommend that you use the tool to study the current state of the market. Even as you read this book, new browser versions may well be coming out, and the drafts of many standards may be updated.

In this chapter, I will try to describe each element of the stack (audio and video, rendering, client databases, and connection) and to provide a couple of useful tips on architecture and styling. In each particular case, we will look at differences in implementation in each browser and discuss fallback options for legacy browsers that lack support for advanced technology.

Rendering

We should start with the basics, as no game is possible without a graphical representation. In the past, the most widely-used option was simple layers, but since the advent of HTML5, developers have been able to choose between two higher-performance technologies: bitmap canvas and vector SVG. Both make high-quality graphics possible in the browser, but they are fundamentally different. It is impossible to say which is better. All you can do is choose the more appropriate option in each individual case.

SVG

SVG stands for Scalable Vector Graphics, an XML-based language for marking up two-dimensional vector and mixed vector bitmap graphics. It is based on PGML created by Adobe, Sun Microsystems, IBM, and Netscape, as well as VML developed by Macromedia and Microsoft.

The World Wide Web Consortium (W3C) began work on the standard back in 1999, and the first stable version, SVG 1.1, appeared in 2003. Development of SVG 1.2 continued for years, and it was recently decided that the drafts needed to be completely redesigned for better integration with the new HTML5, CSS, and WOFF (Web Open Font Format) technologies. The resulting standard would be designated as SVG 2.0.

For a long time, browsers supported SVG with the help of third-party plug-ins, but these days many modern browsers have native SVG support. Even Microsoft abandoned VLM in favor of SVG in its new browser, Internet Explorer 9. Mobile platforms offer decent support, apart from the fact that Android added basic SVG support in version 3.0.

Table 10-1. SVG (basic support): Method of displaying basic Vector Graphics features using the embed or object elements

	IE	Firefox	Safari	Chrome	Opera
Two versions back	~~7.0~~	5.0	4.0	12.0	11.0
Previous version	~~8.0~~	6.0	5.0	13.0	11.1
Current	9.0	7.0	5.1	14.0	11.5
Near future		8.0	6.0	15.0	12.0
Farther future	10.0	9.0		16.0	12.1

Older versions of IE utilized libraries that translated SVG to VML, Raphael being the most popular of these.

As I mentioned, an SVG file is an XML file. It can be viewed separately or added to a page. Listing 10-1 is an example of an SVG image source with gradient, animated ellipse, and image.

Listing 10-1. SVG image source with gradient, animated ellipse, and image

```
<svg version="1.1" width="320" height="320" xmlns="http://www.w3.org/2000/svg">
    <defs>
        <radialGradient id="planet">
            <stop offset="0%"   stop-color="rgb(0, 0, 255)" />
            <stop offset="100%" stop-color="rgb(0, 0, 125)" />
        </radialGradient>
    </defs>
    <ellipse fill="url(#planet)" stroke="#000" cx="256" cy="256" rx="50%" ry="50%">
        <animate attributeName="rx" values="10%;20%;10%" dur="2s"
            repeatCount="indefinite" />
        <animate attributeName="ry" values="10%;20%;10%" dur="2s"
            repeatCount="indefinite" />
    </ellipse>
    <image x="110" y="110" width="100" height="82" xlink:href="ship.png">
        <animate attributeName="x" values="25%;50%;25%" dur="2s"
            repeatCount="indefinite" />
        <animate attributeName="y" values="25%;50%;25%" dur="2s"
            repeatCount="indefinite" />
    </image>
</svg>
```

Figure 10-1 shows what a small image with several primitives looks like.

Figure 10-1. SVG image with gradient, animated ellipse, and image

What benefits does SVG offer?

- Vector graphics are easily scalable with no loss in quality, which is very convenient when building interfaces.

- The format supports animation natively and through JavaScript, making the development process simple and speedy.

- An SVG object model allows assigning familiar events to each object. To obtain similar functionality on canvas, you need to write extra logic for matching object coordinates to click coordinates.

- An XML-based language, SVG provides a familiar DOM API on the page for accessing each element.

What are the drawbacks of SVG?

- The main drawback stems from the fourth advantage. The more complex and larger the document, the slower the rendering—as with any other technology that uses DOM.

Canvas

The way of the canvas element into HTML5 is quite illustrative. It did not arrive from the top as most W3C standards before, which often were good in theory but suffered from problems when applied. It was created by browser developers and approved as a standard after it was popularized. It all began in 2004 after Apple added canvas to one of the WebKit versions, where it was used for rendering certain widgets in Safari. Other browser developers felt a need for a similar tool, so in 2005 canvas appeared in Firefox, and in 2006, was added to Opera.

Canvas is essentially an array of pixels with a special JavaScript API for manipulation: drawing primitive and complex objects, inserting images and text, manipulating pixels, etc. Canvas is a simple tag. For example, Listing 10-2 shows a page with canvas and a little JavaScript, which produces the same image as the SVG sample.

Listing 10-2. An HTML file with canvas tag and JavaScript source code to draw an animated circle and a ship

```
<!DOCTYPE html>
<html>
<head>
<script type="text/javascript"><!--
        window.addEventListener('load', function ()
        {
                // Get the canvas element.
                var canvas = document.getElementById('myCanvas'),
                        w = 64,
                        h = 64,
                        step = 'in';

                if (!canvas || !canvas.getContext) {
                  return;
                }

                // Get the canvas 2d context.
                var ctx = canvas.getContext('2d');
                if (!ctx) {
                  return;
                }

                // Create new img element
                var img = new Image();
                img.src = 'ship.png';

                setInterval(function ()
```

```
                {
                        if (step == 'in')
                        {
                                w++;
                                h++;
                        }
                        else if (step == 'out')
                        {
                                w--;
                                h--;
                        }

                        if (w > 128)
                        {
                                w = 128;
                                step = 'out';
                        } else if (w < 64)
                        {
                                w = 64;
                                step = 'in';
                        }

                        if (h > 128)
                        {
                                h = 128;
                                step = 'out';
                        }
                        else if (h < 64)
                        {
                                h = 64;
                                step = 'in';
                        }

                        // Create the radial gradient
                        var gradient = ctx.createRadialGradient(
                                96+Math.round(w/2),
                                96+Math.round(h/2), 0,
                                96+Math.round(w/2),
                                96+Math.round(h/2),
                                Math.round(Math.min(w, h)/2));

                        gradient.addColorStop(0, "#00f");
                        gradient.addColorStop(1, "#00007d");

                        // Use the gradient for the fillStyle.
                        ctx.fillStyle = gradient;

                        // Ellipse radius and center.
                        var cx = 96 + w/2,
                                cy = 96 + h/2,

                                rx = w/2,
                                ry = h/2;
```

```
                    ctx.setTransform(1, 0, 0, 1, 0, 0);

                    ctx.clearRect(0, 0, canvas.width, canvas.height);

                    ctx.setTransform(1, 0, 0, 1,
                            Math.round((canvas.width - w) / 2),
                            Math.round((canvas.height - h) / 2));


                    // Drawing a circle
                    ctx.beginPath();
                    ctx.arc(cx, cy, rx, ry, Math.PI*2, true);
                    ctx.fill();
                    ctx.stroke();
                    ctx.closePath();

                    // Drawing a ship
                    ctx.drawImage(img, w*2 - 196, h*2 - 196,
                            img.width/2, img.height/2);
                }, 1000/60);

        }, false);
        // -->
        </script>
    </head>
    <body>
        <canvas id="myCanvas" width="320" height="320">
                Your browser does not have support for Canvas.
        </canvas>
    </body>
</html>
```

I would like to emphasize that all of the above applies to the two-dimensional context of canvas. In 2011, we saw the spread of a three-dimensional context, also known as WebGL, which allows adding three-dimensional scenes to a browser natively and manipulating these using JavaScript.

Table 10-2. Canvas (basic support): Method of generating fast, dynamic graphics using JavaScript

	IE	Firefox	Safari	Chrome	Opera
Two versions back	~~7.0~~	5.0	4.0	12.0	11.0
Previous version	~~8.0~~	6.0	5.0	13.0	11.1
Current	9.0	7.0	5.1	14.0	11.5
Near future		8.0	6.0	15.0	12.0
Farther future	10.0	9.0		16.0	12.1

The two-dimensional context has long been supported by every popular browser, with the exception of IE versions below 9.0. Google has created a product called Explorer Canvas, or excanvas, for these older IE versions. Simply by enabling one extra JavaScript file, you get fully functional canvas in the old versions of IE.

What are the benefits of canvas?

- The main advantage is speed. The absence of an object model, a low-level API, and hardware acceleration allows canvas to work really fast!

- Performance is not affected by an increase in the number of objects, because those are simply pixels.

- Results drawn on canvas can be saved as JPG or PNG files.

- The low-level API lets you do whatever you want with the image.

What drawbacks does canvas have?

- The lack of a DOM obliges developers to implement additional logic for storing object information.

- There is absolutely no animation support, which means you have to do the calculations and refresh canvas when needed.

- It has no interactivity whatsoever.

- It has poor text-rendering capabilities.

Choosing a rendering technology

Canvas is good for low-level image editing (cropping, resizing, filters) and generating raster graphics (sprites and fonts in games). SVG works well for creating for resolution-independent and interactive interfaces, and certainly for vector graphics. Therefore, the perfect option is to combine the two by rendering raster graphics on canvas and animating that with SVG.

Audio

Back in 1995, IE2 added the possibility of inserting a sound file into a page using the tag `<bgsound>`, which never became part of the standard. NN3.0 responded by adding the tag `<embed>` for inserting multimedia objects including audio files. That battle of the first browser war ended with the tag `<object>` being added to the HTML 4.0 standard.

The implementation of `<object>` differed significantly from browser to browser and depended on the type of file to be integrated. This is exactly what led to mass use of Flash for displaying multimedia on web sites. However, with the advent of the HTML5 era, we were given the excellent and largely convenient tags `<audio>` and `<video>`.

One of the main challenges of integrating video and audio into browsers is the difference in codec selections in different browsers, which requires us store several copies of content; for example, Ogg Vorbis files for Firefox, Chrome, and Opera, and MP3 files for IE9 and Safari.

Let us take a closer look at cases of using <audio>. These are first, background music, and second, action sounds. Each option has its pitfalls, with some browsers lacking the capability to loop music tracks; whereas the single-channel nature of the sound prevents repeating the track before it ends.

We will talk about this single-channel nature of <audio> in more detail. It means that if we restart the file as it is playing—for instance, when the player is shooting rapidly—the browser will cut off the sound and start again. To prevent that sort of behavior, we can create several audio objects and rotate them, as shown in Listing 10-3.

Listing 10-3. An example of implementing multi-channel sound by rotating audio elements

```
<audio id="sound_fire" src="audio/laser.wav" preload="auto"></audio>
<a href="javascript:play_multi_sound('sound_fire');">Fire</a><br />

<script>
var channel_max = 10;      // number of channels
audiochannels = new Array();

for (a=0;a<channel_max ;a++)
{        // prepare the channels
        audiochannels[a] = new Array();
        audiochannels[a]['channel'] = new Audio();       // create a new audio object
        audiochannels[a]['finished'] = -1; // expected end time for this channel
}

function play_multi_sound(s)
{
        for (a=0;a<audiochannels.length;a++)
        {
                thistime = new Date();
                if (audiochannels[a]['finished'] <thistime.getTime())
                {
                        // is this channel finished?
                        audiochannels[a]['finished'] = thistime.getTime() +
                                        document.getElementById(s).duration*1000;

                        audiochannels[a]['channel'].src = document.getElementById(s).src;
                        audiochannels[a]['channel'].load();
                        audiochannels[a]['channel'].play();
                        break;
                }
        }
}
</script>
```

The tag <audio> is relatively new, and there are a fairly large number of people still using browsers that do not support it. Historical reference makes it clear that it is not always the optimum solution to fall back on <object>, so the best option would be to use a compatible Flash object. One of the easiest ways to do this is to employ an audio.js library to handle the problems.

Connection

Most games are sensitive to network latency. We developers are at a crossroads again today, given a choice of several technologies. Let us look at the advantages of each and figure out what to do about obsolete browsers that do not support them. I will provide a little background, so that we know what we are dealing with.

Everybody knows the internet is built on the HTTP protocol, and being a request–response protocol, it does not preserve the state in between requests or support continuous connection. The first method used in creating pages with live content was to do a simple refresh. It utilized frames and a special META header, and later, JavaScript.

Mid-2000 saw the advent of the XMLHttpRequest API, which allowed sending asynchronous requests to the server. It grew swiftly in popularity, serving as the basis for the widely known AJAX technology. This period is considered to be the beginning of the Web 2.0 era. But let us take a closer look at this technique. Figure 10-2 shows what client–server communication looks like after a page is loaded.

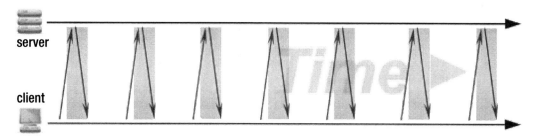

Figure 10-2. Network traffic diagram demonstrating short polling

This type of interaction is called polling. Its advantages over full refresh are obvious, but there are some drawbacks. The worst of these is "no-load" activity: the browser often makes hundreds of requests, only to learn that there is no new data. The answer to this problem is long polling, which fetches results as soon as these appear on the server (see Figure 10-3).

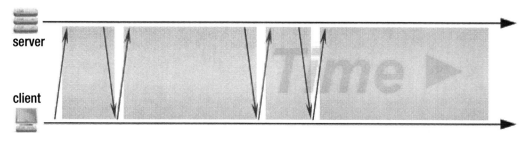

Figure 10-3. Network traffic diagram demonstrating long polling

Long polling is the happy medium between simple AJAX and complex HTTP streaming, also known as HTTP server push or Comet (see Figure 10-4). Its key advantage is that the client creates only one connection, which it uses to receive data from the server in real time. Its drawbacks are complexities with implementation and disharmony with the spirit of HTTP.

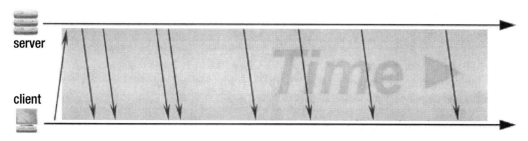

Figure 10-4. Network traffic diagram demonstrating streaming

For a long while, Comet was the only option of receiving real-time data from the server without resorting to third-party plug-ins. With the advent of HTML5, we are given two technologies to do this: WebSockets and Server-Sent Events.

Server-Sent Events

Server-Sent Events builds on the Comet idea and should replace it in the future (or at least displace long polling). The client subscribes to server-side events, receiving notifications and certain event-related data as soon as the event takes place.

As shown in Listing 10-4, simple reception of server messages is organized with just a few strings of code—no comparison to the bulky logic used in Comet.

Listing 10-4. An example of a simple SSE connection

```
// Specify new message source
// Note you are using http
var source = new EventSource('http://sontan.name/stream/');

// Subscribe to messages from the source
source.addEventListener('message', function(e) {
        console.log(e.data);
}, false);
```

The event stream is plain text using text/event-stream as Content-Type. In the simplest case, as shown in Listing 10-5, it is a string that begins with data: followed the body of the message and ending with two newlines: \n\n.

Listing 10-5. A single-line message from the server

```
data: simplest message\n\n
```

To create multi-line messages, use one \n at the end of each line preceding the last one, and two, at the end of the final line, as shown in Listing 10-6.

Listing 10-6. An example of a multi-line message used in JSON transmission

```
data: {\n
data: "msg": "hello server-sent event",\n
data: "id": 42\n
data: }\n\n
```

Besides, SSE can track message numbers, transmitting the last message's identifier to the server whenever the connection is broken. Listing 10-7 shows that this is enabled simply by transmitting the number of the message using a line that begins with `id:`.

Listing 10-7. A server message stating its own ID

```
id: 42\n
data: message\n
data: text\n\n
```

By default, the browser will attempt to reconnect to the server after a three-second time-out expires. We can modify the time-out by adding a line that begins with `retry:` stating the time-out in milliseconds, as shown in Listing 10-8.

Listing 10-8. A message setting reconnection time-out to 5 seconds

```
retry: 5000\n
data: one more hello world\n\n
```

Listing 10-9 provides an example of another feature of SSE: the possibility of naming events by adding a line that begins with `event:` and ends with a unique message name.

Listing 10-9. Naming an event as "playerlogon"

```
event: playerlogon\n
data: {"playername": "Sontan"}\n\n
```

As shown in Listing 10-10, once the event has a unique name, we can subscribe to that event by specifying its name in place of "message" in the client.

Listing 10-10. Subscribing to a message named "playerlogon"

```
source.addEventListener('playerlogon', function(e) {
  console.log(e.data);
}, false);
```

The simplicity and flexibility of the protocol, the possibility of using it over regular HTTP, and support by the majority of modern browsers make Server-Sent Events a highly promising technology.

Table 10-3. Server-Sent Events: Method of continuously sending data from a server to the browser

	IE	Firefox	Safari	Chrome	Opera
Two versions back	~~7.0~~	~~5.0~~	~~4.0~~	12.0	11.0
Previous version	~~8.0~~	6.0	5.0	13.0	11.1
Current	~~9.0~~	7.0	5.1	14.0	11.5
Near future		8.0	6.0	15.0	12.0
Farther future	10.0	9.0		16.0	12.1

What benefits do Server-Sent Events offer?

- The protocol works over HTTP, making adoption very easy and eliminating the need for a dedicated server.
- The reconnection is automatic.
- Events can have numbers, and arbitrary events can be transmitted.

What are the drawbacks of Server-Sent Events?

- The main drawback is unidirectionality of the protocol: a user can receive events, but cannot transmit anything using an open connection.

WebSocket

WebSocket is a completely new protocol that works over TCP, reducing overhead and increasing latency, thanks to absence of HTTP, but requiring a server that supports it. One of the differences between WebSocket and Server-Sent Events is that the former is bi-directional; that is, we can both receive and transmit data in real time.

To connect to a server, you need to enter an address that starts with ws:// or wss:// for secure connections. Listing 10-11 shows what the WebSocket API looks on the client side.

Listing 10-11. Simple example of creating a WebSocket connection; sending and receiving data from the server

```
var connection = new WebSocket('ws://sontan.name/stream/');

// When the connection is open, send some data to the server
connection.onopen = function () {
        connection.send('Ping'); // Send the message 'Ping' to the server
};

// Log messages from the server
connection.onmessage = function (e) {
```

```
            console.log('Server: ' + e.data);
    };
```

A study of the protocol's security in the late November of 2010 revealed that when used with transparent proxy servers, the transmitted data cache can be replaced, and the user will receive a version of the data created by an intruder instead of the actual data. This quite serious issue prompted Firefox and Opera developers to disable WebSocket support. The new draft successfully addressed the vulnerability, and WebSocket support in these browsers was re-enabled.

Table 10-4. WebSocket: Bi-directional communication technology for web apps

	IE	Firefox	Safari	Chrome	Opera
Two versions back	7.0	5.0	4.0	12.0	11.0
Previous version	8.0	6.0	5.0	13.0	11.1
Current	9.0	7.0	5.1	14.0	11.5
Near future		8.0	6.0	15.0	12.0
Farther future	10.0	9.0		16.0	12.1

What are the benefits of WebSocket?

- The special protocol reduces response time by eliminating HTTP overhead.
- Bi-directionality allows both receiving and transmitting.

What are the drawbacks of WebSocket?

- The special protocol requires a dedicated back-end server.

Choosing a connection technology

The bi-directional and fast WebSocket is obviously the option for games, but the temporary lack of support in many browsers and the raw character of existing servers make it a technology of tomorrow. SSE, in turn, easily combines with Comet and has a simple format, which makes it a highly usable option today.

You must have noted that the latest version of the Microsoft browser ignores both of these standards, calling for a special approach.

Client databases

We used to have only cookies to store data in between page refreshes, but as applications grew in complexity, it became apparent that 4 kilobytes was not enough—not to mention that cookies have to be sent to the server every time because of the way they work. The year 2009 saw the appearance of the Web Storage standard, often referred to as DOM Storage.

Web Storage provides a convenient way to store up to 5 megabytes per domain in Firefox, Chrome, and Opera, and up to 10 megabytes in IE. Importantly, the standard has complete browser support, as shown in Table 10-5.

Table 10-5. Web Storage: Method of storing data locally (like cookies)

	IE	Firefox	Safari	Chrome	Opera
Two versions back	~~7.0~~	5.0	4.0	12.0	11.0
Previous version	8.0	6.0	5.0	13.0	11.1
Current	9.0	7.0	5.1	14.0	11.5
Near future		8.0	6.0	15.0	12.0
Farther future	10.0	9.0		16.0	12.1

We have two storage locations available: localStorage and sessionStorage. Quite obviously, the former stores data for the entire web site, while the latter keeps the data during the session only. Let us look at Listing 10-12, an example of using sessionStorage.

Listing 10-12. Example of sessionStorage use

```
// Setting temporary value to sessionStorage
sessionStorage.setItem(yourkey, yourvalue);

// Getting value
var item = sessionStorage.getItem(yourkey);

// Removing key
sessionStorage.removeItem(yourkey);

// Clearing session cache
sessionStorage.clear();
```

It is all very simple and seemingly requires no improvement, but data is stored in the key–value format, and many considered this insufficient in the modern world of relational databases.

This gave rise to new standards: Web SQL Database implemented in Chrome, Opera, and Safari, and Indexed Database promoted by Mozilla in Firefox. The two standards co-existed for some time, but in late 2010, work on Web SQL was stopped in favor of Indexed DB. Seeing how the latter is only implemented in Firefox 4 or newer and Chrome 11 and newer, and that the future of Web SQL implementation in other browsers is unclear, it is worth taking a very careful approach to the selection of a back-end for the client database.

Web fonts

Implementation of original fonts on web pages was planned for a long time. In 1995, the HTML2 standard added the tag <font>, which allowed using a font installed on the user's system, or falling back on a suitable font family if the user did not have any of the required fonts. The CSS2 specification with identical functionality came out in 1998; whereas the first attempts to implement font-face in IE4 and Netscape Navigator were made in 1997, but never became popular. The cause of that may have been the low bandwidth of dial-up access or each browser using its own format, with IE4 and newer utilizing Embedded OpenType (EOT) fonts, and Netscape Navigator supporting TrueDoc (PFR) fonts. On top of that, there were copyright issues with using fonts on the web, as they could simply be downloaded directly from the web site.

Then there was a prolonged lull on that front as designers customized various Flash plug-ins—like sIFR and later, SVG rendering via Cufon—for adding fonts to web sites. It was only quite recently that the font buzz resumed amid dynamic HTML5 development. Mozilla Firefox 3.5+, Opera 10+, Safari 3.1+, Google Chrome 4.0+, and even Internet Explorer 9+, received support for the familiar TrueType (TTF) and OpenType (TTF/OTF) formats. A W3C working group gathered subsequently to approve the Web Open Font Format (WOFF) specification, the prospective unified font format for all browsers.

WOFF is not a new font format but a standard of delivering fonts to the browser. Compression is now part of WOFF, helping reduce file size by more than 40 percent. I would like to note that WOFF uses lossless compression, so the unpacked font is identical to the original OpenType or TrueType font. This allows keeping the rendering mechanism unchanged, thus preserving the quality of fonts. The format also contains additional metadata whereby the author can specify how the font was used. The information will not affect loading but will allow identifying the origins of the font. Hence, it will be easy to trace what font is used on a web page. WOFF compresses, but does not encrypt, fonts because the format was not designed as protection for those who wish to strictly control the use of their fonts.

WOFF is currently supported by all popular browsers: Firefox 3.6+, Google Chrome 6.0+, Opera 11.10+, Internet Explorer 9+, and the new version of Safari for Mac OS X Lion.

Quite obviously, using WOFF is the simplest and most promising way of font styling, but how does one convert a familiar font to a WOFF file, and what about legacy browsers? The easiest way is to use the Font Squirrel generator (www.fontsquirrel.com/fontface/generator) to upload an OTF or TTF font file and obtain an archive containing the complete set of web fonts: TrueType, EOT, SVG, WOFF, and the special "bulletproof" CSS style for quick and smooth integration in a web page, as shown in Listing 10-13.

Listing 10-13. Bulletproof CSS style for almost all browsers

```
@font-face {
        font-family: 'MyFontFamily';
        src: url('myfont-webfont.eot?#iefix') format('embedded-opentype'),
        url('myfont-webfont.woff') format('woff'),
        url('myfont-webfont.ttf') format('truetype'),
        url('myfont-webfont.svg#svgFontName') format('svg');
}
```

This format allows using custom fonts in a vast range of browsers: Safari 5.03, IE 6+, Firefox 3.6+, Chrome 8+, iOS 3.2+, Android 2.2+, and Opera 11+—and that is good!

Conclusion

We have examined the core stack of technologies used for development of modern browser-based games. It is now apparent that selecting the right combination is no trivial task. Every technology has its pros and cons. To achieve the perfect balance, you will have to compensate for the drawbacks of one technology with the benefits of another by combining them.

In my team's project, FAR7, we used the combination of Canvas/SVG+Comet/SSE+WebStorage because this was most adequate to our requirements. Fast canvas rendering and SVG animation, Comet (which works in most browsers), and the stable SSE for next-generation versions—all achieve a sensible balance between performance and complexity, while supporting old browsers and utilizing the advantages of new ones. I hope my research will help you choose the right stack for your game, too.

I would like to note that web technology is developing by leaps and bounds, and things may change drastically within the project development period. Follow trends and news, news feeds and relevant web sites. Keep your sights on possible replacement of core stack elements as you develop web sites. By doing these things, the vortex of new web technology won't run you off course.

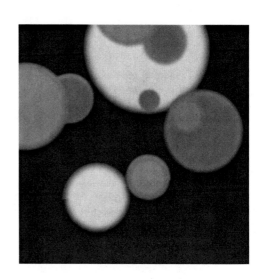

Index

CPSIA information can be obtained at www.ICGtesting.com
Printed in the USA
LVOW111524030412

275987LV00002B/1/P

9 781430 239789